Brothers in Grief

NORA GROSS

BROTHERS
in GRIEF

———

The Hidden Toll of Gun
Violence on Black Boys
and Their Schools

———

THE UNIVERSITY OF CHICAGO PRESS
CHICAGO AND LONDON

The University of Chicago Press, Chicago 60637

The University of Chicago Press, Ltd., London

Published 2024

Printed in the United States of America

33 32 31 30 29 28 27 26 25 24   1 2 3 4 5

ISBN-13: 978-0-226-82087-3 (cloth)

ISBN-13: 978-0-226-83620-1 (e-book)

DOI: https://doi.org/10.7208/chicago/9780226836201.001.0001

Library of Congress Cataloging-in-Publication Data

Names: Gross, Nora, author.

Title: Brothers in grief : the hidden toll of gun violence on black boys and their schools / Nora Gross.

Other titles: Hidden toll of gun violence on black boys and their schools

Description: Chicago ; London : The University of Chicago Press, 2024. | Includes bibliographical references and index.

Identifiers: LCCN 2024009782 | ISBN 9780226820873 (cloth) | ISBN 9780226836201 (ebook)

Subjects: LCSH: African American high school boys—Social conditions. | African American high school boys—Education—Social aspects. | School environment—United States. | Education, Secondary—Social aspects— United States. | Youth and violence—United States. | Grief—Social aspects—United States. | Psychic trauma—United States. | Educational sociology—United States.

Classification: LCC LC2779 .G76 2024 | DDC 373.18211089/96073—dc23/ eng/20240403

LC record available at https://lccn.loc.gov/2024009782

♾ This paper meets the requirements of ANSI/NISO Z39.48-1992 (Permanence of Paper).

To all the boys who grieve, and who are grieved for.
And to my sweet boy, who brings me so much joy.

I don't know if I'm the same without you
It ain't no gang without you
Birthdays ain't the same without you
Christmas ain't the same without you
I'ma represent your name when it's 'bout you

QUAVO, "WITHOUT YOU" (2023)

I'm 18.
I play pick-up basketball games with ghosts.
Is there a reason, I'm making it out of a community that
    has martyred young men
I might be mistaken for?
I.
Don't.
Know.
Will they ever call your death beautiful,
Your life a sacrifice,
A love story to be jealous of?
How many deaths will it take
Before this is considered genocide?

DEMETRIUS AMPARAN (AGE 17), NATE MARSHALL
(AGE 18), AND DIANNA HARRIS (AGE 18), "LOST
COUNT: A LOVE STORY" (2008)
Poem performed at the Brave New Voices youth poetry slam

Contents

Preface

In some sense, this book began in 2008 when, fresh out of college, I was a high school writing teacher on the West Side of Chicago. Two months into my first year, our community was rocked by the drowning deaths of three beloved students, AJ, Jimmy, and Melvin, on an overnight leadership retreat. The local headlines—"Three Chicago teens die in Fox River boating tragedy"—could never convey the impact of their deaths on the tightknit school community. Students, teachers, administrators all mourned together, held each other, and cried at three funerals. For the rest of the school year, most of us wore yellow rubber bracelets bearing the school's mascot, the Phoenix, which symbolized our shared desire to rise from the ashes of what felt at times like unrelenting grief.

Although new to the school, I was already connected to all three boys; many of their friends were peer coaches at my Writing Center. The Monday after the three students' funerals, the principal told me with a sympathetic smile that I had gone through "baptism by fire," as if acknowledging that losing students was an unavoidable rite of passage for an urban teacher; it just didn't usually happen this early in a career, or three at a time.

At twenty-two, I was the youngest teacher at the school. Though I had by no means led a sheltered life, I had experienced extreme privilege—growing up an only child with two professional parents, attending a private elementary school, an elite magnet public high school, an Ivy League college, and being white. I had been raised with an attentiveness to the challenges of poverty, homelessness, and racial injustice in my unequal city (New York) and beyond, and with a sense of responsibility toward bettering my communities. But I had not experienced these hardships myself and had mostly been shielded from the violence and untimely death that were already so familiar to my Black students. For several of these Chicago teens, these were by no means their first lost friends.

Even so, I was at the time grappling with my own first consequential experience of peer loss: the death of a close high school friend in a hiking accident. Perhaps sensitized by the chaos of my own still raw feelings of shock and grief, I became acutely conscious during the course of that year of the enduring, sometimes destructive, aftermath of premature peer deaths on my teenage students, layered on top of the many other injustices that had already shaped their young lives.

Certainly, some students, I noticed, seemed to gain strength and motivation from the losses, growing closer to each other, learning not to take their friends for granted, and feeling more determined to work hard for their futures. But others saw their friends' deaths—especially because they were so unexpected and random—as yet another sign that they ought not to expect to "make it out," that is, escape the risks and challenges of their Chicago neighborhood. The veneer of a college preparatory school could not protect them from either expected or unexpected dangers. Hard as they had striven to imagine and work for bright futures for themselves, many seemed now confirmed in the conviction that an early death likely awaited them too.

For years afterward, I reviewed the terrible days and weeks after AJ, Jimmy, and Melvin's deaths, wondering what more the school, my colleagues, and I could have done to help these beautiful, traumatized children with so much potential, struggling to stabilize themselves after their calamitous loss. I also worried about how much the emotional toll of peer losses was unspoken and unacknowledged each new school year.

In 2013, those gnawing questions traveled with me to graduate school in Philadelphia, where the shooting deaths of young people were becoming a way of life in some parts of the city. Though gun violence was not at the forefront of my mind when I began my studies focused on the social contexts of urban education and adolescent boys' inner lives, my experiences in Chicago had attuned me to the ideas of grief and loss as underexplored subtexts of school life for young people growing up in contexts of poverty and precarity. As the homicide rate steadily rose in my new home, so did the troubling feeling that surviving youth were suffering silently.

I have the tremendous privilege—which I imagine only some of my readers share—of not having to worry about my own risk of dying too early, whether by gun, by police, or by societal neglect of one sort or another. Only when gun violence, particularly mass shootings, dominates the news cycle do I feel its presence in my own life as an everyday potential danger. Will this place be the next target? Could this conversation be my last with this person? Public interactions feel heightened, goodbyes more loaded. But high-profile mass shooting incidents, while terrifying and tragic, account for a tiny fraction of US gun deaths, and I am among the lucky whose acute fears wane as the news cycles move on.[1]

Yet, for so many kids across the country, gun violence has always been an everyday worry. When the headlines dwindle, their worries—and real risks—remain.

The longer I lived in Philadelphia, the more I came to see that reality. One summer day in 2016, I spotted the cover story of the local paper: a shooting that took the life of a fifteen-year-old near a basketball court just a mile or two from my campus. A week later, I heard from a former Chicago student about the gun death of another young man who had been a senior my first year of teaching. On social media, I watched the vigils and memorials, read the anguished posts from his friends, peers, and former classmates (many my former students). I began to ask: How was grief affecting their relationships, their aspirations, their ideas about themselves? My questions grew and expanded: What are peer deaths doing to our young people? What are they doing to their schools, their schooling, and their possibilities for the future?

I began looking for an appropriate site to begin an in-depth study of grief and schooling in the aftermath of neighborhood gun violence. I met with the head of a local Philadelphia nonprofit serving young adult men, who mentioned the basketball court shooting I had seen in the paper and offered to introduce me to a teacher at Boys' Prep, the all-boys charter high school the victim had attended. Coincidentally, the very same day, a colleague made the same connection. Within a week I had a meeting with the school's leader. Like me, Dr. Stephens worried about the Black teen boys who populated his school, many of whom he believed were still suffering deeply after the death of their friend. If I could answer my research questions about how grief shaped their experiences of and in school, I might be able to help. He warmly invited me in.

As my research plans took shape and I began to share them publicly, I was not always met with the same sense of importance and urgency that Dr. Stephens and I felt. I was told by at least one senior scholar that attempting to explain school experiences or achievement by looking at gun violence losses was like looking for a specific piece of hay in a large haystack: With so many challenges in urban education, why focus on this one specifically? Others encouraged me to seek out a white comparison group to strengthen my study. While I valued these perspectives, they missed the depth, breadth, and inequality of this problem. Grief for murdered friends was a form of suffering experienced by thousands of children across Philadelphia, and it impacted myriad dimensions of their social, emotional, and school lives. These impacts were concentrated for groups already marginalized by race and class and, up to this point, largely neglected by prior research. We academics are often quick to seek the bigger picture or a comparison, but there is insight to be gained in sitting with the complexity of individual human experience as it is—especially in corners that generally don't get enough light.

Here I focus on a single school year, 2017–2018, during which one school was shaken to its core by the murders of at least three young people connected to the school, including two active students, one of whom had been a participant in my research. I tell the stories of the teenage boys alongside their teachers and school leaders as they navigated their grief and endeavored to continue pursuing their educational goals. Though this is the story of one year in one school, it represents a set of experiences faced by thousands of other young people and their school communities across the country amid a gun violence crisis that shows no signs of ceasing.

Generally, gun violence research and reporting concentrate on the victims—and, increasingly, those who survive their injuries. Another point of focus is the families. Sometimes, in the case of a school shooting, the school community itself receives public consideration or study. Such perspectives may also include the perpetrator, who may also have been the victim of other kinds of harm. But here, my eyes and ears were trained on another disturbingly large band of vulnerable people in the aftermath of a shooting, who are so often left out of the accounting on injury: the friends—the brothers in grief.

This book does not have all the answers, and certainly it does not have a solution for gun violence—one of the most urgent problems of this century. But, *attention must be paid*, as we know from that classic line in Arthur Miller's play. And, instructively, *attention is the beginning of devotion*, as the poet Mary Oliver wrote. Witnessing and listening to the stories of these young people is a necessary step if we are to respond with compassion and urgency. The boys on these pages are your brothers, sons, nephews, friends, students. We cannot let ourselves be lulled into the feeling that their losses are normal or their grief tolerable. These boys deserve our attention, and our active devotion.

"I'll Never Know My Last Time . . ."

INTRODUCTION

On Saturday afternoon of the long Thanksgiving weekend, Hazeem was in his room enjoying an unusual period of quiet at home and thinking about the future. Tall and a little lanky with dark brown skin and small rectangular glasses, Hazeem had a brooding quality. He would often sit on the margins of groups of boisterous boys in the school cafeteria, lost in thought or in the world of his phone. Now in his junior year, he seemed to enjoy proximity to several peer groups, but privately identified only a handful of close friends. In classrooms, Hazeem sometimes mumbled to himself or made crude jokes, not particularly endearing himself to his teachers. He found the schoolwork hard, regularly wondering if he could cut it.

Hazeem had been at Boys' Prep since ninth grade. As its name implies, Boys' Preparatory Charter High School is a school for boys—more specifically Black boys, mostly from low-income neighborhoods across Philadelphia—with the mission of preparing them for college and the social mobility expected to come from that path.

Hazeem wasn't sure the school was the best fit for him. That afternoon, he made a post to Instagram with his ponderings: "Yoooo I'll be 18 next year wtf ❗ I gotta make my mind up cause I don't even know what college I wanna go to or what I really wanna do." Perhaps he was hoping for encouraging comments or advice. Although he still talked constantly about his frustrations with the school's singular focus on college, the uptight uniform and discipline policies, and the lack of girls—and regularly repeated his desire to transfer to cyber school—Hazeem had a new girlfriend who seemed to be a positive influence and he was starting to develop a more optimistic outlook about what could be next.

Less than an hour later, Hazeem picked up his phone to scroll through his feed and check for messages. He saw a post that confused him. He clicked the link, which took him to a news article. No fluff, straight to the point: police were called to an address; when they arrived, they were taken to the body of eighteen-year-old JahSun. "According to investigators, [he] died from multiple gunshot wounds." JahSun's name was misspelled, but the other facts lined up with what Hazeem had heard about his friend's Thanksgiving plans to visit his sister out of town.

Hazeem didn't know what to think. He clicked over to JahSun's own Instagram page, looking for evidence that this was a mistake. He and JahSun had gotten closer that fall since they shared a lunch period and often sat at the same table. Though Hazeem was not a part of JahSun's close crew of friends (many of them seniors and on the football team), the school was small enough that almost everyone knew each other. Peer hierarchies were limited, so even as a junior who did not play any sports, Hazeem could count on JahSun to give a friendly greeting in the hallway or reply to his online posts with motivating words. JahSun had always seemed happy to play the role of mentor to his younger schoolmates.

On JahSun's Instagram page, Hazeem found corroboration of the news article. Several friends had already started adding comments on JahSun's most recent post—uncertain messages like "this can't be real" and "please text me back," but also "rest up" and "I love you for life." The details were still hazy, but the reality started to set in. JahSun had been shot. Murdered. He was dead.

Hazeem's lazy holiday afternoon pondering the future was over. This moment would launch him, his teenage classmates, and his entire school community into a year of mourning that, for some, led to long-term wounds neither they nor their school had the tools to fully heal.

The Context of a School Year

The school year at Boys' Prep had already been a trying one so far, with a new principal and other administrative changes; ongoing battles with the school board responsible for renewing the school's charter; and the perennial fall challenge of incorporating a new class of freshmen—arriving with a range of levels of preparation for the academic and behavioral expectations—into the school culture. But by Thanksgiving, there was a sense that the school year at Boys' Prep had found its rhythm. Both students and staff welcomed the four-day holiday, expecting it to help everyone rebuild their stamina for the final push to the semester's end. No one expected the break to be interrupted by the shooting death of a student—let alone one like JahSun.

To understand how the school community responded to JahSun's death, I need to explain the gruesome context: at Boys' Prep that awful year, the murder of JahSun was bookended by two more student murders. While technically this was the first time in the school's history that a student was killed *during* the school year, it was only sixteen months earlier that Tyhir, a rising Boys' Prep sophomore, was gunned down after a neighborhood summer-league basketball game not far from the school. Tyhir was a popular and charismatic student, a budding musician, and a talented basketball player. He was shot by another teenager (not from the school) allegedly after a previous game had ended in a dispute over the score. The shooter unloaded into a group of boys affiliated with the team he thought had wronged him, injuring two and hitting fifteen-year-old Tyhir in the face. Tyhir would die within a few hours at a nearby hospital, as several of his friends gathered in the hospital parking lot.

Tyhir was mourned by many friends at school, including Hazeem—and JahSun himself. Teachers and staff also mourned the future Tyhir would never have and wondered if they had done enough to support his grieving friends, several of whom had transferred out of Boys' Prep in the wake of their loss. Some who stayed seemed to have never fully recovered, now over a year later.

And in this new school year, JahSun's death would not be the only loss students would have to cope with. The school would lose another cherished student, Bill, that spring—and this grief layered on top of grief for other loved ones beyond the school community, victims of gun violence as well as numerous other circumstances and illnesses born of systemic racism and the continued structural neglect of Black communities, families, and children. For the boys you will come to know in this book, the presence of early and unnatural death was a social fact of their lives. The tangible awareness of their own and their loved ones' mortality was a given. As poet Claudia Rankine has written, "The condition of Black life is one of mourning," and for Black boys growing up in cities where centuries of racism have birthed decades of gun violence, this mourning is chronic and acute.[1]

At the same time, these boys attended a school that aimed to orient them toward a future of social mobility and mainstream success. Hallways and classrooms were filled with college banners. The staff included two college counselors and an alumni counselor. The school's professional uniform, the Latin classes, and the assemblies and field trips were all designed to point students toward college and the futures it was believed college would make possible.

So what does a school do when its very premise—helping young people prepare for their futures—is turned on its head by the death of a child? And what if his death is not a singular tragedy, an unlikely accident, but part of a larger epidemic with no end in sight? An epidemic to which the Black teen boys at this school know they are especially susceptible? While I am not aware of any databases documenting youth homicide by the victims' school, there is plenty of anecdotal evidence to suggest that many schools experience the particular misfortune of losing multiple students within a single school year.[2]

This book tells the story of one year at Boys' Prep, a year punctuated by loss and overwhelmed by grief: the debates among school leaders, the strategies of disciplinary staff, the decisions of teachers in managing their own classrooms, and the experiences of the adolescent boys facing the unthinkable that somehow became normal. I arrived at the school as a researcher not long after Tyhir's death, with the goal of trying to understand how his friends and classmates were experiencing their loss over the long term, and especially how it might be playing out in their schooling. I never expected to be at the school as a practiced observer, already incorporated into many aspects of the school community, when another gun death happened.

As I narrate the year that followed JahSun's death, I show how the school, at first, responded well—but then, facing an impossible set of choices, took steps that ultimately exacerbated the harm for its students. The losses these teen boys experienced were shared, but the shaping of their emotions in school forced their grief to be experienced largely alone, and eventually to be hidden, so that over time, the continued grief among students became injuries that transformed their social lives, their aspirations, and their report cards. However, long-term harm was also mitigated through relationships and interactions that took shape primarily beyond the school walls, including online. And there are approaches that the school could have taken to help the students channel their grief into hopeful action and see both their pain and its alleviation as part of a collective experience.

JahSun, Lost Too Soon

Always a reliable student, well respected by peers and teachers alike, JahSun had been hitting his stride that fall, his senior year. He had finally earned a starting position on the school's football team. He was experimenting with rapping and had recorded a handful of songs. By Thanksgiving weekend, JahSun had already been accepted to two colleges. Though he hoped to play football in college, he envisioned several career possibilities beyond sports.

JahSun, whose name means "God is the center of all things," was a believer and a deep thinker. He would regularly attend church with his mother, but he also wondered sometimes whether he connected more with Islam, which he learned about through his father's children from another relationship. Though his parents separated when he was very young, JahSun had close relationships with both of them and had spent long stretches living with each parent. At school, he seemed equally comfortable being the center of attention or on the sidelines, thoughtfully observing. Jah, as most of his friends and family called him, had several close friends at Boys' Prep, an extended circle of football teammates, and was friendly with other peers spanning multiple social groups. JahSun's half brother, Bashir, had also just started at Boys' Prep that fall as a freshman.

JahSun's good looks were a regular point of conversation among his friends—he had caramel skin and hazel eyes, and football training was making his 5′9″ frame more muscular. He'd had interest from many girls, and while he projected a certain coyness about his relationships, he told me he was committed to the idea of ultimately marrying one woman for life and having kids only once he had done so.

Though still a teenager, JahSun himself had already lost multiple friends to gun violence. He had mourned the death of Tyhir, and then an even closer friend—one he considered a big brother—killed six months later. This was, in fact, how I came to know JahSun. In the spring of his junior year, soon after his older friend's death, a classmate introduced us, knowing I was looking to interview students about their experiences of peer loss to gun violence. By the time we sat down for an interview in March 2017, I had already been situated at Boys' Prep as an ethnographic researcher for half a year. I had mostly been spending time with Tyhir's close friends—then sophomores—trying to understand the way their continued grief affected their school lives and relationships.

JahSun spoke in long, thoughtful sentences, but did not make much eye contact as he played with the squishy green ball I would bring to interviews to fend off the awkwardness some teen boys felt sharing their emotional lives with a near-stranger. He had recently gotten a memorial tattoo for his honorary big brother across his entire forearm that he was eager to show off. This was one way he had found a sense of healing amid his grief. But he also theorized that grief had manifested in some ongoing physical symptoms.

The deaths of two friends in the past year, layered on memories of the murder of his uncle, gave JahSun an intimate sense of the precarity of life. In a matter-of-fact tone, he told me as we were wrapping up the interview: "Death . . . is like, you never know. I know that I just, like, tell my friends to be safe and stuff because . . . I'll never know my last time talking to them, and it's a scary thing . . . Like I lost somebody every year so far . . . I feel like death is, it's like constant right now." JahSun was anxious about what might await him and his friends, but the frequency and proximity of loss in his life had also given him some purpose. Though he had previously considered becoming a dentist (because they made good money and, he thought, always seemed happy) or a firefighter (because the career would give him stability right out of high school), now he was wondering more and more if he should become a therapist (like his father) to help others make sense of the uncertainties he was experiencing. There is a tragic irony that—just as Hazeem soon would—JahSun linked his ponderings of future possibilities with his experience and fears of death.

The following fall, when Thanksgiving weekend approached, fear was far from JahSun's mind. He was excited by the news he'd just received of a full scholarship to a nearby college. JahSun asked his mother, Maxayn, if he could visit his older half sister a few hours away for the holiday and to celebrate his good news. JahSun's mother obliged and drove him to the train. His left leg was secured in a large knee-immobilizing cast from a football injury that had sidelined him for the past month. After finally getting real playing time on the football team, he was discouraged to be out for the season and crippled in such a pronounced way in his daily life, but JahSun was trying to stay focused on getting healthy in time to play in college. This trip was meant to be a little escape from what had been a difficult month of doctors' appointments and uncertainty about his recovery timeline.

His sister's fiancé had invited his own brother and his girlfriend, all of them quite a bit older than JahSun. The group apparently partied late Friday evening. JahSun kept mostly to himself, stretched out on his sister's couch, texting and scrolling through Instagram. By early Saturday morning, something had gone terribly wrong. An argument between JahSun and the brother of his sister's fiancé escalated. Still limited by his leg cast and unarmed, JahSun was shot seven times and died early that morning on top of a pile of clothes in his sister's bedroom. The substance of the argument remains a mystery, although JahSun's mother insists it stemmed from jealousy.[3]

For years, Maxayn would replay the incongruity of dropping her son off at 30th Street Station and then seeing him again when she picked up the casket holding a body that would never age past eighteen. "30th Street, casket. 30th Street, casket," she would repeat. His friends, too, would revisit their totally normal text conversations just hours before the shooting; they couldn't comprehend how those unremarkable words to each other became their last.

The Unequal Impacts of Gun Violence and the Burden of Peer Loss

JahSun and his friends are not alone in the ways gun violence has taken and transformed their lives. It is indisputable that the United States has a gun violence problem and that young people have suffered most gravely from it. After a significant drop from the homicide peak in the 1990s, rates started rising steadily again in 2015 and have spiked even more since 2020. More than 2,000 children and teens are killed by guns each year; in fact, firearm violence has now overtaken car accidents as the leading cause of death for children and adolescents.[4]

Gun homicides are also a deeply racialized and gendered problem. By some estimates, Black women and girls are four times as likely to be killed by a gun than their white counterparts; for Black males, it is more than twelve times.[5] In Philadelphia alone, the premature killings of Black men and boys in *a single year* account for nearly 10,000 collective years of life lost. Put another way, Philadelphia is said to have 36,000 "missing Black men" due to early death, as well as incarceration.[6]

Violence clusters geographically, often in places with the greatest racial inequality.[7] It is no coincidence that the neighborhoods that have been systemically neglected and disinvested in over decades—resulting in unstable housing, under-resourced schools, environmental threats, absent or abusive policing, and lack of access to living wages, healthy foods, transportation, social services, and political representation—are the same places experiencing the worst gun violence. Concentrated poverty and violence cyclically perpetuate each other, and neighborhood violence itself, separate from other factors, has been shown to contribute to "the intergenerational transmission of economic and social disadvantage."[8]

The magnitude of early death in Black neighborhoods has profound structural implications: violence impacts neighborhood economies and job opportunities, educational access, family structures, parenting decisions, and community trust, just to name a few. And the aftereffects of gun violence and lingering grief can be seen, heard, and felt across the most impacted neighborhoods in street-corner memorials, painted murals, the titles of basketball tournaments, the lyrics of songs on the radio and recorded in amateur basement studios, social media handles, jewelry, t-shirts, tattoos, and more.[9] If you know where to look, memorials to gun violence victims and evidence of enduring grief are all around. "It's as if these communities are piecing together the equivalent of a war memorial," journalist Alex Kotlowitz writes.[10]

There are other ways to measure the scale of the problem. Estimates are that every homicide leaves behind up to ten grieving family members, whose lives are critically rerouted by the loss of a parent, a child, or another close family member.[11]

But as the average count of a youth murder's co-victims or survivors, ten is vastly too small a number. Someone like dear JahSun leaves behind not only his mother, father, siblings, cousins, aunts, uncles, and grandparents. His death also represents a loss for dozens of young people who were his close friends at school, on football teams, in summer camps, not to mention his romantic partners and crushes, his neighborhood friends, his elementary and middle school friends, and the many other peers whose paths he crossed in his short life. These friends and peers are too often forgotten in the hierarchies of grievers. In the modern era and the developed world, the death of a peer is considered highly unusual for young people and has not been adequately captured in scientific measures of healthy development.[12] And yet, the evidence is convincing that youth exposure to community violence, even if not directly experienced or witnessed, has serious academic, cognitive, and even neurological impacts.[13]

. Higher rates of homicide among Black males inflict an "unequal burden of loss" on Black boys and young men who are most likely to be the friends of those killed and to experience multiple losses during adolescence and early adulthood.[14] Not only does the race, gender, class, and age of Black teen boys growing up in and around poverty increase their likelihood of losing a friend to gun homicide, but these identities may also impose social restrictions on their experience of grief. The intersection of racial stereotypes, constrained constructions of masculinity, class-based burdens, and adults' perceptions of adolescent emotionality can limit the ability of boys like Hazeem to grieve publicly and to recover in productive ways from their losses. All the while, our society maintains a "peculiar indifference," as criminologist Elliott Currie frames it, quoting W. E. B. Du Bois, to the suffering of these boys and of their communities.[15]

The News about JahSun Spreads

Saturday afternoon, the reality of JahSun's unexpected, violent death had still not fully sunk in. The guys in the Boys' Prep football team group chat kept waiting for JahSun to chime in to tell them it was all a misunderstanding. One player called JahSun's phone thirty times, hoping he would pick up.

Another of JahSun's circles—communicating on a text chain with twenty-four Boys' Prep seniors—was alternating between disbelief and devastation. A phone call between friends Tony and Ezekiel passed along confirmation from JahSun's cousin. Months later, Tony told me he still remembered the "chilly feeling" that overtook his body once he was sure it wasn't a sick joke. Slowly, they all started to reckon with the reality. Owen, who was used to making fun of JahSun and planning weekend get-togethers, didn't know what to do with himself. Omari clocked out of work early so he could be alone.[16] In his bedroom, Khalil started wailing so loudly his mother heard him from downstairs.

Elsewhere in the city, Emmet was cooking sweet potatoes. He thought they turned out well and was about to, as he put it, "flex in the group chat." But someone else's message informing them about JahSun came through first. Emmet felt anger welling up in him and threw a pot against the wall.

Yaja got the news on that same text chain while on the way to his job at a fast-food restaurant just outside the city. He didn't expect his mostly white coworkers would get it, so he decided not to tell anyone at work. "I kept going to the bathroom and readjusting myself because I kept crying," he recalled. Eventually, his manager came to check on him and surprised Yaja with his understanding, spending the rest of the shift by his side offering comfort.

Hazeem, still alone in his bedroom, flipped to JahSun's page on Instagram and scrolled for a picture, finding one he especially liked from months earlier. Hazeem took a screenshot and put it on his own page with the caption "shxt fucked me up dawg 😥💔💔 #Restupbrodie 💯 we cant even bid at lunch no more yo 🙍🏿." As he refreshed his timeline, more and more posts like his popped up. Some shared recent memories of JahSun. Others posted their raw emotions: a mix of confusion, anger, and deep pain. Social media was one space where JahSun's friends could share and process their immediate reactions, especially if they didn't have someone to talk to right away.

Several boys, particularly those who had felt the most acute impact of Tyhir's death the summer before, referred to other lost loved ones, as if this loss retriggered those memories and pain. This was not the first time their day had been interrupted by the devastating news of a gun murder and a friend's death. "I lost another one," they would say. "We don't get no breaks." Herc, a junior, immediately connected JahSun's death to the loss of other friends: "So many of my homies dead. I feel like I post them every day," he wrote on social media. For Herc, at sixteen, JahSun was the seventh close friend or young family member who had died. By age twenty-two, he would have to add seven more to the list, including one of his best friends and his older brother.

What does it mean to be a teenager who has already lost multiple friends to sudden, violent deaths? And what does it mean for a school to have dozens and dozens of such teens walking its hallways? Every year, and with increasing frequency, hundreds of schools go through what Boys' Prep was about to: the return to hallways and classrooms, cafeteria tables and stairwells, alongside a ghost. And too many schools, as would be Boys' Prep's fate too, experience the sting of untimely death more than once in a single year. What would it be like back at school on Monday? And over the course of the rest of the year? How would Herc's, Hazeem's, and all the other boys' grief shape and be shaped by the unique goals and culture of their school?

Schooling Poor Black Boys in a Prep School Package

Boys' Preparatory Charter High School, where these boys would return on Monday without JahSun, is housed in a three-story gray stone building on a small hill set off from the street of a residential Philadelphia neighborhood. Inside the refurbished church school, bland floor tiles and tan lockers are brightened by walls with colorful murals, student art, and college banners. The school complex covers an entire city block, with the building itself sitting between a parking lot and a large fenced-in field, recently restored at great expense for use by the football team. The neighborhood is 93 percent Black, with a median annual household income of $29,000 to $32,000 during the time of this study.[17] About a third of the 30,000 residents live below the federal poverty line, and 8.5 percent have a college degree. The neighborhood's crime index is twice the national average, though it is not one of the city's neighborhoods most notorious for violence.

Boys' Prep opened in 2007 with the mission of preparing low-income Black boys for college. The single-sex high school serves approximately 450 students (grades 9–12), 97 percent of whom are Black. Students are selected by lottery; the school typically receives applications from three times the number of students it can admit. According to the school's charter renewal, just under half the student body officially qualifies for free/reduced-price lunch, but to accommodate any ratio of economic disadvantage, the cafeteria offers free breakfast and lunch to all students.

The school's founders aimed to provide an elite prep-school-style education, including four years of Latin, not because of its utility, but "because it is hard." The boys wear school-branded blazers and neckties, along with a tightly restricted palette and style for pants, dress shirts, and all the way down to their belts, shoes, and socks. Boys' Prep boasts sending more Black males to college than any other high school in the state, with an advertised 98 percent college-acceptance rate, an 85 percent college-enrollment rate, and a 77 percent persistence rate—though numbers had been dropping as the school neared its ten-year anniversary.[18]

As a charter school, Boys' Prep is both publicly and privately funded, but managed independently, operating mostly outside the regulation and oversight of the Philadelphia School District.[19] Unlike larger networks of charter schools with multiple locations (e.g., KIPP), Boys' Prep is a freestanding school with a single middle school and high school location, about a mile apart. A board of trustees makes most schoolwide decisions and supervises a CEO, who directs the principals of the two campuses.

"No-excuses" urban charter schools have become notorious for prioritizing student compliance to behavioral standards by "sweating the small stuff" and employing complex systems of punishment and reward. In these schools, poverty or trauma is *no excuse* for bad behavior or school failure. They set high standards and emphasize "academic achievement as a means to an end: to set students on a path to college and the middle class."[20] Though Boys' Prep does not neatly fit the no-excuses charter school model, it shares some characteristics, including the use of "small stuff," like the school uniform, as a proxy for broader behavioral compliance. Discipline is also an area around which students and school adults experience daily power struggles as students vie for more behavioral and bodily freedom and the school generally prioritizes order—though there was also an emphasis on educating through strong relationships.

Boys' Prep is part of a growing movement of public single-sex educational programs designed specifically to serve low-income boys of color and to counter the persistent educational inequities this group faces.[21] This movement has grown in popularity since the 1990s, with supporters in both liberal and conservative education-reform camps. Early motivation for race- and gender-(re)segregated schools centered around "saving" Black boys "in crisis"—and presumed to be fatherless—through exposure to male teachers and positive role models.[22] More recent marketing of these schools focuses instead on the need to "reverse abysmal graduation and college completion rates among boys in urban centers."[23] Embedded in the visions of success at many of these schools—"Black Male Academies," as they've been called—is a very particular image of Black male respectability. As sociologist Freeden Blume Oeur explains, this school-reform strategy "seeks to institutionalize respectability and to lift up and reform Black men."[24] To do so, these schools often accentuate their differences from other local schools and promote the respectable identities of their students in contrast to the stereotypical "deviant features of Black masculinity and Black urban life."[25] Boys' Prep used the Classics curriculum and professional uniform to mark their students as having disciplined minds and disciplined bodies, substantively and sartorially separating them from other boys in the neighborhood.[26]

The perception of access to social and cultural capital through the school's approach was, in part, what attracted many families to Boys' Prep. The school was seen as a bright spot in Philadelphia's troubled public education landscape and a very good option for families who could not afford private school and whose sons were not accepted into one of the city's handful of magnet high schools.[27] For most parents, the draw was the school's focus on college preparation, the emphasis on behavioral respectability, and Boys' Prep's reputation as a caring, safe institution. Some parents especially appreciated the school's small size, which they felt created opportunities for students to be supported in a more individualized way. As one mother put it, "Boys'

Prep has been a saving grace because they're willing to work with [my son] and they're not disparaging him and throwing him away," which she had experienced in bigger public schools. Students also generally appreciated the smaller student body and potential for close relationships with teachers, while acknowledging that this made it more difficult for them to get away with petty rule-breaking or acts of rebellion. "I'm going to transfer" was a common refrain, especially when students found themselves in trouble.

However, Boys' Prep's positive reputation did not mask the poverty of the school. The schools on which Boys' Prep was modeled—for the children of the wealthy, privileged classes and a chosen few others—boast sprawling green suburban campuses that rival elite private colleges. In addition to abundant academic and extracurricular options for students, these institutions have their own athletic fields and facilities, rich and varied arts offerings, and a wealth of full-time staff to enrich their students' mental and physical health. In contrast, the 450 Boys' Prep students had access to one half-time nurse, a single social worker, an understaffed Special Education department, very limited arts classes or extracurriculars, and a simple fenced-in field that only the football team got to enjoy.

Further, many Boys' Prep students enrolled having been woefully underserved in their first decade of schooling. Freshman English teachers reported having students reading at the second- and third-grade levels. Compared to their peers at the elite prep schools, most Boys' Prep students attended elementary and middle schools with less experienced teachers, older buildings and learning materials, and fewer resources across the board. The "educational neglect and underperformance" this produces can lead to students' disengagement from school and behavior issues.[28] In addition, these boys, growing up in the poorest major city in the country,[29] faced a multitude of other sources of precarity throughout their childhoods, including hunger or malnutrition, lack of access to adequate healthcare, housing instability, and exposure to violence and trauma. These facts have become so normalized that we can sometimes forget to maintain our outrage about the way society continues to fail Black and low-income youth both in their schools and on the streets, where their lives are extinguished with barely a headline.

Despite Boys' Prep's lofty educational vision, the school could not escape the reality of a criminally unequal society that betrays Black boys at every turn. Within this context, Boys' Prep's mission to launch its students to college "and beyond" required considered effort. In my observations, their efforts were guided by three pillars I call the *urgency to compensate*, the *compulsion to prepare*, and the *responsibility to protect*. These priorities steered the school's daily activities as well as their response in the aftermath of JahSun's death.

Boys' Prep's *urgency to compensate* for the poverty and racism that shaped students' lives came from both the fact and the feeling that students were entering high school behind where they should have been and behind their more privileged peers. The need to catch students up academically was reflected in the longer school day (students participating in extracurriculars stay until 5 p.m. three days a week), double English classes for freshmen, and almost no room in students' packed schedules for "extras" like art or gym. Students regularly had to recite a pledge committing to pursuing education as their "full-time job."[30]

Alongside—and sometimes conflicting with—the urgency to compensate was the school's sense of the *compulsion to prepare*. Despite some students' lack of preparation for rigorous high school work, Boys' Prep still expected all students to strive for college. School assemblies, presentations to parents, and marketing to the public stressed the college-going statistics of Black males in Philadelphia and nationally, and framed Boys' Prep as a salve to these low numbers. There was no time to waste, the school's founder would say, if they were going to reverse these abysmal statistics. College talk was constant in the building; multiple checkpoints and events throughout the school year reminded students of the importance of college and assured them of their ability to succeed there. Students were tracked into two different levels: honors classes or the lower level, called "college prep." The compulsion to prepare also included ideas about behavioral compliance and respectable bodily comportment, viewed as additional preparation for the middle-class life college would enable.[31]

Finally, both Boys' Prep as an institution and its leaders as individuals felt a deep sense of *responsibility to protect*: to protect their young students from the dangers of the neighborhood, the struggles of poverty, and temptations that could steer them off their path. Central to the ethos of these "Black Male Academies" is the hope that in separating boys from their less focused or ambitious peers and their troubled neighborhoods, they can inoculate and insulate them from the perceived dangers of the streets. This viewpoint necessarily involves the construction of a hierarchy of Black manhood and the school's sense of preparing *these* Black boys for a hardworking, honorable, respectable life while *other kinds* of Black boys continue to enact the worst negative stereotypes of urban Black masculinity.[32]

In the pages that follow, we will be tracking the powerful pull of these three guiding principles as they informed each school decision following JahSun's death and shaped the efforts toward recovery for his friends and classmates.

Studying the Aftermath at Boys' Prep

An hour after his first memorial post, Hazeem shared another expression of his grief. Alongside a photo of JahSun, he described memories of their time together in the school cafeteria: "💔💔 the streets took another one of my brothers. wtf that shxt hurts dawg 🙏 . . . you always would tell me to chill if I was drawn at lunch. we just was together dawg bidding. remember u threw milk on Owen. shxt was the bid dawg. ima miss u bro love you too 💯." Then he posted a series of Instagram stories—temporary posts that disappear after twenty-four hours—including one that marked the death dates of both Tyhir and JahSun.

The cafeteria was where Hazeem had bonded with both the friends he now memorialized online. Freshman year, he had been part of a large crew of friends that included Tyhir. Most lunch periods, they spanned two long rectangular tables with students and conversations regularly moving between them. Sophomore year, with Tyhir gone and several other members of the group transferred out or moved away, the tables downsized. Hazeem made a new lunchtime home with Herc, Kaliq, Latrell, and Jonquett. The five shared their often too-small meals of processed proteins and canned corn or green beans, usually leaving the vegetable untouched in its partition on the Styrofoam plate. They made a basketball hoop out of the trash can and competed for distance. They shared quarters when one of them was short and wanted to supplement the free meal with chips or cookies. They swapped stories of teachers who were annoying them, friends who were being dumb, girls they were talking to. Sometimes they scrambled to finish homework for the next period. They played 8 Ball Pool with each other on their phones, initiated satirical rap battles, and when someone remembered to bring the deck, played (or cheated at) Uno.

The cafeteria was also where I, as an ethnographer, differentiated myself from teachers and developed relationships with the boys. During the three lunch periods each day, the cafeteria was loud, chaotic, and often smelled of sweat mixed with processed meat and chocolate chip cookies. Generally, the only adults who spent time in the cafeteria were there to supervise and discipline students. Teachers generally passed through as quickly as possible to get to the adjoining teachers' lounge. By joining students at their red lunch tables to eat my mediocre home-cooked leftovers, I signaled that I was not a teacher. When I didn't flinch at curse words, banned cell phones, or homework copying, I proved that I had no intention of disciplining or snitching on them. And when I joined Uno games and learned to mimic their cheating strategies, I showed the boys that I was someone they could teach about their lives.

I arrived at the school in the fall of 2016, a few months after the basketball court shooting that resulted in Tyhir's death. I embarked on this ethnographic research journey to examine the interrelations between violence, grief, and schooling for adolescent Black boys. I wanted to understand how the students at Boys' Prep were making sense of the loss of friends and peers, and how their experience of grief and grieving was both shaped by and shaped their interactions in school. I focused my attention primarily on the students and adults most directly affected by Tyhir's loss, which included multiple lunch periods a week with Hazeem, Herc, and their table of sophomores in the cafeteria.

I also observed students and adults in classrooms, hallways, the teachers' lounge, the main office, and at major school events and activities. While I was initially introduced to Tyhir's circle of friends through the school's social worker, over time I struck up conversations and built relationships with students across social circles just by being around. Sometimes I was the one to find a student alone fuming in the stairwell just needing to vent; other times I probably bothered kids by expressing too much interest in chatting as they waited at the bus stop. As the students I was coming to know continued to mourn Tyhir, as well as other losses in their lives, I attended school memorial events, candlelight vigils in the neighborhood, balloon releases, funerals, and visits to the cemetery. Ultimately, I conducted official semi-structured interviews with sixty-five students as well as the majority of school faculty and staff (thirty-five in total, a combination of focus groups and one-on-one interviews) and a handful of parents (two focus groups of three parents each, and attendance at PTA meetings). With their permission, I learned about students' lives by observing their activity on social media and accessing their schoolwork and official school records. I also sometimes exchanged text messages or social media direct messages with students, which some seemed to find more comfortable than face-to-face interviews or informal in-person interactions. I write in more detail about my methodological approach, the consent process, my positionality as a researcher and caring adult in a school community in crisis, and some of the methodological and representational dilemmas I faced in the Author's Note.

JahSun was killed during my second research year at Boys' Prep. I was one of the first adults connected to the school to find out about his death. On Saturday afternoon, Yaja, the senior who had introduced me to JahSun nine months earlier, sent a brief text: "Hey Nora . . . I don't know if you got the news . . . But JahSun died earlier today."

Yaja's text is still on my phone. I stared at it uncomprehendingly that day, and many times since. JahSun's words from our interview eight months earlier were ringing in my ears: "You never know [your] last time talking to [someone]." I had come to the school to understand how the gun murder of one teen boy, Tyhir, affected his friends—including JahSun. I was getting to know JahSun as a *brother in grief*, someone whose sense of loss I was trying to understand. JahSun and I had been trying to schedule a follow-up interview. Now suddenly he was dead, lost, gone. JahSun himself would become the epicenter of more circles of grief.

The cafeteria had been the last place I had spoken to JahSun. A week or two earlier, I had joined him and his best friend, Ezekiel, at their table so JahSun could update me on his injury. He told me he wasn't worried about whether the long recovery would mean missing the rest of the football season because he was focused on college. Now he would never get to attend.

As a researcher, I felt the best I could do in these horrible circumstances was to faithfully document what I was witnessing, what people were telling me, and what I felt and experienced as a member of the school community, in the hope that the outcome of this work will provide useful insights. At the same time, I too was grieving for JahSun and for the loss of innocence and childhood so many of his friends were facing: the pathways to a safe life, an engaging and dignifying career, a loving family, a comfortable home that increasingly felt foreclosed to them because of this loss and so many others. I also grieved for the teachers and administrators who had pursued careers meant to inspire and prepare Black boys for bright futures, only to find themselves playing roles they had not trained for, making decisions they were unprepared for, and holding on to memories of lost students.

Grief in Context

This is the story of grief over the hard days, weeks, and months that followed JahSun's death. It is about the way grief is shared among friends and within a school community. The way grief is both shouted and whispered. How it is carried, embodied, displayed, hidden, policed. How grief can be tamped down by policy and freed through relationships and technology, and the weight with which it bears down on people as it is heaped on itself. Yet this book is also about the potential for grief to be generative and constructive, if bravely supported. It is a story about friendship, brotherhood, and the unexpected kinds of community that form in the wake of shared loss. Despite the odds stacked against them, so many boys found creative, relational ways to support their own and each other's healing.

American culture has trained us to think of grieving as a private experience, but it is in fact, like most emotions, deeply social.[33] Our experiences of grief are shaped within social interactions and filtered through cultural norms. Stubborn gendered and racialized social rules—"feeling rules," as sociologists have described them[34]—often dictate who can publicly grieve, in what ways, and for how long. Inequalities in our society further limit outlets for emotional expression or access to resources for recovery for some marginalized groups. Thus, the bereaved may find their grief pathologized, minimized, or encouraged to move on (too) quickly—what some scholars have called the disenfranchisement or suffocation of grief.[35]

In short, grief derives its emotional weight from both the magnitude of the loss itself, and the burden of carrying it through the constraints of one's social world.[36] For the boys you will come to know in this book, grief is a complex, evolving experience, not a singular emotion. The boys grieved for their friends' abbreviated lives and all the experiences they would never have. Equally, they mourned the erasures in their own life of a missing friend, a supportive companion in their social circle, whose loss would haunt all future milestones that ought to have been shared. Inevitably, along with outward-turned grief, there was for many a sad sense of lost innocence along with a diminished feeling, if they ever had it, of present safety or a secure future. With every peer death feeling like a death threat and encroaching on the dream of unencumbered futures, their grief was inextricably bound up with their social identities as Black boys and their social context within a city battling both a gun violence epidemic and a profoundly flawed education system. And so too were the boys' public expressions of grief interpreted by others through the lens of their Blackness and maleness—and all of the attendant social expectations and restrictions.

In addition to their experiences of profound grief, many of the boys whose stories are shared in this book also experienced what experts—and often the boys themselves—would call *trauma*. JahSun's murder, like many of the gun violence incidents they were exposed to, was traumatic to those who knew him. Trauma is defined as resulting "from an event, series of events, or set of circumstances that is experienced by an individual as physically or emotionally harmful or life threatening and that has lasting adverse effects on the individual's functioning and mental, physical, social, emotional, or spiritual well-being."[37] Over the decades, definitions of trauma have evolved to emphasize the individual's level of distress rather than any objective measure of an event's severity, as well as to include secondhand experiences or witnessing of traumatic events and not just direct exposure. Scholars have also found utility in thinking about how some forms of trauma are cultural or collective and can shape the identity of an entire group or population in meaningful ways—including the way the history of chattel slavery has impacted Black identity.[38]

There has been an increasing interest—among educators, academics, and the general public—in understanding the frequency and short- and long-term effects of traumatic experiences for youth. An entire therapeutic niche has emerged around trauma-informed or trauma-sensitive workshops, trainings, consultants, books, and more—especially for schools.[39] It is encouraging that so much attention has turned to understanding how young people and their communities are shaped by histories of trauma and how institutions can better respond to their needs. At the same time, there are legitimate worries that the word and concept, *trauma*, have become so widespread and "watered down" as to hinder a helpful analysis and response.[40] In fact, *trauma* became the word of the year in 2018, and *The Body Keeps the Score*, a book about the effects of trauma on the body, spent most of 2021 at the top of the *New York Times* bestseller list. "TraumaTok" is booming, and one scholar has gone as far as to propose that we rename the generation of Americans enrolled in school since 2001 Generation T (or Gen T) for trauma.[41] "By relying on trauma to understand our modern lives," one journalist writes, "we're undercutting the very real impacts of stress and overwhelm. We're flattening all hardships, conflating the horrific and life-shattering with the merely unpleasant."[42]

Grief and trauma are, of course, linked, but they are not the same. A traumatic event can result in grief, but it does not have to; and one can grieve a loss that may or may not have been traumatic. But, compared to trauma, grief remains relatively neglected in our popular understanding and focus, especially as it relates to adolescents in their schools. Despite the clear and important overlaps between the concepts and experiences of trauma and grief, here I aim to highlight grief—in both its specificity and universality—for a group whose emotional lives are too often pushed into the shadows.

Just as I deliberately shift the focus from trauma to grief, I also intend to keep our attention on the aftermath of violent events for those in mourning rather than the more sensational stories of the violence itself. There is much valuable work by sociologists, criminologists, and others on the perpetrators of these shootings as well as effective violence prevention strategies, and I hope this strain of research continues to proliferate—especially given the stranglehold that existed for so long against federal funding for gun violence research.[43] But here I tell a quieter, more tender story of the grief that lingers and hides long after crime scenes are cleared.

The Book Ahead

This book presents a chronology of school life beginning on the Monday JahSun's friends and teachers returned to school after his death through the end of that school year. It is intended to be read in order and in full. I show the ways the grief of JahSun's friends and classmates played out in hallways, classrooms, conversations with friends in school and online, relationships with teachers, interactions with discipline policies and disciplinarians, grades and academic prospects. I observed these institutional experiences of and interactions around grief moving through three stages—the *easy hard*, the *hard hard*, and the *hidden hard*. In each stage, a set of competing expectations and pressures shaped the way boys experienced and expressed their grief and how their grief impacted their schooling, their relationships in school, and their ideas about themselves.

Faced with so much loss at so young an age, how would the boys cope? Would they have the space and the tools to grieve? And who would help them recover? Would their school and teachers—already tasked with compensating for structural inequalities that extend far beyond the domain of education—be able to build them back up as the losses and the violence in their lives kept mounting? And if the adults at school couldn't fully recognize the depths of their students' grief, how could they prepare them for their promised futures?

The book opens on the first Monday back at school after JahSun's death, which is seen from two perspectives, the students' and the adults'. In chapter 2, we see the acuteness of students' pain that day as they navigate school hallways and classrooms without JahSun. I tell the story of Hazeem and other boys as they interact with peers and teachers and memorialize JahSun. In chapter 3, after reviewing the staff's preparations for the resumption of school, we witness the day unfolding from the viewpoint of a school staff with no prior plans in place, limited resources, and who are pushing through an already challenging school year. Only in hindsight was it apparent that this was both the worst of times and the best of times, as the community came together to share their grief.

If Monday was the *easy hard*, what follows is the *hard hard*, as the school continues to grapple with ongoing grief for JahSun and a steady pattern of continued losses. Chapter 4 examines the expectations that bear down on the school, shaping the decisions to return to "normal" after just one day of collective grief. Facing pressures from multiple directions, administrators, teachers, and disciplinarians prioritize the school's college preparatory mission, leading to the neglect of some students' unresolved grief and a fractured, chaotic winter in school. In chapter 5, I document the *hidden hard* stage as grief moves further into the background of Boys' Prep daily life. The exclusion of critical aspects of students' emotional lives from school and the assumptions projected onto them of stoic resilience compels the boys to develop creative, yet furtive, modes of grieving out of view of many of the adults in their lives—often expressed through bodily practices and in peer-driven digital spaces. Yet for many, grief continues to show up in their peer relationships, on their report cards, and in the ways they engage with school and college planning. Nearing the end of an already devastating year, Boys' Prep is beset by two more deaths— sophomore Bill's murder during spring break and a former student murdered at a senior's Prom send-off party—reflecting a *repeated hard*. Chapter 6 details the way recurring losses take a toll on students' optimism for the future and lead to what I call social injuries, which are exacerbated by Boys' Prep's decontextualized education model that precludes opportunities for students' critical analysis of their social circumstances.

Did it have to unfold this way? In chapter 7, I consider responses to gun violence that occurred elsewhere in the country during the same year. A mass shooting that February at Marjory Stoneman Douglas School in Parkland, Florida, reframed the national conversation around gun violence—and put young people at the center. The transformation of adolescent grief into meaningful political grievance in communities across the country highlights an opportunity schools have to alleviate student suffering by enriching their political understanding and offering students a role in their communities and broader justice movements. Though this did not happen at Boys' Prep, the relationships some boys formed with their deceased friends' mothers illustrate another way that finding a purpose and a communal role to play can support healing. I close the book with reflections on possible ways forward, along with a brief update on some of the central characters you will meet.

It is easy from the outside (and even from within) to place blame, to see some people as part of the problem and others as victims, but the reality I saw was never that simple. The school and the people you will come to know on these pages were faced with a catastrophic, impossibly difficult set of circumstances. They did their utmost to stabilize themselves and support each other, but this is not really a redemptive story. It is a tale within a tale: of our society's stubborn failure to acknowledge the hidden toll of urban gun violence, and of the children whose lives it takes and transforms.[44] Ultimately, it invites us all to wrestle with the consequences of shooting deaths for Black boys, who experience so much loss, yet are denied the spaces to grieve; and to consider the role that our schools can and should play for them.

Some Final Notes for the Reader

Close readers may notice a few, perhaps unconventional, writing choices I have made, which I will address briefly here. First, I refer to the teenage students as *boys* rather than, for example, young men. Given the sordid history of the word *boy* being used to demean and humiliate Black men, I feel conflicted about this choice. Yet there is an equally wretched pattern of Black children being viewed as older than they are in ways that cause them harm.[45] Something is very wrong when a young person experiences the deaths of multiple peers. At the risk of turning off some readers (and I hope I'll win you back), I use the word *boy* to avoid the trap of adultification and to remind us constantly that it is *not normal* for *children* to die or for *children* to grieve each other.[46]

Second, to honor the memory of the deceased, JahSun's name has not been changed. Nor have Tyhir's and Bill's. I write in detail about how I came to this decision, in consultation with their parents, in the Author's Note. As is the custom in ethnographic work, however, all other proper names—including the names of students, teachers, and the school itself—have been altered. In images taken from participants' social media, names and Instagram handles have been changed to reflect those pseudonyms (all altered text is in yellow).[47]

Third, throughout the text, I quote from students' posts and messages on Instagram. In some cases, I have made minor edits to spelling, grammar, capitalization, or punctuation to increase legibility to a wider audience, but the majority of quotations are untouched. A glossary in appendix A includes contextual definitions of internet shorthand, local slang, and emojis.

Finally, I attempt in the pages ahead to offer a view of the experiences of the school community collectively—both students and adults—though I focus most on the boys because their critical formative years are most deeply etched by these losses, and their brave, vulnerable voices are often missing from our understanding of this problem. But schools never have a singular story. At any given time, hundreds if not thousands of interactions are taking place in classrooms, hallways, and offices, and among and between students, teachers, administrators, staff, and parents. Everyone's experiences in the days, weeks, and months following JahSun's death were different—and I only had one view—but I have tried to present the fullness, richness, and contradictions of a school filled with complex humans and layered interactions. Most scenes in the book come from my own observations, though some have been reconstructed through interviews with participants, social media posts, text and email exchanges, and other artifacts. I shared sections of this text with many participants to confirm my memories and reconstructions with theirs. All text in quotes represents words I heard or read directly.

*

Sunday night, less than two days after JahSun was killed, Hazeem was in his room trying to will himself to get some sleep. For him, and all the other boys at school, Monday would mean facing classrooms and hallways and cafeteria tables without their classmate. Before putting his phone down, Hazeem posted a final story to his Instagram: "tomorrow gonna be hard 💔😩."

Chapter Two

Silent Hallways, Shared Sorrow

For its students, Boys' Prep must often have felt rife with contradictions. Walking through the hallways, they were just as likely to see a student and teacher sitting together on the gray carpet having a heart-to-heart as to bump into a peer being kicked out of a classroom by a frustrated teacher. A building as full of warmth and care as it was of short tempers and *having it up to here*. Teachers would tell students they were committed to the school's mission and loved their "kids"; yet day to day they often felt overworked, underappreciated, unsure they were making a difference. For their part, most students didn't pick Boys' Prep (their parents did)—they would have been much happier attending a co-ed school without a uniform. But in private moments many admitted, begrudgingly, that they felt safe and loved, and that the real sense of brotherhood and close relationships with teachers made tolerable the imposition of the uniform and the gender isolation.

Typical Mondays bustled with boisterous adolescent energy and lots of noise: playful singing and laughing in the hallway, lockers screeching open and slamming shut. Adults would be shouting about untucked shirts and missing belts. In return, boys might suck their teeth, or talk back, or make the half-hearted sartorial adjustment, or run away giggling because they have this back-and-forth with Ms. So-and-So every day and they both know that compliance now will only be followed by an untucked shirt by the next period.

But this Monday morning, November 27, 2017, as the building re-

filled with teenage boys after the long Thanksgiving weekend, Boys'
Prep was eerily quiet. The expected animated greetings and lively
conversations about the holiday weekend were replaced with bowed
heads or nods, sometimes a long firm hug. Were the boys wondering what school could possibly provide when their feelings were so
immense? For months, memories of that morning would stick with
students. One senior recalled, "This school is never quiet. Everywhere,
there's some people being rowdy, big fighting, yelling . . . an all-boys
school type atmosphere," but on this day there was a "gloomy," "ghost
town" quiet in the building, unsettling and ominous.

The boys would find the day unbearably hard. But, as I will show in
this chapter, it was made easier by being together, by the leniency and
tenderness of school staff, and the ways the isolating experience of
grief was made collective. In this way, it was a day of contradictions.

Arriving at School

Hazeem had been alone in his room on Saturday when he learned
of JahSun's death. On Monday, grappling with ideas about mortality usually reserved for people decades older, he worried that being
at school would be difficult, but, he reasoned, stewing in his own
thoughts alone for another day would be far worse.

The late November morning was unseasonably warm. Hazeem
wore only a hooded sweatshirt over his school uniform. On the worn
strap of his backpack, #RIPTyhir was scribbled in Sharpie to mark the
memory of his first close friend who'd died, just after freshman year.
With both lost friends likely on his mind, Hazeem silently entered the
Boys' Prep building.

He was startled to see Bashir, JahSun's freshman brother.[1] Bashir
had spent the weekend watching his dad (the parent he shared with
JahSun) cycle through anger, sadness, and a multitude of unpleasant tasks, so even though Bashir did not have many close friends at
Boys' Prep, he thought being at school would be easier than spending
more time at home. He took the bus alone, arriving at his usual early

hour: 6:50 a.m. He was in perfect uniform, his compact body sway-
ing back and forth as he wandered the hallways, his eyes filled with
tears. Friends or teachers periodically stopped him with words or ges-
tures of condolence—as well as surprise that he was in school. One
teacher spent time comforting him before leaving to find the school
social worker, Ms. Rivera, hoping she had a plan for him.

Owen, JahSun's football teammate and close friend, arrived a full
hour before classes would begin. Normally the two boys would travel
part of the way to school together. Today, Owen headed to JahSun's
locker, near the end of the third-floor hallway: "It just felt, like, weird
for me to go to school on Monday. So when I came in and I went past
the locker, I just broke down." On Sunday, the locker had been fashioned into a memorial by a group of JahSun's friends. It would become
a site of gathering throughout the day. Memorial messages would
cover not only JahSun's locker, but the one below—and Owen's locker
several feet away: "I love you man," "rest easy, bro," "long live the general" (JahSun's nickname). Photographs of JahSun were interspersed
with slogans referencing the football team and JahSun's jersey number
18 (fig. 2.1). In the coming days and weeks, daily rituals developed
around the lockers; dozens of photos would be taken there and posted
to social media; meals would be eaten on the hallway floor.

But now, early Monday morning, Owen was alone, leaning against
the wall in tears. A faint hip-hop beat emanated from his earbuds. Earlier that morning, he had written a message to JahSun as a comment on
JahSun's final Instagram post: "Good morning bro 🖤 today gonna be
hard as hit but ima make it through for you 💯 nbs i miss you like crazy.
it's driving me insane. i just wanna wake up from this nightmare 🧎 💔
i told you ima come talk to you everyday and tell you how life going
💯 i love you bro 🖤." Owen vowed to talk to JahSun every day by
meditating at the locker and posting on social media.

Over the weekend, other students had used Instagram to begin
putting into words the depth and complexity of their confusion, shock,
anger, and sadness: "I'm lost, I don't know how to move past this" or
"I feel crazy, trying to be sane in a world full of fucked up shit."

Some reflected on recent memories of JahSun: "you always gave

Figure 2.1. JahSun's locker (and the one below it) covered in photographs and memorializing text. See Author's Note for a discussion of the related book cover image.

me advice," "we were just rapping," "I was just watching your football highlights," "you just dapped me up last week." Others looked ahead to experiences they would not get to share with their friend—"we don't get to graduate together"—and ways they would honor JahSun: "you'll live through me," "I'm gonna take [football] to a whole new level for you," "I'm not going to do anything dumb," "we gonna keep your name alive."

The School Day Begins

When the bell signaled the official start of the school day, Owen reluctantly pulled himself away from the locker and walked slowly down the hallway to the homeroom he'd shared with JahSun. This happened to be the first day of the second trimester, which meant new classes and teachers and often the chance for a fresh start. But today didn't have the energy of something beginning. In the classroom, a first-year science teacher awkwardly passed out the students' new printed schedules, deciding not to disturb students whose heads were down.

Homeroom was the first time students would hear an official acknowledgment from the school. The clear voice of Dr. Stephens, the school's CEO, came over the PA: "We lost a warrior over the weekend." In a tempered monotone he honored JahSun, sharing details of his achievements in school, sports, and art, and the mark he left on his friends and teachers. He encouraged everyone to look out for each other as a "supportive community of brothers." Dr. Stephens continued: "Some of you may find peace in the routine of the normal school day today. Others may need to talk with counselors and/or friends. Different people grieve differently, and we will have avenues for those differences throughout the day." After sharing logistics and the plan for a memorial vigil at the end of the day, he led a moment of silent reflection.

Slumped on a stool in the corner of the room, Owen's head was already bowed, his eyes closed, and his earbuds still in. A few minutes passed after the end of the announcements, and in this classroom, feeling JahSun's absence most acutely, these minutes were filled with total silence, interrupted only by Owen's sniffles. When the bell finally rang for first period, most students stayed glued to their chairs, many still with their heads down as if taking in the full sight of the room would confirm the reality that JahSun was gone. Eventually, I stood up and walked slowly toward the front of the classroom, prompting movement from the rest of the class. The guys wearily gathered their things and headed to the door, many leaving their new schedules behind untouched.

In his homeroom, Hazeem had listened intently to the announcements and now wasn't sure he was ready to focus on his classes. On his way downstairs, he again ran into Bashir, deciding in that moment to take him under his slightly older wing. Helping Bashir through the day might give him a sense of purpose and fill the seemingly endless hours until the afternoon vigil. In a message to me later that day, Hazeem reasoned that perhaps he and his friend Kaliq might, together, show Bashir ways to cope, keep him on track, and motivate him. Playing this role for JahSun's younger brother might "naturally motivate" them too. Together, Hazeem and Bashir ventured to the temporary grief counseling room in the basement.

An Empty Seat in Class

Meanwhile, classes were getting underway. It is unlikely that anyone expected much teaching or learning to happen, but there was a schedule to follow and eight periods to fill. I joined the Latin class JahSun would have been in. Most students were already in their seats, staring silently straight ahead or with their heads on their desks; some covered their ears with headphones or their eyes with sunglasses.

Ms. Kallum walked slowly to the front of the room, holding a thermos of coffee, and gently closed the door. Though only in her midthirties, with youthful blond hair reaching down her back, Ms. Kallum's wisdom, calm, and maternal energy made her seem older. She walked the aisles, checking in on each of her students: "You guys think we should have class today? It's up to you." Hearing no response, she returned to the back of the room, took out a big box of cookies, and began walking the aisles again. During the few seconds it took each student to grab cookies from the box, Ms. Kallum seemed to be gauging his mood.

Addressing the class, she asked: "How was your Thanksgiving? What did you eat?" A few guys started responding, and she nudged the conversation forward with more questions, keeping an eye on the quieter students. At one point, noticing tears in the eyes of a student in the back row, she grabbed a box of tissues and walked it back to him without missing a beat in the exchange.

"Want to talk or watch a movie?" Ms. Kallum finally suggested. "The silence is kinda weird," offered one student opting for the movie. Ms. Kallum started running through options from her Netflix account;

the few talkative students agreed on the kids' movie *Sing*. Some students moved closer to the front to see the screen better, while others remained occupied by their own inner worlds of sorrow. Even Ms. Kallum's tenderness and care could not break through to them that morning.

Though Ms. Kallum was no doubt one of the most sensitive and thoughtful teachers JahSun's friends encountered that day, cookies and tissues could only do so much. In one of the many contradictions they faced that day, the boys in a school dedicated to preparing them for promising academic futures were also now acutely attuned to the threat of gun violence cutting their futures short.

Social Support

One floor below, a basement classroom had been designated as the counseling room, likely because it was relatively private, sharing a hallway with only one other classroom, and relatively tranquil, with carpeting and dark curtains covering several of the windowless walls. Ms. Rivera, the school social worker, and Ms. Gallo, a college counselor, took shifts, but two therapists from a local anti-violence organization ran the show. Their job was to travel the city, visiting schools after tragedies. Their services were offered free or low-cost to the schools, but in a city with up to forty youth homicides a year, they were stretched thin, their visits generally limited to just a day, with continued counseling available to only a handful of students identified by Ms. Rivera.[2]

The therapists, white women in their twenties, were kind and empathetic, but they were strangers to the students and the school. Their plan was to assess whoever arrived each period and either run a grief circle or talk informally with individual boys. Hazeem and Bashir arrived during first period and stayed for several periods. Just a trickle of other students came throughout the day—mostly younger students for whom JahSun's death had triggered lingering feelings of grief about another loss, rather than JahSun's closest friends.

The therapists asked each student to share how they knew JahSun—though mispronouncing his name as Ja-Shun, like the misspelling in the initial news stories. Unfazed by the mistake, Bashir talked at length about his father's reaction to JahSun's death and his own retreat into his journal where he sometimes wrote poetry. Bashir could vacillate quickly between being shy and soft-spoken to very talkative, depending on the topic. He mentioned that he'd just seen a classmate's Instagram post commenting on how "depressed" everyone was at school. Bashir was hurt; didn't this student know he was grieving the murder of his big brother? The therapists nodded empathetically.

Hazeem also shared how he was processing the death of his friend. Not knowing either boy, all the therapists could offer was generic advice like "things will get more challenging" or three critical coping strategies: talk to people, drink water, and get sleep. One therapist suggested staying off social media if they found it too upsetting or triggering.

As the group circle started winding down, one of the therapists showed Hazeem an exercise he could use when he "blacked out," as he described it: "Notice three things you see, three things you feel, one thing you taste, and one thing you smell. You try. What are three things you see?" Hazeem smiled: "I see therapists, teachers, and a desk." With a bit of prodding, he got through the rest of the list of sensations. Then Hazeem shrugged, "I probably won't use it."

One of the most destructive effects of rigid ideas of masculinity for Black boys is the stigma around sharing complex emotions, asking for help, or engaging with mental health support.[3] Growing up in neighborhoods with socioeconomic deprivation can necessitate the performance of a "cool pose," adherence to the "code of the street," or other strategies of "emotional suppression," but Black boys and men of all class backgrounds are often expected to be invulnerable, to project toughness and emotional stoicism, and to be strong—even in grief.[4] Hazeem and Bashir's willingness to engage with the visiting counselors, share their own emotional experience, and at least listen to therapeutic advice shows an alternative to these masculine codes is possible. It also signals that, despite the pressures of Black masculinity, there are many boys willing and wanting to share deeply and vulnerably, even with a stranger, if offered the opportunity.[5]

Though Hazeem had been undeterred by the stigma of the counseling room, the counselors' attention and advice had failed to ease the acuteness of his anguish. By late morning, his worst fears about the day seemed to be panning out. He started tuning out the counselors who continued to offer him coping skills to practice. Shaking and tensing up, he abruptly stood and walked into the hallway. All the loneliness and confusion of facing his grief with just the network of peers through his phone, the fears of being back in school without his friend, the anger that this seemed to keep happening, and the frustration that well-meaning counselors and teachers couldn't take away his pain finally exploded. He threw all his body weight behind his fist into a metal locker.

Jolted by the noise of the reverberating metal, the team of women back in the classroom got to their feet. Within seconds, Hazeem was surrounded by the two visiting counselors, Ms. Gallo, and Ms. Rivera, who ushered him back to a seat and began comforting him and tending to his bruised and bleeding knuckles. An hour or so later, Hazeem messaged me through Instagram, asking me to find him. Perhaps because I was an outsider in a school where he often felt marginalized and I regularly had the time to listen, Hazeem had come to rely on me as a safe person he could open up to. He was one of the few students who regularly called or texted me on weekends or evenings to update me on something that had happened when I was not in school, or to vent about a problem. Every couple of weeks he would ask if we could do another "interview," which he seemed to find therapeutic. That morning he wrote, "I'm really losing it" and told me he had punched the lockers again. I found him in the counseling room, where he lamented, "I was just getting myself together then this happened." Switching gears from his own grief to JahSun, he continued, "If you do the right things, it seem like it's still hard to survive."

Hazeem hoped his friend Kaliq could cheer him up. He and Kaliq lived near each other, shared a lunch table nearly every day their freshman and sophomore years, and had grieved Tyhir's loss together. When I met the pair, Kaliq seemed to have more social status at Boys' Prep, but was a loyal friend to Hazeem. Kaliq has the look of a football player, stocky but yet to grow into his full height, and always had intentions to try out for the school's team to play with JahSun, but work and home responsibilities kept him from it.

That day Kaliq was going through his own complicated emotional journey. Just a few months earlier, he had learned that JahSun was a distant cousin, which had tremendously strengthened their bond. In recent weeks, Kaliq had come to play a protective role for JahSun, who had been nursing a knee injury that made him somewhat immobile; at JahSun's request, Kaliq had traveled home with him a few times to "watch his back." With five younger siblings, Kaliq was practiced in the protector role. He was known to most of his friends, especially Hazeem, as a dependable guy in a pinch.

Today, Hazeem was craving that protection. His hand bruised from punching the lockers, Hazeem went to look for Kaliq. He found his friend in a classroom, head on the table, his blazer pulled up, fully covering his close-cropped hair.

Kaliq had voiced his grief and anger through online posts over the weekend, describing the way this loss, on top of other recent losses, put him "back in pieces." He wrote, "Idk how to recuperate from this shit dawg! I'm really broken all up man! Back to back to back losses 🧍🏾 tell me when Ima win god 😮‍💨." He had begun the day trying to keep a normal routine, staying emotionally strong and focused, but found himself needing time alone before he could get there. As he recounted later,

I came in, I'm like, alright, they gave us the option of going in the [counseling] room and like being around like a bunch of friends and stuff like that, talking about it and all that, or go to class and try to be normal and go through it like that. So I said, "I can't sit around and cry and stuff, and then fall back on school, so I'm gonna go to class." So I tried to go to class. Then it was just like, the teachers are looking sad, they was saying his name and stuff, "rest in peace, we lost JahSun" on the loudspeaker, it just hit me like, "yo, this is really real." So I started crying in class, I just had to step out first two periods . . . I sat in the office, you know, clearing my mind . . . Wipe my tears all away, clear my head, all of that. Right back to class, and just finish my day out like that.

Kaliq didn't want to sit around talking about his feelings. Hazeem needed his friend, but he understood that Kaliq needed something different. Hazeem sulked back to the counseling room, resisting his urge to punch the lockers again.

Comfort in Community

Elsewhere in the building, students were gathering comfort from being in community with peers. In the empty mid-morning cafeteria, a group of seniors were in study hall in a lighter mood. Some were on their laptops doing schoolwork, while others had given up on the prospect of productivity and were just chatting. One proudly passed out tissues from a stack he had stealthily procured. Two students grabbed the precious resource to blow their noses. Eric took a single tissue from his friend, neatly folded it, and placed it in his pocket as he said with a cautious smile, "I'm saving this for the candlelight"—referring to his expectation of sadness at the afternoon vigil.

Another group of seniors were back at JahSun's locker planning the final components of the event, unsure who might give a speech. Khalil worried he would not be able to keep it together. Rajae had already started rehearsing things he might say to honor JahSun and cheer up his friends. He had lived too far away to come the day before to help with the locker decorations, but visited JahSun's mom on Sunday instead.

The ghost-town atmosphere of the morning gradually gave way to more energy. Ezekiel, one of several boys who described themselves as JahSun's "best friend," had taken off his tie, a compulsory part of the Boys' Prep uniform, and turned it into a headband. His grief seemed to be manifesting in silliness as he, Rajae, Khalil, and Theo hung around by the locker pulling up funny pictures and videos of JahSun on their phones. As this core group stood watch over the decorated locker and tried to lighten the mood, Owen continued staring into space and listening to music, not ready to make his grief social.

Theo, a football teammate, was thinking about the unfairness of what they were going through. Over the last six months, he had also lost two young cousins and an uncle. He thought about other people his age who might get to celebrate an older family member's ninety-third birthday, while his friend wouldn't graduate from high school and his cousin wouldn't see the birth of his daughter. Since learning about JahSun, Theo had been getting headaches and having trouble falling asleep, but reminiscing about the good times was providing some solace.

The boys found humor in these moments too. At one point, Bashir came by on a mission to correct a message he had written earlier on the locker; his mom had pointed out a misspelling when he sent her a picture. JahSun's friends greeted him warmly, calling him "little brother." He accepted their affection with a hearty smile, and then turned to the task at hand: he had written to his brother, "you're still not a better raper than me," though he had meant to write "rapper," referring to JahSun's budding musical career and Bashir's interest in poetry. The older boys hadn't noticed the error, but laughed heartily once they saw Bashir correcting it.

Emerging School Rituals of Mourning

At some point, word spread that Ms. Kallum had candy in her room. After migrating to procure the sweets, the group from JahSun's locker discovered that she had set up a small memorial, with a split-open football labeled "Notes for JahSun." On the table beside a lit candle was a stack of small note papers. Whereas early in the morning the classroom had been almost completely silent, now the crowded room had new energy. The lights were off and cartoons were playing at low volume on the big screen at the front, but about a dozen boys were bunched in the back eating candy and dropping messages into the football.

Boys scribbled notes like "I remember when I first met you . . . at summer academy. Ever since then you've been a brother to me. Gone but never forgotten." And "Rest in peace Jah. I'm going to miss bidding with you in class." Theo confessed to those in earshot, "it's like my 11th note" as he gracefully folded a piece of paper and put it inside the football.

In a science classroom upstairs, two young teachers, Ms. Thompson and Ms. Abadi, set up a shrine-like table with candles and colorful writing supplies. Students used the construction paper to write longer messages to JahSun's family or directly to their friend. They recalled memories of JahSun and acknowledged their own grief. They described JahSun as a "beloved person [and] a lovable friend," "the most positive and outgoing guy I've known," and "a role model . . . even though he was younger than me." In a simultaneously amusing and poignant "sidenote" at the end of one letter, a student committed to stop cheating on his girlfriend because that is what JahSun, while alive, had told him to do.

Some students shared messages acknowledging that, though they had not personally known JahSun, they still felt his loss deeply and wanted to offer sincere condolences to his family. One said JahSun's death made him think "that it could be any one of us that can be killed. It is also sad—and hard understanding and comprehending that you can be killed even in the most safest place." That student committed to look out for Bashir since he no longer had an older brother. Other boys offered advice to the family: "I hope that you guys don't put the blame on yourselves," "I just want you to know it's okay to be sad," or "I hope that through all this pain that you think about all the good times and keep hope alive."

A few students put JahSun's death in the context of other losses, or shared their views on how the community could better support and protect each other. Some even blamed themselves or their peers: "As a school, I feel as though we need to do better at helping people become better men. Over the summer of last year, two people died, then someone got arrested, and now more people are being killed. It is sad to watch family die. I have seen so many people die and it make me feel bad that I can't do anything about it. We need to keep up with each other as students because teachers can't keep up with every student after school." The boys' analyses of what had happened to JahSun and how efforts by the school community could make a difference were rich and nuanced. Held inside, their grief, confusion, and fear could fester, but perhaps the chance to write offered some immediate relief. Across the school, space and time devoted to collective mourning seemed to be helping in the moment. Students took advantage of the range of options: to be alone, talk with counselors or friends, or attempt some sliver of normal routines.

Yet the plans for Monday and beyond did not include space for students' critical analysis—the kind just beginning to emerge in these written messages—to be shared out loud or shaped through discussion. While students expressed somber feelings of powerlessness to prevent the violence that took their friends away, the impromptu school rituals of mourning prioritized immediate comfort.

A Rite of Passage

At lunchtime, the building itself seemed to exhale. Though the hallways and classrooms still lacked the typical Monday chatter and buzz, the freedom of movement and the large gatherings of both students and adults over lunch started to shift the mood. I found Yaja standing surreptitiously outside the teachers' lounge—a large kitchenette off the cafeteria—waiting for an adult to offer to microwave the Ramen noodle cup he'd brought from home. I heated Yaja's noodles and my own lunch and then rejoined him.

Yaja had been the one to introduce me to JahSun a year earlier and was the first to text me the news of his death. We leaned against the wall as we ate, looking out across the sea of students. "I never cried so much in my life," he said about finding out about JahSun. Yaja had recently lost another close friend in a road rage shooting that garnered a lot of local press. The two losses seemed to blend, each magnifying the devastation of the other. Thanks to an invitation from the school social worker, Yaja participated in a weekly counseling session led by a pair of Black male counselors from a local nonprofit. Though the men spent a lot of time talking *at* the boys—and sometimes Yaja didn't really feel like talking—he found it helpful and reassuring, and was looking forward to their meeting on Wednesday to help him process.

A small group joined us. Larry looked dazed. He told us this was his first real loss, the "first person I really connected to who died . . . It makes me cherish moments more, not want to walk around all angry." Though teenagers growing up in contexts of more privilege may never experience the death of a peer until adulthood, for Black boys in neighborhoods where gun violence is prevalent, the first loss is a kind of rite of passage. And most youth don't expect only one.[6]

Emmet explained that he was "all cried out by 4th period." Yaja countered: "There's more crying in me, actually . . . At the vigil, I'm gonna die." Earlier that morning, Dr. Stephens had showed him the slideshow they would be playing during the vigil. Seeing a photograph of JahSun with angel wings, his costume for a school play, "I just lost it."

This was a group of seniors not as visibly associated with JahSun as the crew camped out by the lockers, but they still felt close to their lost friend (see appendix B.1 for a visualization of the students' friendship circles). Yet, already it was apparent that Yaja and his friends would not be receiving the same public recognition of their loss. They had not been invited to the school the day before to decorate the locker. Nor had any of them been asked to speak at the vigil. On Monday, the school was experiencing collective grief, but a nascent division between recognized and unrecognized grievers was beginning to surface, which later would prove more consequential.

Varied, but Shared, Burdens

After lunch, Yaja, Larry, and Emmet made their way to Ms. Cain's Honors Philosophy class—a class they had shared with JahSun. With no standard curriculum for high school philosophy and no statewide test, Ms. Cain had freedom to teach in innovative ways and engage topics that connected directly to students' daily lives. They held weekly Socratic seminars on such topics as masculinity, happiness, and memory. Some students reflected that it was the only class where they actually had to *think*.

As the students took their seats, Ms. Cain sat on a desk facing the class, a more informal post than usual. She acknowledged that it probably was not easy for most of them to get to school, but she appreciated them being there, in part, because it was helping her: "Being alone was hard and I was looking forward to being back at school and seeing all of you." A few boys noticed that a tear fell down her cheek as she spoke. They had seen more teachers cry that day than ever before.

Ms. Cain's classroom had become a community. The teacher from the room next door did not want to spend her free period alone and sat in the last row. When Bashir and Hazeem wandered in, knowing it had been one of JahSun's favorite classes, Ms. Cain gestured that they could stay.

As the students listened quietly and compassionately, Ms. Cain shared her impressions of JahSun as a kind, thoughtful, and understated person and a good writer, and then asked the class if it was okay to read a piece of his writing from a recent assignment. "That's perfectly fine," one student called out from the back. The room fell silent as she read from JahSun's handwritten essay about his commitment to picking up others when they were down.

When she finished, Ms. Cain emphasized the gift of his words, but also shared her view that right now "It's okay to be down, it's okay to be sad." With no formal lesson for the day, she was, in a sense, modeling for them how to grieve. She continued, "This is a tough time for me, and I know it's a tough time for you. And we're sharing those burdens together." Despite her empathy, she could not relate to the identity threats and vulnerability this kind of loss produced for the students. But to her credit, Ms. Cain was committed to learning. "One of the things I want to find out is how do we want to—how are we gonna take care of each other this week, how are we going to take care of ourselves?" She had created a short survey for her students about how they were feeling and what they might need from her and the class. She offered them the option to work on it silently or talk to each other, whatever felt good to them.

Students' survey responses represented a range of reactions to loss, from one who would "appreciate if we discussed dealing with the death of a loved one," to another who preferred that they "went along business as usual." One wanted to "hang around in groups more so that I won't have to be alone during this time," while another requested "individual work instead of working in groups." Some wanted people to check in on them and ask how they were doing; others preferred not to be asked too many questions. Many expressed that they might find it harder than usual to "focus," "concentrate," share openly, or have their usual energy or good humor. Several requested that their positive memories of JahSun be incorporated into the class and that they all find ways to keep him present in the classroom. The distinction between Yaja's and Larry's experience was echoed here, with some boys saying they felt especially overwhelmed because of multiple back-to-back losses while others were not sure what they needed because this was new to them. Despite these differences, sharing their desires with others made their grief communal, a burden to be supported by their teacher and the classroom community.

The Vigil

When the last period ended, students ventured downstairs to find the cafeteria transformed. The large basement space, which doubled as the school's auditorium and sports practice facility, was set up for the vigil. All sports and club meetings had been canceled; this was the only afternoon activity, open to anyone who wanted to participate. A hundred or so chairs faced the makeshift stage and screen. A perimeter of cafeteria tables held poster boards, white paper bags, and

markers. Fluorescent lights that just a few hours earlier had energized
the lunch periods had been selectively turned off, giving the cavernous
space a sense of calm. The projector looped a slideshow of photographs of JahSun as the room began to fill with students, teachers, and
several of JahSun's family members. Some began writing messages on
the large poster paper, but most quietly took their seats. An overflow of
at least thirty people stood in the back. One student found it especially
gratifying "to see how many people actually cared about [JahSun]."

Mr. Donaldson, the principal, welcomed JahSun's family and acknowledged the heaviness of why everyone had gathered: "We have
lost a special part of our community. We come here today to honor
JahSun, to celebrate his light that shines here today despite our darkness . . . We are here to acknowledge we will need each other in the
days and weeks ahead and find strength in the community where
JahSun loved his brothers well and was loved by them in return." Mr.
Donaldson passed the microphone to Dr. Stephens, the CEO, who
echoed similar sentiments and introduced a Philadelphia state senator who had reached out to the school. A Black man in his sixties, he
spoke directly to the boys, trying to motivate them to use this tragedy
to drive their own futures. He reminded them that JahSun's death was
not an isolated incident, but connected to bigger structural issues and
the social conditions they all faced:

Black men . . . die in record numbers, but they also don't talk to one another in moments of pain. They don't bond together, lean on one another.
But, by definition, that's what makes us stronger, when we bond together,
when we lean on each other . . . That expression of tears or whatever you
may have, the emotion that you are filled with, will make you a man.
And that moment will allow you to go forward as a man, amongst men,
to lead them.

This may have been the first time all day an adult had publicly connected JahSun's death to larger patterns of racialized violence and
oppression—and encouraged students to do something with their

pain. The senator concluded by encouraging the boys to deal with whatever anger they felt "in ways the rest of the country doesn't expect." The senator's words made explicit the messages boys had been getting implicitly throughout the day about community, brotherhood, and support—as well as the value of processing grief intentionally so it does not emerge later in destructive ways.

The formal event concluded with an invitation to write messages on white luminary bags. Knowing that staying busy was his best bet for keeping himself together, Kaliq had volunteered to help two teachers fill each bag with sand and a tea light.

Attendees formed a line out of the cafeteria and onto the school's field. The sun was setting, and the temperature had dropped. As the mourners gathered, they placed their candlelit bags on the grass forming a large "J." JahSun's family and dozens of students and faculty encircled the glowing initial. Rajae bravely entered the circle to give a short speech about what JahSun meant to him and his friends. A few others followed, after which a few of JahSun's family members spoke. As the sun dipped behind the low Philadelphia rowhouses and the sky filled with pinks and purples, a few mourners released balloons in JahSun's favorite colors. Dozens of boys raised their phones to capture the scene in photos and videos, many of them uploading their images directly to Instagram with versions of the rallying cry, Long Live Jah.

A long moment of silence was punctuated by audible crying from the crowd and honking from cars driving by. Emmet, who had thrown a pot at the wall when he got the news a few days earlier, told me, "The vigil was crazy. [My friend] was holding on to me, and he was hugging me, and when I'm crying the worst thing somebody can do is touch me—it just all comes out . . . and it overflows." Upon reflection, the release was good for him, making the pain "slowly start to become smaller and smaller." Another student echoed that "it felt a lot better after the candlelight."

After a day of small memorials embedded into the usual school structures—lockers, PA announcements, classroom reflections—this ritual was separate from the school day. As successful communal rituals do, it produced a renewed sense of brotherhood and positive emotions, even as it marked a tragic occasion.[7] The gathering made most students feel comforted and more deeply connected to each other and the school.

When the ceremony concluded, students slowly made their way back into the building to gather their things. Yaja went to the bathroom to change into his Chick-fil-A uniform—he had to go straight to work. Hazeem and Kaliq headed to the bus stop; staying together was important since it was late for their long trek home.

One group of JahSun's friends remained on the field, drawing comfort from the solidarity and shared emotional energy. All the contradictions of the day encapsulated in this small moment between Owen, Ezekiel, Khalil, Rajae, Theo, and a handful of others: sorrow and release; the isolation and community of grief; the desire to stay in the moment, even in acute pain. They took pictures, sang and rapped songs that reminded them of JahSun, and grasped each other tightly. One would start the Boys' Prep football chant, and they all huddled close as they repeated it. Each time the revelry seemed to be dying down, someone would revive it with an inside joke, a new song, or a suggestion for another group photo. Perhaps they intuitively knew that once this evening concluded and they went home, tomorrow would be a different kind of day.

*

Though this late November Monday began with a convergence of students' fears, anxieties, and devastation, as the day progressed, the possibilities of what a school can be for its community came into view as the networks of students, teachers, and administrators united in hallways, classrooms, and out on the field. They shared the horror of what had happened and the challenges of figuring out how to move forward. They showed up to be together in a place that was about more than just learning and was, at least for the day, focused primarily on what was going on in students' hearts. The strengths of this small community were visible in the spaces students carved out for their grief, and in the messages they wrote on cards, luminary bags, and lockers. They could be felt in the prolonged hugs and hands held in a circle at the vigil. And heard in students' conversations about loss and confessions about grief that countered conventional expectations of Black boys as stoic and numb to emotion. Despite what the boys might have feared about the difficulty of the day, they showed up at school and the school showed up for them.

Chapter Three

A School Prepared— And Not

THE EASY HARD

Although it only became clear to me later how progressively difficult things would get, Mr. Hopkins, the vice principal, seemed to have realized it right away. As I waited to microwave Yaja's instant noodles that Monday lunch, I thought Mr. Hopkins looked frazzled. This was not unusual: he often scurried out of the teachers' lounge once his lunch was hot and nibbled at it while pacing the cafeteria to monitor student behavior. Now, as he watched the digital countdown on his Tupperware of leftovers circling inside the microwave, he reflected— half to himself and half to the handful of teachers in earshot—that today would be "the *easy* hard day, tomorrow the *hard* hard day . . . and beyond is the hardest."

Did any of us in the room fully appreciate the profundity of his prediction? Certainly, in that moment, I did not.

New to Boys' Prep, with only three months under his belt, Mr. Hopkins had, upon hearing of JahSun's death that weekend, felt "hopelessness" mixed with "wanting to feel useful." He had already experienced untimely student death at previous institutions, but never a murder or death by gunfire. The best he could find, ransacking his files for guidance, were two crisis plans for student/staff deaths, both shared with him years ago: one from Fairbanks, Alaska; the other, more than a decade old, from Madison, Wisconsin.[1] It is likely that such manuals exist for every school district, on file somewhere at every school.

They provide generic instructions for handling "critical incidents" and protocols for securing "safety and security," the "dissemination of accurate information" to various stakeholders, and supporting "the emotional and psychological needs of all parties."[2]

At first, the documents gave Mr. Hopkins a sense of order and structure, but they were not the road map he needed for handling this unspeakable tragedy. Neither manual said anything about the specific experience of boys like Hazeem, Yaja, Owen, or Kaliq, grappling with the sudden, violent death of a peer in a city where their own race, gender, and class situate them to fear the same fate.

In the previous chapter, I narrated the return to school in the fog of loss from the perspective of JahSun's grieving friends and classmates. This chapter will look at the day from the perspective of school leaders and teachers to better understand how Monday unfolded as it did, and how the school staff reflected on it as they planned for the harder days ahead.

The Slow Trickle of Information

The initial news of JahSun's death moved much more slowly through the networks of adults at Boys' Prep than among the students. A handful of teachers with especially close connections to students heard, as I did, through a direct text message or call. A few younger millennial teachers who followed the Instagram pages of students or alumni found out—like most of their students—when they opened Instagram for a casual scroll or to share their own Thanksgiving photos. Among senior staff—administrators, counselors, and several longtime teachers—a phone tree spread the news, abruptly terminating the holiday weekend. It was time to plan the school's response.

Even as administrators were still gathering information about JahSun, they felt a pressing need to alert the school community in a systematic way. Dr. Stephens, the recently promoted CEO, and the new principal, Mr. Donaldson, traded drafts of an email to faculty, a separate message to the parent and student community, and an announcement for the school website. A light-skinned biracial Black man, Dr. Stephens has an imposing presence at well over six feet tall, but his sweet demeanor becomes apparent as soon as he smiles or begins to converse. Mr. Donaldson, white and in his late thirties, was the school's first non-Black principal; before his promotion, he had been chair of the math department and a basketball coach. The two men contemplated opening the school on Sunday for an impromptu community gathering but nixed the idea when they could not immediately reach JahSun's family.

At the same time, a small group of veteran teachers who had been at the school between four and ten years was processing the rapidly evolving story. Ms. Cain, Ms. Finn, Ms. Neal, and Ms. Redmond communicated regularly through an iMessage group affectionately titled "Work Ladies." White women in their thirties, they taught history, English, and Latin, and usually used their text thread to vent about teaching frustrations, celebrate wins in the classroom, swap funny stories about students or colleagues, or simply share personal updates. But Saturday afternoon they were talking about the news— noting the misspelling of JahSun's name in the paper, seething at racist comments from anonymous online posters speculating on what gang activity JahSun might have engaged in to bring on his murder, and wondering when the administration would share something official.

Fresh in their minds was Tyhir's death two summers earlier. Each of them had watched their young students work through grief at the loss of this spirited and well-liked boy who had barely begun high school. Since he'd died in summer, they had not had to develop lesson plans for the rawest days and weeks that followed, but they had all observed the impact on Tyhir's friends in the fall: increased anger, hopelessness, and worry about their own deaths; disengagement from and disinvestment in school; and difficulty communicating their feelings.

Ms. Cain remembered JahSun's own vulnerable reaction to Tyhir's death. JahSun's openness, his willingness to bring himself honestly into the classroom, was one of the things many teachers admired about him. He was the kind of student about whom teachers passed on praise and insight to colleagues who would have him the following year. Ms. Finn, JahSun's tenth-grade World History teacher, had given Ms. Cain the heads-up to look out for him in eleventh-grade US History: an especially thoughtful and smart student who might fly under the radar because he was not boastful or showy about his intelligence. As Ms. Cain had gotten to know JahSun, she had come to understand the central role the deaths of friends played in his life. Now the rest of her students were facing *his* untimely death.

It was almost evening when Principal Donaldson finally hit send on the official message to the Boys' Prep students and their parents. He had not yet had time to process the loss emotionally himself, but the message needed to go out. The letter was empathetic, acknowledging that this would surely be a difficult time for the whole community and that emotional responses of any kind were okay. Perhaps betraying his own insecurity about how to handle the crisis, as well as how he might be perceived as the school's first white leader, the new principal wrote much of the letter in the passive voice, even avoiding the first person to describe his own role in planning the school's response. Just three months into his new position, and replacing a beloved Black predecessor, it would be understandable to be uncertain of his readiness to lead 450 Black boys through this moment of unexpected tragedy—on top of the challenges he was already juggling at the helm of a school with ambition that often far exceeded its resources.

In the message to his staff, Mr. Donaldson projected more confidence but few specifics. The principal encouraged his colleagues to care for and support each other, conveying the idea that there was no right way to grieve and no specific expectation of how they should conduct themselves or their classes on Monday. To the extent that he offered details about Monday's plan, they were about basic school-wide logistics rather than advice for lesson planning or forecasts of the specific needs of JahSun's friends. Mr. Donaldson concluded with a request that the entire staff gather for an emergency meeting at 7:30 a.m. on Monday.

Making It Up as They Went Along

The school leadership was not prepared to deal with tragedy like this. The very premise of the school was to keep neighborhood events of this kind *out* of school life; to give poor kids a prep-school-style education divorced from the social suffering that too often accompanies urban poverty. The hope of the school's founders was to provide Black boys from Philly the tools and opportunities to go to college and build an upwardly mobile life where street violence was no longer a concern. At Boys' Prep, and other Black Male Academies like it, a "repeated refrain [was] that 'we are in a struggle with the streets.'"[3] The school's policies and practices tried to shut out the problems of the neighborhood, decontextualizing the education happening in the building from the students' daily lives outside school in an effort to help them focus on the future.[4]

Mr. Hopkins lamented to me later that the handbooks he consulted contained protocols for administrative actions rather than strategies for supporting a school community's emotional needs. One handbook encouraged administrators to "determine friends impacted," but said nothing about what to do for them. Other guidance countered his instincts—like the suggestion that schools "discourage any dramatization, memorial services, PA announcements, or closing the school for the funeral."[5]

For all the sensitivity and concern they brought to the moment, most Boys' Prep staff had no direct experience with the violent death of a current student during the school year—a "long stretch of luck" in the school's ten-year history, as Dr. Stephens later reflected. Now they would have to deal with the immediate emotional aftermath and consider both short- and long-term curricular and policy plans. With little relevant professional guidance, and no plans already in place, the team had to figure it out in the moment.

Ms. Gallo, for example, a young white college counselor, was just a few years into her tenure at the school. Though initially trained as a guidance counselor, she was hired at Boys' Prep as one of two college counselors to support students' college preparation, applications, and decisions. In this moment of schoolwide crisis, she felt needed, but also nervous to be thrust into a role she had never previously assumed. Scouring her notes from graduate school and the internet for helpful resources, she found, on a website managed by the Coalition to Support Grieving Students, a four-page handout with suggestions for things teachers might say to comfort students. The document reminded teachers to "expect a range of responses" and to "be present and authentic . . . listen more, talk less . . . avoid trying to 'cheer up' students . . . accept expressions of emotion . . . [and] show empathy."

Cutting their weekend short, a team of administrators and teachers gathered at the school on Sunday morning. A skeletal outline for Monday was already taking shape, but now they had to scramble to flesh it out. Dr. Stephens took charge of the meeting. Though it gave him what he described as a "false . . . sense of control over something that is totally out of control," he was glad to be with colleagues after spending the previous day working the phones, planning and fretting alone.

Dr. Stephens began delegating grim tasks like removing JahSun from class rosters and online school records, as well as notifying his coaches and the colleges to which he had applied. One person volunteered to collect pictures of JahSun for a memorial page in the yearbook. The group scripted the Monday PA announcements and kept a running list of issues to be discussed at the morning faculty meeting. Someone had to rearrange the complex schedule of classes and classrooms to free up a room for grief counselors. Ms. Rivera—the school's social worker and only staff member devoted to students' emotional well-being, though not a certified counselor—communicated with several local nonprofits that offered these services. Ms. Gallo photocopied the handout she had found to pass out to her colleagues.

The administrative team began envisioning the vigil. This was one way, the group decided, the school could involve JahSun's family in what JahSun's mother wished would be a "celebration" with JahSun's "Boys' Prep family." The team prioritized creating physical and temporal spaces for the collective recognition of loss and expressions of grief. They developed one-time rituals, but did not have the time, experience, or guidance to think much more than a day ahead in terms of students' needs.

Ms. Redmond had been sharing updates all morning in the "Work Ladies" chat, since her long tenure at the school and her role as alumni coordinator made her an honorary administrator and a part of the group gathered at the school Sunday. She asked the text group for help coming up with a reading for the vigil, one of her delegated tasks. By afternoon, the four women were sharing ideas of what they would do in their classes on Monday. Ms. Neal was brainstorming ways to support another English teacher who was new to the school and had been teaching both JahSun and his younger brother.

Ms. Cain was quiet on the group chat, allowing herself space to grieve. That morning she had poked around PowerSchool, the online platform used for student grading and administrative records, to piece together JahSun's life at Boys' Prep: his ID picture, his past teachers, his grades. She discovered she had misremembered his performance in her class the year before, thinking he had done better than he had. She was also worrying about how to navigate her philosophy class, which was supposed to start a new unit on the philosophy of happiness on Monday.

Other teachers were planning for Monday in different ways. Ms. Kallum, JahSun's Latin teacher and an advisor to the senior class, took an extra trip to the grocery store to have boxes of cookies on hand for Monday. Two young science teachers, who shared a classroom on the second floor, coordinated to bring candles and writing supplies for their memorial table.

Even with all these preparations, most teachers felt apprehensive about Monday. They had chosen a profession dedicated to the bright future of children. How, then, to get through a day that darkened it?

The Final Stages of Planning

Ms. Bloom, a science teacher, thought to connect with JahSun's closest friends right away—both to find out what they needed and to include them in planning the vigil. Although she held no formal administrative role, Ms. Bloom had likely been invited to the Sunday meeting as a liaison to the seniors. She had come to Boys' Prep four years earlier through Teach For America and had quickly developed a reputation as a caring and involved teacher. Ms. Bloom is white and grew up in a working-class neighborhood in Philadelphia that she described as somewhat similar to the neighborhood where Boys' Prep is located. Young, hip, and utterly devoted to her students, Ms. Bloom would decorate her classroom each year with a new collage of photos of students and alumni, regularly attend Boys' Prep sports games to cheer on her students, and generously offer rides or meals when students were in a pinch. (It was these practices that made her the favorite teacher of many students, though some of her colleagues thought it was too much.) Ms. Bloom had remained a critical support for Tyhir's friends over the year and a half since his death and thought often about their continued grief. She still had a birthday card Tyhir had made for her as the background image on her phone.

Ms. Bloom felt a similarly deep connection to JahSun and several of his close friends. On Saturday, Ms. Bloom had sent a group text message to about a dozen seniors she thought to be his core friendship circle,[6] letting them know she'd be in the building on Sunday; to her surprise, nine of them showed up to join her. Ms. Bloom's third-floor classroom was already a regular gathering spot for the students in her close orbit, and was only a few doors from JahSun's locker. As the boys gathered somberly, some of them flipped through a stack of photos of JahSun she had printed up.

One of the boys grabbed the tape dispenser and a Sharpie and walked into the hallway with a few of the photographs. Gathered around JahSun's locker, the boys began taping the pictures to the tan metal, covering nearly the entire locker. Then they passed around the Sharpie and began writing messages between the photos.[7] Ms. Bloom reported later that the impromptu gathering of friends "started off pretty somber, but they started talking and goofing around. I [could] tell they [were] having a hard time." While they took photos of each other by the locker, the boys shared memories of JahSun and ideas for the Monday vigil. Ms. Bloom was especially glad to have a role to play with students to help her with—or, perhaps, distract her from—her own grief. She didn't always feel colleagues appreciated her investment in students' lives, so under these circumstances, she preferred being with the boys upstairs to the administrative meeting downstairs. Once the locker was decorated, Ms. Bloom headed out, offering a few boys a ride home and treating them to pizza on the way.

In the administrative offices, purchasing candles, sand, white paper bags, and markers for the vigil was the final logistical step for the day. Already this planning was dipping into the principal's discretionary budget for the year, which he also intended to use to offer JahSun's family help with funeral expenses, as they had for Tyhir the year before. As Mr. Donaldson reflected later about the costs, "It's one of those [things], where it's like, you just do it. You'll figure it out later, and if it means something else doesn't get covered, it doesn't get covered."

Sunday evening, Mr. Donaldson sent a final email to his staff with updated details. Separately, he reached out to each of JahSun's teachers to make sure they felt ready and supported for Monday and were planning to come to work; he was not sure that he himself was up to the task, but he knew he had to give it his best effort.

Dr. Stephens anticipated that many students would want the regular routine of the school day, but also worried that this might be a sign the boys were internalizing their emotions in troubling ways. He wondered what the school could do to help in the weeks and months to come. But most of all, Dr. Stephens worried about Monday. Although JahSun's teachers had assured him and Mr. Donaldson that they would be there, what if they changed their minds? Would the students come? Would they get what they needed? Had he and his team prepared enough?

Heading to Work on Monday

Ms. Cain hitched a ride with me Monday morning, grateful to shorten the extra-long day by cutting out her usual public transit commute. It was a relief for both of us not to be alone as we steeled ourselves for the sadness of the day. Ms. Cain rehearsed what she would say to her students when they were gathered in the room they used to share with JahSun, growing increasingly nervous about whether she could keep herself together. She was eager to get to her office to look through the stack of student work she'd left sitting on her desk before the break. An essay JahSun had written a few weeks earlier was somewhere in that stack; Ms. Cain remembered it as an especially poignant reflection she wanted to reread.

Like the students, the school staff made their way into the building with an unfamiliar somberness. Generally, a Monday morning would bring a combination of excitement for the possibilities of a new week and regret for a weekend gone by too quickly with neither enough preparation nor enough rest. Under normal circumstances, teachers would be annoyed by an early morning faculty meeting, especially with all the other administrative changes this year—new principal and vice principal, and discipline policies that seemed to change every week.

But today the faculty gathered obligingly, many stone-faced or sniffling, for the 7:30 a.m. emergency meeting. Those who greeted each other did so almost in a whisper. Some sat at student desks, others opting to stand along the wall as if not quite committed to the gathering. For many, this was one of the first times they would be witnessing Mr. Donaldson, their former colleague, in his new leadership role managing a crisis.

When a critical mass had arrived, Mr. Donaldson closed the door. After a long pause, he acknowledged what had happened and described the plans for the day. Just for today, the principal advised, teachers should be lenient about student absences or lateness. He also requested that everyone check in on each other and support each other, as well as their students, and that every adult try to be out and about in the hallways when possible: "We want to make sure there isn't a student alone in the stairwell feeling sad." Facing several dozen weary, teary teachers, Mr. Donaldson seemed calm and pulled together, and projected both sweetness and empathy—traits I confess

I had not fully expected, given previous interactions in which he had been quite stoic and serious.

Referring to some notes on a folded sheet of paper, he suggested faculty try for some sense of normalcy for those who might need it and then offered gently: "Do your best to be a genuine version of yourself and understand that not everyone is going to make perfect decisions as we're trying to figure this out. Give yourself that forgiveness and understand that there's no right or wrong way to move forward in that." Mr. Donaldson asked Ms. Gallo to share her handouts. In the past, teachers had told me they longed for more professional guidance and training on how to handle these kinds of events, which felt increasingly common. But in the moment, it was unclear how much help a handout could provide when swarms of students were just outside the door.

Some students peered curiously through the small window in the door of the classroom where the teachers were assembled. Before the meeting closed, Mr. Donaldson solicited the names of students who might be most affected, including JahSun's friends and his brother Bashir's social network.[8] As he wrote down the names, Ms. Estevez, JahSun's math teacher from freshman year, was audibly crying. Mr. Donaldson reminded the staff that a loss like this might trigger memories of other losses for everyone, even if they had not personally been close to JahSun.

After several moments of uneasy silence, Mr. Donaldson officially dismissed the faculty. While some teachers rushed back to their classrooms and offices, others moved deliberately slowly, taking a few extra moments to compose themselves before venturing into the sea of students.

Teachers Worry about Preparedness and Their Own Grief

JahSun's homeroom teacher had just returned from a short leave to visit his ailing father in India and had only learned the news on Sunday. In an email that night, he confessed to me that he had no idea how to handle a classroom full of JahSun's friends. It showed. Facing a room of silent, sad seniors, all he could do was smile sympathetically as he passed out their trimester schedules and not take it personally when most didn't even make eye contact.

In JahSun's first-period class, Ms. Kallum felt slightly more ready to interact with grieving boys. She had been out on maternity leave for the first two months of school, so didn't yet know her new students as well as she would have liked. "I still feel like I hadn't gotten to know JahSun too well," she wrote me in an email Sunday night. "So I'm mostly just sad that he's gone and feeling like I missed a chance to get to know a good kid, you know?" Ms. Kallum predicted that in class on Monday she would "mostly be the officiant and tissue/hug/chocolate provider." During her midday prep period when she usually ate lunch, she realized her stash of cookies was almost out. She hopped in her car, drove to the nearest grocery store, and bought several bags of candy to keep the students satiated through the afternoon.

In freshman classes, where students generally hadn't known JahSun and were less likely to be acutely affected, teachers felt conflicted. Ms. Bloom felt pressure to keep herself together since she imagined her freshman students craved normalcy—even as she also was keeping her eye on the intensely grieving seniors who spent most of the day at JahSun's locker just outside her classroom door.

In contrast, Mr. Khan chose to open up to his freshman students and give them a window into his own experience of grief. At the end of the day, he reflected: "This was the hardest day of teaching of my life. I thought I could teach, but I couldn't stand in front of the class, I couldn't get through it . . . I thought I should just use the time to demonstrate what I'm going through and that it's okay to shed a tear, or many tears . . . Sometimes I can't tell when I'm teaching if kids are really getting it or paying attention, but I've never seen a class so enthralled . . . you could hear a pin drop in the room." Mr. Khan is South Asian, one of only three male classroom teachers of color. He was often hyperaware of this additional responsibility and, in this case, hoped that witnessing a man of color express vulnerable emotions would be a good learning experience, even if most of his students had not known JahSun and were not personally impacted.

Midday in the teachers' lounge, many teachers—like the students during their study hall around the same time—seemed to have given up on what would usually be productive time for grading, lesson planning, or disciplinary reports. Instead, they were checking in with each other and sharing reflections on which students were genuinely struggling and which they worried were "skipping all their classes because they can."

Ms. Estevez had not touched her packed lunch. She wondered how any day could be harder than this. "That's my boy," she repeated several times in a melancholy tone. "My one question was, why was he alone? And he wasn't even able to put up a fight because he was broken," she lamented, referring to JahSun's recent knee injury. "I got up in front of my seniors this morning. I thought I would be okay, but I was like, 'I can't even look at you guys . . . this is your space, just do what you need.' . . . I can't teach today." But, she added with a sigh, she would have to figure out a way: she had freshmen in the afternoon.

Afternoon also brought the class Ms. Cain had been preparing for: JahSun's philosophy class. For several hours she had been rehearsing what she would say when the time came to greet her class with a conspicuous empty seat. She had found JahSun's writing and prepared some notes.

For Ms. Cain, JahSun's death changed everything about her class and her approach to teaching. She felt it used to be possible to "compartmentalize," to talk about death as an abstract thing. Naturally, death came up often in a philosophy class. Ms. Cain believed it was helpful for students to be able to talk openly about death, but also to come to school and "be silly" because "this was a place . . . untouched by that." But now things were different: "It's like a mask dropping off . . . This place is no longer death-free . . . It's just another place where you're going to have to anticipate losses." Of course, for so many of the students, JahSun's death was not their first time coping with the early death of a friend and, perhaps, no part of their life had ever felt "death-free." But for so many of their teachers, this loss was a first and necessitated new ways of thinking about their work and their students.

Relaxed Discipline

Outside the classrooms, in the less structured spaces of the school, staff were also navigating a necessarily changed environment. Discipline and control were usually the hallmarks of interactions between students and teachers in the hallways, particularly during passing periods between classes. This was the moment to attend to school uniforms, to make sure the energy wasn't too rowdy, to check for compliance with the school's cell phone and headphone policies.

But today called for a different set of disciplinary priorities: a complete, if temporary, suspension of monitoring and punishment. Across the building, students were finding extra leniency and permissiveness. Behaviors that would normally have provoked a disciplinary response were overlooked. Students were not chastised for sloppy uniforms—or even complete flouting of the Boys' Prep dress code, like Ezekiel's tie wrapped around his head. A student found wandering in the hallway was asked how he was doing before he was asked where he was going or where he was supposed to be. No one bothered students who had their phones out or their earbuds in during class. In the college office, the filtered water cooler was notoriously off-limits to students, but today there were no restrictions. The students who were most closely identified with JahSun understood that they had the unfamiliar freedom to be where they wanted to be with no adults directing them to get back to class.

To be sure, all this was a sharp departure from the school's usual emphasis on the regulation of students' bodies and behaviors; but it was in keeping with the principal's instructions that adults offer students the latitude to experience this day of mourning however they needed.

The Day's Conclusion

Despite the school's lack of prior preparation and limited resources, Monday went as well as it could. An abundance of tenderness and permissiveness throughout the building created emotional latitude for struggling students. Teachers who were experiencing their own personal grief also felt the warmth of community. The vigil on the school's field provided a reflective communal moment for students and adults to be together and grieve together, using cultural rituals familiar to most students (candles and a balloon release). Dr. Stephens, Mr. Donaldson, Mr. Hopkins, and the other school leaders who had been working tirelessly for nearly three days on these plans took pride in having created an event that was also welcoming for JahSun's family.

On Monday, institutional and informal supports worked in conjunction as members of the community relied on both grief rituals and personal relationships to get through the day. During this brief period of collective mourning and profound unity, the strengths of Boys' Prep as a small, tightly knit community with limited bureaucratic oversight shone.

Especially during times like these, school is more than just a site of education. It is a community, a home, a meeting place of the generations—a space where young minds get attention from adults beyond their family, where adults care for and love other people's children. Small schools like Boys' Prep can also be a brotherhood, with closeness felt between students across differences in age, family background, and friend groups. And in neighborhoods burdened by the tumult of gun violence, school is positioned to be a potential bedrock, a solid and dependable constant for students.

While our story concerns the aftermath of one student's death at one school, the frequency of youth murder in American life suggests that it is a recurrent tale. Recurrent, too—although I can only attest to it based on this close study—is a cycle of schoolwide grieving that began with what I call, to borrow Mr. Hopkins's terminology, the "easy hard," or the brief period of communal grieving immediately following a shared loss.

Why *hard*? This is the easy part to understand: the devastating difficulty of the day was visible in the students' bowed heads, teary eyes, and aimless wandering. It was audible in the quiet hallways, the somber PA announcements, the slam of Hazeem's hand colliding with a locker, Ms. Estevez's sobs at the faculty meeting, the anguished groans during the vigil.

Why *easy*? This part is, perhaps, more surprising: I witnessed a school culture so often organized by the need for control and order replaced by a culture of care and a temporary leveling of the adult authority students often fought so hard to resist or undermine. Already it was possible on Monday to see how intergenerational rituals, breaks from usual routines and disciplinary constraints, and both peer- and adult-driven creative practices forged a kind of collective grief that may have lightened everyone's load. As Ms. Cain said so poignantly in her class, "We're sharing those burdens together." Shared, public mourning made each person's sorrow feel less insurmountable—at least for the time being.

But, just as quickly as the school had rallied to support students in their shared grief on Monday, did it shift by Tuesday. In an effort to refocus both students and staff on the mission of Boys' Prep, policies and practices were enacted that individualized the emotional experience of grief, launching the school into a new phase of mourning.

Policing Grief

THE HARD HARD

"Algebra feels weird without my boy Jah in here," Herc posted to his social media page alongside a tilted desk-eye view of the whiteboard. This Tuesday morning class was one of three the charismatic junior had shared with JahSun. Herc's favorite teacher, Ms. Jordan, was trying to transition the boys back into some semblance of learning math, but in the back of the classroom, Herc was distracted, posting "If I could talk to god one on one I'd ask for my n***as back."

Across the school, many students were still actively and visibly grieving, unready to return to their routines. Hazeem, who had been part of JahSun's peripheral circle, was still icing his swollen hand from punching a locker the day before. Although on Monday he had seemed to draw strength from his emergent feelings of responsibility toward Bashir, on Tuesday he was wandering the hallways, not quite ready to return to class, but unsure where else to go.

Though comforted by being together, most of JahSun's closest senior friends were struggling to motivate themselves. Ezekiel had shared so many classroom spaces with JahSun over the years that he couldn't bring himself to reenter any of those rooms now. Instead, the senior started his Tuesday in the vice principal's office, where teachers planned to rotate throughout the day to supervise, checking students in and out. Ezekiel and six others made themselves comfortable in the conference-room-sized office, some sitting around the oval conference table, others atop Mr. Hopkins's desk, one stretched out on the floor.

Their conversation moved haphazardly: the suspect in JahSun's murder, whose picture had just been released by the media, but was not yet in custody; their plans for the weekend; where the school should put a mural for JahSun; and gossip about girls. One student passed around his basketball shoes and a Sharpie for everyone to add RIP messages. Looking up from his phone, Ezekiel exclaimed: "I finally know what my first tattoo gonna be. I didn't want to put any dumb thing on my body, but now I know what I want to do . . . cuz my man," referring to JahSun. He pointed to a spot on his arm: "Put my man on there."

Though the staff was allowing this group of boys to skip class, the school's disciplinary machine had started to flip back on; as if by reflex, teachers were returning to their roles as behavior monitors, beginning with the baseline symbol of students' subordinate status: the uniform. The reminders were gentle at first—a nudge to tuck in a shirt, an innocent query about a missing belt. One teacher adopted a playful approach, admonishing a student for wearing mismatched socks by calling to him with a smile in a singsong tone, "I hope you find your other black sock by the *next* time I see you."

Other teachers were on guard, anticipating that students might take advantage of the leniency. In the teachers' lounge, one wondered aloud how long JahSun's friends would continue cutting all their classes: "Yesterday I gave them a break. But today, if they don't come to me to at least check in, I'm writing them up for skipping." Charged with setting the tone for discipline in the school, head disciplinarian Mr. Pratt theorized that some students would surely be thinking, "So, I don't know the student that passed away, but I see that everybody else is going through something, I'm gonna utilize this opportunity to be lazy . . . to not do work . . . to slack."

Disciplinary repercussions had returned. Herc was summoned to serve an in-school suspension the following day for accumulating too many "tardies" and class absences in recent weeks. Now in his third year at Boys' Prep, Herc had managed to avoid serious trouble so far this year; but the school's point-based disciplinary system also tallied minor infractions, triggering a form letter requiring him to clear the slate by attending the half-day suspension. It was irritating to Herc to receive the letter in homeroom that day; none of this seemed important in the context of what had just happened.

It was only Tuesday, but already the school had moved into a new stage of shared grief that I call the *hard hard*. JahSun's death was still a regular topic of conversation at all levels of the school; students still felt they had permission to announce their grief; and adults still factored the loss into their decision-making about seeking order in their classrooms and throughout the building. But collective mourning was no longer a school-sponsored activity. Responding to the high stakes of their educational mission, school leaders shifted their focus from grief support to academic restabilization—and in the process privatized the emotional experience of grief. The initial sense of community and in-it-togetherness gave way to a fracturing into factions across the school.

Pressures to Return to Normal

To understand this abrupt shift, we need to step back and examine the multiple pressures Boys' Prep was facing. Two sets of institutional forces, long predating the tragedy of JahSun's murder, shaped both administrative and faculty decision-making around continued support for student grief. First was the pressure on the board of directors, CEO, and principal to boost test scores and college numbers to restore the reputation and ensure the future of the school. Second were stresses felt throughout the school from a transitional year under a new administration. Each complicated the school's response in the aftermath of JahSun's death.

Though mostly unspoken, these forces were certainly at play Monday evening when Dr. Stephens and Mr. Donaldson convened a small team of teachers and administrators after the candlelight vigil. They gathered in the first-floor classroom where they had started the day ten hours earlier. Despite the darkness, Dr. Stephens could make out the outlines of JahSun's friends through the window, still clasping each other on the dimly lit field. He was pleased that he and his team had created a memorial event that honored JahSun, gave space to his family, deepened community in the school, and gave JahSun's friends a sense of "ownership." But he was nervous about what would come next.

Though the shadow of gun violence and grief hung over the group, another ongoing educational crisis loomed. Before the phone call last Saturday jolted Dr. Stephens out of a relaxed family Thanksgiving weekend, he had imagined that this Monday would be devoted to motivating students to start the new academic trimester off right. A large banner in the cafeteria introduced his new "Black Degrees Matter" initiative of college-focused assemblies. Monday might have been a day to spark students' excitement about college.

Dr. Stephens was also dealing with the *conditional* charter renewal Boys' Prep had just been given. Boys' Prep receives public funding from the city and oversight from the district's charter school office, but is managed by and accountable to a board of directors. The board was understandably unhappy about a recent damning report identifying the school as not meeting academic standards on all but a handful of dimensions, and failing on several administrative and organizational metrics. Boys' Prep's charter was renewed for an additional five years only on the condition of specific improvements. The school's board of directors had to have been worried about the recent spate of school closings in Philadelphia, and that Black-led schools seemed to be targeted.[1]

Dr. Stephens had been working hard to correct some errors in the report and make the case that college matriculation rates ought to be included since they mattered as much as standardized test scores. This view certainly matched the mission of the school, which centered college preparation above all else, but also seemed like a good strategy given the low scores. To make this case, Dr. Stephens needed to be sure he could back it up. The senior class had already dropped from 150 students three years earlier to 94 before the Thanksgiving holiday.[2] Now his top concern was getting the remaining group—93 without JahSun—across the graduation stage and enrolled in college. The boys would need to do well on the SAT, submit college applications, apply for and receive financial aid, continue mastering academic skills, and prepare themselves and their families for a major life transition.

The already emotionally drained staff was burdened by these urgent tasks, especially those veteran teachers whose careers and life missions were wrapped up in the school's success—like Ms. Redmond, the school's founding Latin teacher, who was widely seen as part of the school's emotional core. In her free time, she served as a hospice chaplain, and students often pointed to her as a teacher they could go to for emotional support. But even she felt the weight of this precarious moment in the school's history competing with the need to mourn. At one point she filled a silent moment in the Monday evening meeting with a worry on her mind: the Pennsylvania statewide exams would begin in a week. "The timing . . . is making me so nervous." As she spoke, she almost censored herself: "I can't believe I'm even saying this! The SATs are on Saturday too . . . it's real." Her sentence dropped off into nervous laughter. She knew, as did everyone in the room, that this would be most seniors' last chance to improve their SAT scores before application deadlines. They also knew that the charter renewal report listed Boys' Prep as not meeting the standard for SAT readiness.

Ms. Redmond joked that the colleague who managed the school's testing program would be proud of her for raising this point—but her face bore embarrassment that *she* was talking about tests with such somber and existential matters at hand. Her unease was met with tentative laughter, a moment of bonding and release as everyone wrestled with the impossibilities of the moment. The boys in their care were supposed to be stressing about state tests, not grappling with teenage mortality. And as teachers, they should be debating pedagogy—were they teaching to the test too much, or not enough?—not brushing up their grief counseling skills.

The room was also feeling the internal institutional stress of a year that had already been rife with change and instability, including a new leadership team, the turnover of one-quarter of the faculty,[3] a set of experimental but so far unrealized new discipline initiatives, and a shifting school culture.

Mr. Donaldson was an experienced teacher, but a brand-new principal. In a candid moment toward the end of the year, he reflected: "When you're in a classroom, you're controlling only that classroom. When you're in charge of the school, [you] feel the weight of everything that happens." He could barely eat his first few months on the job because he was so overwhelmed:

I had this extensive notebook of everything I wanted to accomplish . . . Then it quickly gets thrown out the window because it's like this job isn't even remotely what I thought it was gonna be. It very quickly became survival. Like, you survive this, figure this out, you get through the day. Solve the problems in front of you today. The ones you can't solve, try and get to tomorrow. It's so hard with the amount of daily work that you have to be able to see things big picture because you just get so pressed into the day-to-day of what's happening. Then . . . a pipe busts, and then the next five hours are gone. So whatever you were planning to get done is not gonna get done.

For a new principal, just making it through the year, learning the ropes, and setting realistic goals for the next year would have been enough. Losing a student and dealing with the aftermath for an entire school was more than he signed up for.

The same could be said for Mr. Hopkins, hired as vice principal just three days before the school year began. Despite the late start, Mr. Hopkins had begun the year with big ideas for a restorative discipline approach, developing an honor council where peers would evaluate each other's disciplinary infractions, and trying to limit student suspensions. He was heading up the "climate team," which included the two disciplinarians, Mr. Pratt and Mr. Adams, both Black men who had been at the school for ten and two years, respectively. Together, they attempted to overhaul disciplinary procedures to improve school culture. In Mr. Pratt's words, "We tried to do a lot of little creative things" to avoid suspending students in favor of restorative justice practices that would keep students in school. They focused on students' exterior displays such as uniforms and cell phone use in the hope that their respectable look and behavior would engender a readiness to learn. By Thanksgiving break, just before the school was stunned by JahSun's murder, the disciplinary team had become overwhelmed by policing minor infractions and the challenge of implementing a restorative approach to bigger disciplinary issues, and had shifted their priorities again, deciding to lay off some of the small stuff but reinstitute suspensions for larger breaches.

Teachers struggled to keep up. The "flip-floppy [approach of] detentions/no detentions, suspensions/no suspensions," as one teacher described it, made it challenging for them to manage disruptive behavior, not knowing what kind of support and backup they would get from above. While some teachers felt the consequences for bad behavior were too lenient, others worried about the effects of emphasizing students' compliance with rules over developing critical thinking. These administrative "growing pains," as one teacher framed it, had created a chaotic first trimester.

So that Monday night, when the group of school leaders gathered—some with eyes still wet from the memorial, and all weary from a very long day—they must have been feeling all the demands of educating students deemed already behind in a city that was consistently failing Black boys. They were surely feeling the urgency to *compensate* for what their students were deprived of because of their race and class, to *prepare* them for college and positive futures, and to *protect* the ones they still could from a fate like JahSun's—the three underlying pillars of Boys' Prep's education I described in chapter 1. The complications of this particular year heightened these urgencies. This was the context for the decision to pull back on leniency and extra supports come Tuesday, to try to usher students out of their brief moment of acute grieving and back to the regular business of learning in classrooms, preparing for tests, and performing respectable behavior in hallways.

Dissenting Voices

Some adults in the school building foresaw that this quick return to business as usual might backfire. Monday night, just as the group was preparing to pack up and head home after the long day, Ms. Gallo, the young college counselor, posed a tentative question to her colleagues: "I just have a slight concern about, I guess, like I had mentioned this to some people before, but like, there being a lot of services you know today and a lot of supports, you know like we brought in the counselors, but not, but then just like dropping it off. And I just want to make sure there's like—and I'm sure you've already thought about this and there's people in place—but just like to have people, you know, just so that there's a constant." Her worries were quickly shut down with the assurance from her boss that "we"—those in the room and all the other staff—"are the constants" for the boys. Indeed, Boys' Prep had always prided itself on strong student-teacher relationships. The bigger concern was what Mr. Donaldson had expressed earlier: that "there will be kids who will use [grief resources or accommodations] to avoid class that really aren't trying to process things" and who need to be focusing on school. The decision to start "taking a step back toward the norm" meant that those students would be expected to resume learning and behaving as usual. School staff would handle continued support for any boys who were deemed to really need it on a case-by-case basis.

In small schools like Boys' Prep, teachers and other staff do often play vital emotional support roles for students, but Ms. Gallo was not appeased by the idea that this was the administration's best plan. Nor was Ms. Bloom, who I suspect was imagining that she would once again be left on her own to provide mentorship and support to the dozens of students who already saw her as their go-to adult in the building. Ms. Bloom had arrived late, delayed by a conversation out on the field with JahSun's mother about driving a group of boys to the family home that weekend for a visit. By the time she got to the meeting, decisions to pull back extra supports for students—like counseling services, free spaces outside classrooms where grieving students could gather, and disciplinary leniency—had already been made.

Barely twelve hours later, as the bell rang for first period on Tuesday morning, I saw Ms. Bloom outside her third-floor classroom; she seemed to want a listening ear. The decision to return to normal was a grave mistake, she believed, although she had not expressed this view to her colleagues the night before. The seniors who were closest to JahSun were still in desperate need of time to process and be together. "They never listen to me here," she added under her breath as she headed into her classroom.

Students' Coping and Emotion Management

Some students didn't need the push to return to normal. Despite his frustration with the school discipline policies and his upcoming in-school suspension, Herc was doing his best to keep his feelings under control and attend all his classes. When I met him the year before as a sophomore, Herc stood out not only for his particular mix of sweet, silly, and thoughtful, but also for the immense grief he bore after the death of Tyhir, one of his best friends, the summer after their first year at Boys' Prep. Herc's silent struggle in the months that followed led him to attempt suicide during the winter of his sophomore year, when he felt completely unable to cope with his emotions. One year later, he was grieving his friend JahSun, whom he'd just gotten close to in the past few months. Herc found JahSun's death "shocking" because "it's not like he made his own bed." In other words, JahSun wasn't involved in activities that put him at a particular risk for violence. But Herc felt he had learned how to manage his emotions after loss: "After having a couple, a lot of friends pass, like I try to cry when he died but no tears is coming up . . . I lost too many people, it's like I'm used to it now . . . [It's] horrible. He's still not here. [But] you got to move forward regardless . . . I don't really cope with it no more . . . It's like the same thing, and I know they not going to be the last one." For Herc, JahSun's death was a reminder of his other losses, but he already felt practiced at pushing through his pain without expending extra energy on what he considered "coping."

Kaliq, too, was dealing with multiple layers of grief: still mourning Tyhir, thinking frequently about his grandfather's sudden death years earlier, and now confronting the loss of a friend he'd only recently learned was family. Kaliq spoke of his ability to manage grief as being "all out of fear," numb to loss because of so many prior experiences. Years later, Kaliq would acknowledge that he had been responding to the spoken and unspoken societal expectations that Black males remain stoic in the face of loss and vulnerability, and that although his numbness helped him get through the new normal of the school day, it might have inhibited some long-term healing.[4]

Kaliq's tactics of emotion management kept him determined to be in the classroom. After a brief bout of tears Monday morning, he had attended all his classes and planned to continue doing so. Kaliq resolved not to use JahSun's death as an excuse to fall behind, but to "use it as motivation." His grades had not been great, but he thought he could push himself to do better to honor JahSun. One stumbling block, though: to his surprise and disappointment, Kaliq had, like Herc, received a notification of an in-school suspension, a carryover from some infraction before the Thanksgiving holiday that he had all but forgotten.

Teachers' Closed-Door Decision-Making

Over the course of the week, most teachers tried their best to balance the expectations to teach course material and enforce school rules with the need to respond to the emotional devastation they witnessed among some students—and, they imagined, that were beneath others' tough exterior displays. Despite the official directive to return to business as usual, the truth was that, once teachers closed their doors, they had a lot of freedom to run their classrooms as they wished and be responsive to the moods of their students.

In a sophomore and junior social studies classroom, Ms. Finn turned off the fluorescent lights; the natural light coming in from the windows made the room feel calm and restful. She instructed her class to work silently at their own pace, taking notes from their textbook onto a worksheet. Ms. Finn described the scene: it was "amazing—I fully walked out of the room to get tea and came back and everyone was still quiet and working."

In JahSun's senior Honors Philosophy class, Ms. Cain's priority was helping JahSun's friends find ways to begin healing. With that in mind, she took her class outside for a "field day" of team-building games on Tuesday. They began with "magic carpet": the guys had to flip over a sheet lying on the grass while they all remained standing on top of it. Even Omari and Jahmir, typically too-cool-for-school, were game—no eye rolls or protests or requests to sit out. Many channeled a childlike, playful side they rarely got the chance to bring out in school. Like their choice of an animated children's movie in Ms. Kallum's class on Monday, in this moment of extreme vulnerability, if allowed, the boys wanted to access their childhood and perhaps feel like kids who were safe and protected by adults. Given the space and freedom to grieve, they revealed their youth, not their stoicism.

Ms. Cain offered up a football, a frisbee, and a hula hoop and invited the class to use the rest of the period however they wished. Over the course of the next two hours, the usually empty grass field became a vibrant playground. More students joined the gathering than left it—many claiming to have a free period or to be skipping their lunch. A handful of teachers also made their way outside, perhaps spotting the gathering from a window or learning about it by word of mouth. Soon there were enough boys to start two separate football games. A circle of students and teachers threw a frisbee. Bashir tried to get the hula hoop to stay on his hips.

Though all the participants seemed to enjoy themselves, Ms. Cain later took some heat from colleagues for the schoolwide distraction and felt compelled to send out an email apology. The following day she attempted to ease her class back into regular course material with a game of logic puzzles connected to their new unit. Even with the return to formal learning, JahSun's presence remained palpably strong. As the students arranged themselves into competing teams to answer questions on the Smartboard, one group of four students kept referring to themselves as a five-man team: they had included the empty desk where JahSun used to sit as part of their cluster and put his name up on the board as their team name. Ms. Cain neither questioned nor commented on this, and the other students seemed to appreciate the continued acknowledgment of their lost peer's presence.

For other teachers balancing a mission- and emotion-driven perspective, the transition back to their lesson plans felt more fraught. Ms. Kallum, who had put a lot of thought into the memorial objects in her classroom on Monday, began Wednesday's senior Latin class with "Let's try to get back to before Thanksgiving, what we were learning then," and put up a translation they had been working on as a class. She allowed one of the students she knew to be JahSun's close friend to keep his head down, two others to wear headphones, and another to keep his sunglasses on—usually prohibited behaviors—but kept the lesson going. About fifteen minutes into class, two students started bickering, and Ms. Kallum became visibly frustrated. The disruption prevented the class from settling into an academic rhythm; by the end of the period, they had only gotten through four lines of translation.

One period at a time, students and faculty negotiated what they needed from each other—sometimes distinct from official school policies. Teachers were largely left on their own to decide exactly how to impose the expectations of a return to normalcy and how to respond to the needs they perceived among their students. Compared to the united front of Monday, as early as Tuesday it was evident that there was no longer a shared adult perspective on how to support the grieving boys. In retrospect, I have come to realize that the beginning of this *hard hard* stage of institutional mourning meant not only a widening split between teachers' approaches, but also a conflicting set of expectations on students that left them unsure what to expect from classroom to classroom.

Disciplinary Contradictions

The disciplinary team also faced the challenge of balancing sensitivity to the impact of the tragedy with their desire to maintain a respectable, orderly school culture. While grief led many students to retreat inward and become quieter, others became more disruptive. JahSun's circle of senior friends, in particular, started getting more physical—chasing each other through the hallways, putting each other in headlocks. Their roughhousing dirtied school walls, put dents in lockers, and sometimes ensnared unsuspecting underclassmen just trying to get to class.

At the end of the school year, disciplinarian Mr. Adams reflected that JahSun's death "threw a monkey wrench" in his team's efforts to hold students accountable for their behavior. The climate team realized that, given what had happened, if they "pushed too much," the students might "snap off." So, Mr. Adams explained,

it became one of those things where we still enforced the rules, but it had to be a little loose just for the sake of maintaining the peace in the school . . . It depends on the situation and then sometimes we're like, "Yo, man." [Me and Mr. Pratt] look at each other and we're like, "Yo, what's the plan for today?" He's like, "Well, let's just stay observant. Don't force nothing. Let the kids that's going through what they going through be. If you're going to enforce the rules, enforce it loosely. If [their misbehavior is] not too overboard then leave it alone," because the main thing here is to allow kids to be able to deal with their emotions and not hassle them to a point where it becomes more of an issue than what it needs to be.

Mr. Adams recognized that pushing discipline on an emotionally vulnerable young person might end up creating "more of an issue." He and Mr. Pratt decided to "stay observant," "enforce school rules loosely," and focus only on infractions that were "overboard"—at least in theory.

This looser approach to enforcement was tested on Wednesday at the in-school suspension in the cafeteria. Herc, Kaliq, and two dozen others were required to come to school, on time and in full uniform, to spend the half day (on Wednesdays, school let out before lunch) in the cafeteria in silence. This was essentially a four-hour study hall, with the added expectation of helping with chores around the building.

Herc begrudgingly got himself to school on time and smoothed out his uniform over his tall, lanky frame, but he was already in a bad mood, annoyed to be getting an extreme punishment for what felt like nothing: being late to school a handful of times. Plus, he felt he had a pretty good excuse. As soon as he had turned sixteen and was able to work legally, Herc had started a job at McDonald's to pay for food, clothes, getting around the city, and saving; he felt good having money. He had been working thirty hours a week, weekday afternoons and evenings, sometimes until 11 p.m. His closest friends, Latrell and Jonquett, who had recently transferred out of Boys' Prep, worked at the same McDonald's. When they were lucky enough to be on the same shift, the self-described "three musketeers" liked to hang out together after work, sometimes until 3 a.m. Waking up after those late nights was a struggle. Worse, if Herc was fighting with his mom, she might lock him out, and he would have to go to his sister's apartment much farther from school. He quickly began accumulating class absences and tardies.

Herc spent the first hour of his suspension dozing off. He was then excused from the cafeteria to attend the group counseling session the social worker had set up for him and two other students earlier that fall. The three boys met weekly with two Black male counselors to discuss their lives, focused on a specific topic each week. This week's topic, coincidentally, was grief. The counselors did most of the talking, but Herc offered one reflection that mirrored thoughts he'd shared with me several times: "Losing people, I'm used to it . . . I want to cry, but I don't . . . It's a feeling I don't want to feel no more." One of the counselors advised the teens that they "don't have to hide shit for nobody, dog. Doing that will kill you or make you kill someone." The other counselor added: "You need goals, something that matters. It's dangerous if you don't have that."

When Herc returned to the cafeteria after the session, he was immediately handed a broom and asked to clean alongside the other suspended students. But Herc had a lot on his mind and found the request demeaning. He quietly ducked out and wandered to the third floor, where he planned to hide until he could blend in with the rush of students leaving school; he wasn't too concerned about the consequences if he was caught. The moment his iPhone—with Tyhir's face as the home screen—showed 12:00, he was gone.

Thursday, the school's disciplinary procedures caught up to him when a small misunderstanding in the cafeteria quickly escalated to a shouting match between Herc and Mr. Adams, who was known to have a temper. Herc lashed out verbally at the disciplinarian, then tried to leave the building. "I'm not going to give you respect if you're going to disrespect me," he recalled later. Of course, this only resulted in more trouble: by afternoon, Herc had been suspended and promptly sent home. The administration believed the suspension had Herc "shook." After so many disciplinary infractions over the years, Herc and his parents worried that perhaps this could mean expulsion.

Mr. Pratt, the head disciplinarian, reflected later in the day while sweeping the cafeteria floor that he had tried to give Herc space, knowing what he was going through. But in threatening to punch Mr. Adams, he had gone too far: "That attitude will get him eaten alive out there. We care here, but not out there," he said, pointing to the cafeteria doors that opened onto the street. "I know stuff's going on, but [if] he don't want to be here, he gotta figure it out or his parent has to figure it out." Mr. Pratt, who'd grown up just across the street from the school and had been working there for ten years, knew the educational alternatives if Herc left Boys' Prep. In his view, Herc needed to learn to deal with authority in this building if he wanted to have options in the future. Mr. Pratt was sympathetic to his grief—he was, himself, still devastated by JahSun's death—but maintained that it was no excuse for Herc's behavior.

82

Grief and Support Move Underground

By Thursday, a stranger entering the Boys' Prep building might perceive nothing unusual about the school atmosphere. The volume and energy in the hallways and the cafeteria had mostly returned to its usual exuberance. Most students were back in their classroom seats, no longer ducking out in large numbers to gather in groups. But to a shrewd observer of the in-between moments, the signs of grief were still everywhere: daily rituals around JahSun's locker, solitary students wandering the hallways without a place to be, friends who could tolerate the memories of shared spaces only by numbing themselves.

As students swapped their jackets for binders at their lockers and headed to class, some would steal a long glance at JahSun's memorial. Kaliq developed a ritual of touching the locker on his way in and out of the building as he greeted JahSun in his head. He would remember the interactions they used to have: "I'd be like, 'yo, bro' and he'd be like, 'yo, fat ass.'"

Bashir was still bringing his breakfast and lunch from the cafeteria to eat in front of his brother's locker, usually alone, a practice he would continue for weeks. JahSun's friends would call him "brother" and sometimes drop him a few dollars as a token of respect and condolence.

In math class, as Ms. Jordan grabbed some papers off her desk, she was overtaken by the memory of JahSun co-opting her desk as his seat when his injured leg required extra space for elevation. She had to take a few seconds to gather herself before she could face her students.

Downstairs, Rajae wandered in to talk to his English teacher and broke down about losing JahSun. "So much stuff just came out, he was shaking," the teacher told me later. She tried to comfort him but worried she hadn't done enough.

On the steps leading to the school's entrance, a small group of JahSun's friends were quietly whisked out of their classrooms to be interviewed by ABC News for a two-minute story about JahSun's death.

In the cafeteria, instead of eating, Hazeem snapped a photo of the chair where JahSun used to sit and posted it to Instagram with the caption "💔💔💔💔 can't sit next to me 😤😤😤." The emojis expressed his simultaneous feelings of heartbreak and anger. Then he walked up to the lobby, where he sat, head in his hands, in front of the main office until the school secretary alerted Ms. Rivera to check on him.

In the college office, whenever she had a free moment, Ms. Redmond refreshed her Google search for updated information about the murder. She was also rewatching a video Ms. Estevez posted to Facebook of JahSun and Ezekiel as freshmen: it's "like watching a ghost," she whispered.

Ezekiel himself was reluctantly getting himself back into some of his classrooms by Thursday. He told me, "My first class, *he* was in there with me, so . . ." His sentence trailed off and he looked away as if pondering the fact that just a week earlier, he and JahSun had sat in that classroom together. He confessed later that being in class was so difficult he had to get high in order to tolerate it.[5]

Ms. Bloom was exhausted, worried that she hadn't yet given herself space to process the devastating loss. Wednesday after school she had taken seven of JahSun's friends bowling. That weekend she would be proctoring the SATs and had offered to take more students to visit with JahSun's mom, so it wasn't clear when she would have that time.

The school's decision to retreat quickly from the communal grief support and permissiveness of Monday meant that caring for particularly troubled students now happened in the nooks and crannies of the school days. The *urgency to compensate*, the *compulsion to prepare*, and the *responsibility to protect* all compelled the schoolwide policy of moving on, even while many students and teachers were clearly unable to do so.

An Attempt to Reset

As the exhausting week finally drew to a close, Principal Donaldson hoped he could help his faculty and students reset and prepare for a better next week. In a Friday early morning faculty meeting, he relayed information about funeral plans and shared schoolwide target dates for students to turn in missed work. Later that morning, he gathered JahSun's core friend group to check in and convey his expectations.

Ms. Bloom retrieved the thirteen seniors from their classes. Mr. Donaldson perched at the front of the classroom, sitting on a student desk with his feet on the seat. Ms. Bloom sat toward the back; she wanted to be there, she told me, just in case the principal said something "insensitive" as he tried to usher them back into the fold. Mr. Donaldson began by acknowledging what a hard week it had been and thanking the boys for being such great supports to each other, since "as teachers, we know we can't always be everything that you guys need us to be."

While Mr. Donaldson talked, the guys sat silently, staring straight ahead or down at their desks. Khalil was having a visibly hard time, and Ms. Bloom reached out to rest her hand on his arm. Mr. Donaldson continued with his core message:

We want to make sure that you guys are getting the opportunity to get back into the things you need to do, because we don't want you getting to a place where you're really far behind in your senior year. You guys gotta be moving on towards graduation. We don't want that to get lost in what's going on. Obviously, there's going to be challenges with that. We get that. It's not going to be straightforward and easy. But we want you guys to start moving in that direction. We are hopeful that on Monday the expectation is that you're back in class as normal.

Mr. Donaldson went on to say that he expected there would be days when "normal" wouldn't be possible, and that was okay. But during those times, he offered firmly, they needed to follow the "normal routines" of telling their teacher they'd like to see the social worker because "that's her role in the school." Mr. Donaldson suggested that the boys not overwhelm Ms. Bloom and make sure to give her the space to take care of herself too. He reiterated the deadline to submit missed work and encouraged them to communicate with their teachers because, starting Monday, they would be expected back in all their classes. After making space for the boys to share, which none of them did, Mr. Donaldson encouraged them to find inspiration in the memory of their friend, rhetorically asking: "How do I take the way that JahSun impacted my life and make that part of my every day and the routine and the normal?" His message to the boys was compassionate but forward looking.

Ms. Bloom was close to tears. She was sad for her students and nervous that they might misinterpret what they were being told. She chimed in:

I don't want you to think that we're putting a timeline—like on Monday that you have to stop feeling. Like, it's going to stay with you for a while. I think what we're trying to message to you is that there's no words that's going to make you feel better . . . nothing we say is going to help make sense of it. But if we're learning anything from it, it's that you have to value your own life and the life that you have left . . . I think you've done a really good job of keeping each other close. And I'm always going to be here if you need me. But you guys, like all of you in this room, have been working really hard for four years to get your GPAs right and go to college . . . We want you to keep going with that because that's what Jah would have wanted because he had the same goals. So everything you do, you have to do it for him because he doesn't get the chance to do it. Okay? And if you need me, I'm here. I love all of you.

The boys remained silent, several almost tearing up, as Ms. Bloom's words landed on them. Mr. Donaldson echoed her message: "I think that's exactly where my heart's at too." Then he reiterated his earlier points about the plans for next week, and officially closed the meeting. It was not entirely clear what meaning came through to the boys, since none of them uttered a word.

Friday afternoon also brought the hope for a resolution to Herc's difficult week. At 3:30, he was invited back into the building with his father for the reinstatement hearing to determine if he could return to school. The meeting was led by Mr. Hopkins, who invited Ms. Bloom and me to join as "advocates" for Herc. Herc wore the most impec-

cably pulled-together version of the school uniform I had ever seen
on him as he entered the school with his father, a man in his late forties to whom he bore a striking resemblance.

The vice principal laid out his interpretation of the events of the
week, asking Herc to acknowledge the consequences of his actions—
specifically his very public fight with Mr. Adams and his attempt to
flee the building—and to identify his goals so they could map out
a plan to get him back on track. Herc's dad tried to mediate, acknowledging that his son certainly needed to apologize to the staff member
he'd threatened but also earnestly asking whether the altercation that
led to his son's suspension could have been prevented if the disciplinarian had not egged Herc on. Herc's dad wondered why Mr. Adams
was not at the meeting.

Mr. Hopkins asked Ms. Bloom and me to share our view of the incident (we felt both parties had escalated a minor situation unneces-
sarily). Then Herc offered a very roundabout apology. When they
circled back to next steps and how Herc could improve his grades and
attendance, Herc looked down at his hands. "I live day to day, I'm not
thinking about the future." Given that one of Herc's friends had been
murdered less than a week earlier, this was not unreasonable.

Like many conversations Herc had with authority figures, this one
was like pulling teeth to get beyond one-word answers. Mr. Hopkins
encouraged Herc to share his perspective on his year so far. The new
trimester had just begun and, with the week he (and everyone) had
had, it was unlikely Herc had completed any assignments. All of us
were well aware that Herc's grades this year had been far below his
potential. In the first trimester, he failed four of his seven classes and
received Cs in the other three. On his report card, his teachers expressed disappointment about his attendance and inconsistency, but
also shared their genuine affection for him with comments like Herc
is "polite and engaged," "a strong student when in class," or "such
a special student—he is earnest, thoughtful, and kind. I have really
loved working with him." The paradox of Herc was how genuinely
likable he remained even as he flouted school norms.

Mr. Hopkins continued prodding Herc to commit to making

changes for his own betterment. After about forty minutes with little headway, Mr. Hopkins reinstated Herc, ending his suspension. Though in some sense this outcome was never in question, it still brought relief. While his father waited outside the main office, Herc went to each of his teachers to get his missed work, which he promised to complete by Monday.

No one in the meeting acknowledged that Herc's frustration with the in-school suspension and subsequent public argument occurred just days after the terrifying murder of a friend with whom he shared several classes. Nor did Herc himself make this point at the time—though in the years that followed he would often speak of how dramatically his high school experience was interrupted by the deaths of friends. Herc's week, from the notice about his in-school suspension to this reinstatement meeting, highlighted the tensions of the return to regular discipline in the midst of acute pain. Though Herc would likely not have used this language himself, in my observations, the disciplinarians, in their efforts to settle the chaos of the school, inadvertently suffocated Herc's grief and intensified his despair.[6]

A Split in the Building

Ms. Bloom's attendance at both of the Friday meetings—with JahSun's friend group and the principal, and with Herc and the vice principal—was telling. More than just her own self-appointed role as a student advocate, her presence signaled a larger split that was beginning to form among the adults at Boys' Prep.

Teachers often served as mediators of the administration, bringing institutional policies and values to bear on students through their pedagogy, classroom management, and general interactions with students. Teachers experienced the dual pressures of their desire to be sensitive to students' needs *and* their awareness that they were being evaluated and policed by those above them, based on how well their students met various benchmarks. In the middle of this disconnect between the students who were still in grief and the school-level policy about returning to work, a difference of philosophy surfaced. Without explicit discussion or debate, two camps of teachers emerged over the weeks that followed JahSun's death. Each felt they knew what was best for their students, and each felt the other group of teachers was doing it wrong.

One faction saw themselves as caring, compassionate, and deeply attuned to students' needs. They were critical, though mostly quietly, of the turn school policies had taken, and felt they had a duty to provide the care to students individually that was no longer being offered institutionally. Even before this moment, students regularly pointed out these teachers as their favorites, because they were seen as "getting it"—and perhaps also because they tended to be more lenient and accommodating. In the privacy of their own classrooms or through individual relationships with students, these teachers allowed for and recognized a range of expressions of grief and offered explicit and implicit emotional support. They enacted their form of care by negotiating alternate homework deadlines, allowing students to disengage from class without penalty, and checking in regularly and persistently with boys (in person as well as, in some cases, over text). Though these teachers' own personal cultural styles of coping were often different from their students' (most were white women[7] and followed a typical middle-class white feminine approach to expressiveness, emotional sharing, and help-seeking), some of them still engaged in the boys' culturally specific mourning rituals, such as wearing RIP t-shirts and jewelry and attending candlelight vigils and balloon releases outside of school.

The other group of teachers and administrators also viewed their approach to be one of care and compassion, but subscribed to something closer to a "tough love" style. This cluster of staff was more racially and gender diverse, and included the Black male disciplinarians, most of the male teachers in the building, and women teachers from a range of racial backgrounds. They saw their responsibility as helping students develop skills and dispositions that would serve them throughout their lives—in contrast to the "coddling" (and sometimes even boundary-crossing) they viewed among some colleagues. From the perspective of these adults, students should have made the transition back to regular school life by the end of the week: no more need for hand-holding or the extra tenderness of that first Monday. No more excuses for skipping class, wandering hallways lost in thought, or getting distracted in class.

This second group worried that masses of students were taking advantage of the situation, exaggerating their own grief to get out of full participation in school. To this group, the important thing was to distinguish the students genuinely in need of additional grief-related support from the emotional free-riders whose expressions of grief were insincere, for whom they had little patience. In their view, grieving students needed to learn how to explicitly articulate their specific needs and then go through proper school channels to receive accommodations or resources. Other forms of expression were subject to penalty through the regular disciplinary procedures.

This discourse, even among teachers known for creative pedagogical practices that responded to the individuality of each student, informed a general sense of grief as a binary state—someone is either legitimately grieving or not. For instance, Mr. Gilbert, a veteran English teacher known to go above and beyond in connecting with students beyond the classroom, put it this way: "[After JahSun's death,] there was a lot of taking advantage of the grace that was provided. I think some students needed that grace, but . . . there were also students who didn't. And they definitely pushed beyond boundaries . . . So then the question is, are you trying to take advantage of something? Are you just trying to get out of class? Is [the continued accommodation] something you really need?" Mr. Gilbert and other teachers questioned how many students were *really* continuing to experience debilitating grief weeks after JahSun's death and therefore needed continued "grace" from the Boys' Prep community. He felt a responsibility to usher students back to learning.

But Mr. Gilbert was equally concerned about supporting truly suffering students as about identifying possible fakers. He asked, "If [a student] needs [support] for that long, what do we all do to help [him] to be a fully functioning student at this school? Is there outside counseling we can get for [him], or [can he] eat lunch with someone and talk once a week or something like that?" In a group interview at the end of the year, several faculty members echoed the frustration that larger conversations among school staff never took place about how to help students who were still in active mourning after normal school life generally resumed. It wasn't that the "tough love" teachers wanted to ignore students' continued troubles, but they had hoped for a top-down schoolwide solution to guide them in their support of diverse student experiences and needs.

For the administrators, juggling pressures from all sides, concern over fissures among the staff sometimes obscured their focus on students' well-being. Reflecting at the end of the year on JahSun's circle of friends and the way teachers responded to them, the principal offered:

I think some of them became sort of *against* people in the building. One of the challenging pieces of all of it is that when kids are going through that, you have teachers that are going to extremes to care for them. Unintentionally, it creates sides, and so if you're [a teacher] who would do whatever to help a student, anybody that's not willing to do that is all of a sudden not a good teacher or not a caring person. It's sort of like camped people into those groups . . . When someone like Ramell was acting out, and somebody like Ms. Woo that knows him will handle it in a way of like being concerned and caring, but then another teacher just as lovingly was like, "You can't continue to do this. You need to get yourself together." In the student's mind, it sort of became: these are the people that are good, these are the people that are bad.

Mr. Donaldson acknowledged that although every teacher might have good intentions, the students interpreted their actions differently, latching on to some teachers and rejecting others.

During the *easy hard* day, forms of institutional and informal adult support for students worked in tandem. During the weeks of the *hard hard* period, students were exposed to differential and conflicting sets of norms or expectations about their continued grief, sometimes alternating hourly between classrooms run by teachers they viewed as callous and uncaring and those who they felt "got it." Getting through the school day entailed negotiating at least two sets of clashing expectations and required that boys learn to manage their own expressions of grief to avoid institutional penalty.

Identifying Fake Grief

Later on in the year, after yet another student's death (discussed further in chapter 6), I observed one extreme incident that speaks to the suspicion among staff that their leniency would backfire and that students might take advantage of prolonged tolerance of public grieving. In the immediate aftermath of the loss, sophomore Noble emerged as a particularly suffering student. He claimed to be grieving not only for his classmate, but also, at the same time, for his brother, who had apparently been shot in front of him.

In a conversation with me, Noble described what had happened in great detail. I was caught off guard by the casualness of his storytelling, surprised he was in school at all. But what really stood out was the point Noble made that he had lost *two* people over the weekend: "I'm dealing with two great deaths, everyone else here is just dealing with one." He worried people would think he was "overreacting" if they didn't know about his brother, and also asserted that he couldn't "just talk about one," since both losses were consuming him.

Over the course of the day, Noble shared different versions of this story with other adults, who conveyed their concern up the leadership ladder. Eventually a call home exposed Noble's lie. Perhaps to differentiate himself from his grieving peers and get the individual attention he craved, he had completely fabricated the story about his brother.

According to Mr. Adams, with whom he had a close relationship, this wasn't the first time Noble's pattern of lying had surfaced. "He's always making up stories," Mr. Adams relayed to me. "He wants attention and sympathy. But it's okay, you just have to listen and be there for him." While Mr. Adams understood that Noble's lies signaled a deeper need, for some others, the story cemented their abiding worries that they were being played by students only pretending to grieve. The major takeaway among school staff after Noble's lies came to light was that students might be dishonest about grief, rather than that students were desperate for attention to their grief.

The Unique Challenges of the Hard Hard

The swift transition from the collective, institutionally sanctioned and structured grief practices of the *easy hard* day to the *hard hard* period's attempts at institutional normalcy reflects larger patterns within modern society and American culture. We have become increasingly uncomfortable with death, pushing a natural occurrence that was once a public feature of communal life into the shadows. Death is now "compartmentalized from everyday life . . . [it] is clean, sterile, sanitized," and along with it, "grief has shifted from the everyday realm and no longer has a place in our society."[8] Shared grief rituals have become progressively shorter, and people are forced to do most of their mourning in private. Grief that spills out into public view might be regarded as pathological or in need of clinical intervention.[9] In the United States, our "denial of death" has meant nominal bereavement leave policies for workers and often no formal policies for students in schools.[10]

As an educational institution, Boys' Prep faced many pressures and incentives to return to business as usual. Guided by the sense of urgency in educating Black male students in a fundamentally unequal society that left them perpetually behind, school policies produced official timelines for grief that resulted in the enforcement of exacting academic and disciplinary protocols. These institutional timetables were fixed around school year schedules, testing calendars, and external evaluation deadlines rather than on the unscheduled and unpredictable nature of human emotion—and therefore existed at odds with many students' individual timelines of grief. For so many of the students, ghosts lingered in the school building for weeks and months. Grief continued to manifest in the form of physical ailments, bad dreams, daily distractions. It was impossible for students to fully turn off their grief and move on.

It is my sense that Mr. Donaldson and Dr. Stephens would have wanted to do more: give their students more time to process their loss; provide them with more resources and supports for coping with grief; take more time themselves to carefully think through next steps, consult with experts, or get more input from their staff. These unrealized wishes join an even longer list of wishes I suspect most leaders of schools like Boys' Prep have—all the resources and safety nets they long to provide their young students to ensure a rigorous education, robust and healthy personal development, and social and economic mobility.

Given what they had and the constraints they had to work within, Boys' Prep leadership made the decision to manage their students' grief alongside weighty academic expectations by a hurried return to normalcy. While Monday's decisions had highlighted all the good of the school, the transition into the *hard hard* period exposed one of the underlying tensions of the school's premise—namely, that it was laser-focused on students' futures even as those futures faced constant threats. There was probably no way to prevent the time after a student's death from being hard for everyone in the school community, but the *hard hard* happened when the school tried to transition too quickly, when the necessary resources and supports were not already in place, and when the school's mission and the pressures it faced from above seemed to neglect students' lived realities.

*

As the weeks went by, JahSun's friends continued trying to balance their own emotional processing, the school's expectations, and the day-to-day joys and struggles of teenage boyhood. On the last day before winter break, several seniors attended the varsity basketball game. Most arrived at the nearby recreation center about halfway through the game to find the Boys' Prep team already fifteen points behind. As the game continued, the score disparity widened. Among the fans, good humor mixed with the disappointment: lots of playful mocking of their friends on the court and some slightly less playful criticism of the coaching. When one of the seniors on the team, part of JahSun's circle, blatantly fouled another player, his friends laughed heartily and one turned to the group with a smirk: "Hope Jah don't see this."

The moment passed as fleetingly as it arose, but indicated to me that even when things appeared most back to normal, JahSun was never far from his friends' thoughts. The banner hanging above the court, which read "remembering the past, living in the present, planning for the future," was a stirring reminder that every time the boys remembered their friend, they also experienced the pang of planning for a future without him.

As we will see in the next chapter, when the limited opportunities for students' grief expression in school became even more restricted over time, mourning moved out of the school building and into the peer-driven spaces of social media and the boys' own inner worlds.

Chapter Five

Disenfranchised Grief

THE HIDDEN HARD

At first glance, Ms. Bloom's classroom looks like any other: twenty-five metal desks with attached chairs arranged in tight clusters. Two small whiteboards and a Smartboard in between. A cabinet storing student laptops and a wheeled cart with lab materials. Heavy textbooks, often frayed at the binding, piled up on the windowsills. The trash bin near the door brimming with empty bags of snack food. In the back corner, Ms. Bloom's desk is almost invisible beneath stacks of lab reports and quizzes. Taped to the wall above her desk are handwritten or hand-drawn cards from students. Nearby, a bulletin board she painstakingly collaged with photographs of students to mimic the *Wins & Losses* album cover by Philadelphia rapper Meek Mill.

Behind the Smartboard, the wall is painted with red chalkboard paint, covered with white chalk messages. A few scribblings honor Ms. Bloom as the "best" teacher; some boast that a certain student "was here"; but largely, it is a wall of grief for the dead, covered in RIP messages and hashtags for JahSun and Tyhir and others (fig. 5.1). How long, I wondered, could one ignore the wallpaper-like background to focus on homework instructions or biological concepts? How deeply would the scrawls on the thirty-foot memorial seep each day into the students' consciousness as they studied science?

Figure 5.1. The red chalkboard wall of Ms. Bloom's classroom covered in signatures, doodles, and messages, including several "Rest in Peace" memorials to deceased classmates.

Grief Becomes the Wallpaper

Metaphors are rarely embodied quite so literally. But the idea of grief becoming the wallpaper represents the period I call the *hidden hard*, which continued through the remainder of the school year. After winter break, the most visible tensions of the *hard hard* period had begun to recede. To all appearances, JahSun's death had been absorbed into the fabric of the school, repackaged as a kind of sad asterisk in its history that the students and staff could put aside as they got caught up in the tasks, worries, and excitement of their days. Possibly for some, but not so for many of JahSun's close friends. For them, it was only the beginning of what would become years of painful, ongoing grief.

Students would come to Ms. Bloom's classroom during lunch or free periods—even during teaching hours—to be near her and per-haps also to be near the memorial wall. They would sit on the window-sill or at her desk browsing social media on their phones, listening to music on their headphones, working on homework, or sometimes just sleeping while another class went on around them. This had be-come the accepted culture of the classroom, though there were other adults in the building who were critical and a handful of freshmen who requested to switch into another class with fewer distractions. Ms. Bloom herself would periodically express frustration if the older boys were disrupting the learning experience for her freshmen.

Some students who regularly hung out in Ms. Bloom's classroom explicitly made the connection between their comfort and the chalk-board wall, the programs from students' funerals by her desk, and the wall of pictures of former students. One friend described the class-room as a place that "makes everyone feel better."

JahSun's decorated locker also remained a memorial site holding profound meaning for some, even as it simply became part of the daily school scenery for others. Students' private memorial rituals, like the one Kaliq developed at the locker, were generally silent and invis-ible. Even Bashir, who continued keeping his watch throughout the winter—eating breakfast and lunch on the hallway floor, legs out-stretched toward his brother's locker—may have eventually come to blend in as a fixture of the hallway.

As the school year continued, collective references to shared losses would reemerge around key events on the calendar—birthdays, an-niversaries, preparations for Prom and graduation. But broadly, stu-dents' sustained grief was far less visible in school during this *hidden hard* period of winter and early spring. Most students continued to grieve silently and on their phones. Social media became their pri-mary space for self-expression. Significantly, grief would also show up at the year's end on their report cards and, in interviews with me, in their expressions about the future. In this chapter, I narrate the *hidden hard* period when students' unresolved grief was pushed into private spaces by the schoolwide expectation of normalcy and the mythology around the boys' resilience.

Unrecognized and Disenfranchised Grief

Anyone who has lost someone knows that grief doesn't end after a few weeks. The acute, debilitating pain may lessen, but for many of us it never fully goes away. People talk about grief coming in waves, rising unexpectedly out of nowhere. "Sometimes it just hits me," one boy told me. "One month/year down, a lifetime to go" was a common refrain when the boys posted online about a death anniversary; the mourners believed they would feel the loss as long as they lived.

Social pressures to move on from grief are strong: recover, focus on positive outcomes, "find closure," and avoid dwelling on loss in public conversation.[1] Though the existence of a linear progression of grief has been largely discredited in academic literature, popular views of orderly individual pathways, like the five stages of grief made famous by Elisabeth Kübler-Ross, continue to have influence. The social expectation that most of us will move predictably through our grief and, within a short period of time, be ready to function as normal again remains in many cases.[2] Grief that is "prolonged" or disruptive to daily life is subject to a mental illness diagnosis.[3]

Social cues around what expressions of grief are allowable vary across different groups of people. Some mourners are given space to cry, wail, and be hysterical, while others might be punished for the same behaviors.[4] Some mourners are offered services and supports, while others are expected to quickly recover through their own fortitude.[5] Black and Brown communities experience the greatest social restrictions around grief expression and the least access to social supports—even while experiencing the most loss.[6]

Young Black murder victims are often assumed by the media or the public to have been participating in illegal activities, stigmatizing their families and friends in their most vulnerable moments and delegitimizing their emotional pain.[7] Black families who have lost a child to homicide are less likely than white families to receive notification of the death from the police in an empathetic or emotionally supportive way.[8] Cultural norms also play a role in structuring grief responses: within Black communities, the common expectation to "be strong in grief" can compel the bereaved to conceal their suffering and to avoid triggering someone else's pain by discussing a loss.[9]

The boys grieving JahSun also had to contend with cultural norms around masculinity. Dominant ideas of masculinity and traditional gender socialization of boys create social costs to expressing vulnerability or seeking help.[10] Male grievers who prefer affective or expressive modes often find that "intense feelings of grief are more than a mere inconvenience; they represent a threat to the self" and to their very idea of masculinity.[11] Restrictions around emotional expression are magnified for Black boys, who may face additional penalties for perceived weakness or receive social rewards for projecting toughness.[12]

Dr. Stephens recognized that for his Black male students, gendered and racialized expectations to "have a stiff upper lip and recover" from the devastation of losing a friend would likely create conditions where their grief might "*seem* short-lived," but probably wouldn't be. He knew this as an educator, having been in school leadership at the time of five prior students' deaths, and as a Black man himself who had recently lost his father and was expected to persevere through his pain when he returned to work a few days later.

Social rules around who can grieve, for what kinds of losses, and for how long can result in what is known as *disenfranchised grief*. Lacking a "socially recognized right [or] role," a person so deprived has "little or no opportunity to mourn publicly."[13] And for mourners already devalued by racism and oppression, their grief is further "illegitimated," made to "feel invalid" or "illegible" to others.[14] Some mourners may even be sanctioned for their grieving behaviors, leading to what has been called "suffocated grief."[15] In the context of disenfranchisement and the expectation of hasty recovery, tremendous inner strength and skills of emotion management are required simply to grieve in the open.[16]

The Mythology of Black Boys' Resilience

At Boys' Prep, a critical driver of the disenfranchisement of student grief was the school's (mis)understanding of the boys' resilience. Resilience, or the capacity to withstand or recover quickly from adversity, is a foundational virtue promoted by Black Male Academies like Boys' Prep, part of the DNA of the school-reform effort that brought them about. This approach to schooling aims to equip poor students to respond to "the challenges and risks that arise from neighborhood experiences." Yet, in practice, many do so by "shut[ting] out a desolate urban landscape" from school life or, in this case, trying to move students quickly past outside-of-school traumas or losses.[17]

Following JahSun's death, the idea of resilience took on mythological properties. To be clear, the students' resilience itself was not a myth; without a doubt, they demonstrated remarkable inner fortitude in the wake of losses no one ought ever to face at their age. But a convenient fiction had begun to form in the school's framing of student grit and hardiness in the face of loss.[18] The view of Black boys as inherently resilient derives from a broader racialized and classed normalization of Black death and suffering, gendered stereotypes of masculine emotional stoicism, and societal devaluations of the complexity of youths' emotional lives. This myth of resilience took pressure off already stretched-thin teachers and staff to make student support a continued priority. It played out in the ways adults discussed students' continued grief and the implicit—and sometimes quite explicit—expectations of how and when they should be moving on.

One afternoon in mid-December, two young teachers, both white and in their first year at Boys' Prep, were chatting in the hallway about a recently suspended student. The topic reminded Mr. Leonard, an English teacher in his late twenties, of issues he was having with the handful of seniors in his elective class, some of whom were part of JahSun's close circle. Their grief, he ventured, was "going too far." His colleague nodded in agreement.

Mr. Leonard worried that students were starting to use grief as an excuse not to work and to skip class. The night before, returning to the building around 8 p.m. after coaching an athletic event, he'd been surprised to find several students still at school hanging out with a teacher and eating food she'd bought them. His tone was a little disparaging when he suggested she was "buying [her students] gourmet meals" and, I felt he implied, coddling them.

Mr. Leonard became more impassioned: "The system is tough on young Black men and they are going to face a lot of trauma, so they have to learn to keep moving after trauma." He didn't want students to become dependent on their teachers—or take advantage of them. Mr. Leonard still had several students regularly skipping class or their sports practice; he would find them laughing and playing in the hallway. He reenacted a scene of coming upon a student "looking at snap videos on his phone," who would barely look up from his device to tell his teacher almost flippantly, "I'm grieving."[19]

The teacher standing in the hallway with Mr. Leonard was sympathetic to his view. She added: "It's been two weeks already. I tell them they need to go to Ms. Rivera [the social worker] if they say they're grieving and then I check in with her to see if they went, and if they didn't, then they're skipping class."

These two teachers' assessments may very well have been fair—there certainly are adolescents who might "take advantage" of school-wide lenience. But Black boys are a group that have historically been denied the right to the benefit of the doubt or to an understanding of their emotional complexity. These casual hallway conversations are how school norms take hold, and in the weeks following JahSun's death, many teachers found themselves having to take on the undesirable role of investigator of authentic emotion. They had to decipher between "real" and "fake" grief, often treating them as objective, distinct categories. And even for the non-"fakers," this line of thinking went, these Black boys ought to be learning how to bounce back as quickly as possible. The school's expectations of how and how long to grieve, refined and passed along through staff conversations like the one between Mr. Leonard and his colleague, were fully loaded with ideas about Black invulnerability and stereotypes of Black men's need for emotional stoicism in the face of trauma or loss.

This was not just the domain of white faculty. Stereotype-informed expectations of Black boyhood had shaped Mr. Pratt's reflections on

Herc's suspension, described in the last chapter. Though he prided himself on having the "pulse" of the student body, especially given his own background that mirrored so many of the students', Mr. Pratt sometimes worried about being too "soft" on the boys. The boys needed to be prepared for the real world outside the safe space of the school—so if the real world contained trauma and loss and people not accommodating their pain, then that's what they needed to learn now.

The unspoken assumption seemed to be that because this probably wasn't the first or last loss the boys would face, less tenderness was required. Because they experienced so much trauma, perhaps there was no room (or time) for grief. This echoes observations from research in other school contexts that Black boys coping with peer homicide were viewed by some school adults as "professional grievers" who could be expected to get over their loss with limited external supports.[20] This mythology of Black boys' strength and resilience seemed to neglect their status as children, and perhaps their childhood itself.[21] Worse, assuming the boys ought to be able to recover quickly risks placing blame for continued struggle on the most vulnerable among them—rather than identifying the problem as the structural factors that produce so many teen murders in the first place.[22]

With their grief increasingly sanctioned and therefore forced into hiding inside the school building, the boys responded in a range of ways. I've identified the five most prevalent approaches as: closing in, checking out, standing still, puffing out, and checking in.

Closing In: Friendship Gatekeeping

In the aftermath of JahSun's death, social boundaries among Boys' Prep seniors began to re-form and solidify. A clique of about a dozen seniors, publicly recognized as JahSun's closest friends, became much tighter, supporting each other through the difficult time. This group included Ezekiel, Omari, Owen, Rajae, Khalil, Tony, and Theo (see appendix B.1). But it also excluded students who had felt close to JahSun and whose mourning, without social recognition, became much more difficult. As grief became an individual, rather than communal, activity at Boys' Prep, only some individuals were permitted to remain publicly in a state of grieving.

School staff had played a role in solidifying the boundaries of the group. Ms. Bloom initially identified them by her invitation to decorate JahSun's locker and help plan the vigil. Ms. Rivera used a slightly different list to recommend students for additional counseling. Ms. Bloom and Ms. Woo, another science teacher with close relationships with many students, helped facilitate trips for the primary clique to JahSun's mother's house on Sundays throughout the winter and spring. Ms. Kallum and some colleagues organized a trip to a local college for seniors embarking on senior projects related to gun violence or criminal justice, a group that heavily overlapped with this friendship circle.

According to the boys, this group had not existed in such a formal way before their shared loss, but as Omari put it, "I think . . . it drove us closer. 'Cause, like, before this year . . . I didn't hang out with [some of them], but now . . . we actually meet up and go places." Boys' Prep had long been promoting the idea of "brotherhood," but Ramell acknowledged he never felt that until now: "People dying just bring everybody closer together. It really makes us a brotherhood, like, how the [the school] was trying to in freshman year."

But JahSun had traveled in many social circles and befriended a range of peers across the school. He had been on the football team as well as in the school play. He was described by some peers as "street"—although, to be sure, *not* to the extent that anyone expected him to get killed. JahSun's grades were good (but not great), which placed him in a mix of honors and regular classes. The small senior class was roughly split across two loosely formed social circles that might crudely map onto stereotypical binaries of high school coolness. Though JahSun was more closely associated with the "cooler" crowd, his diverse interests meant that several senior boys from the *other* group—higher achieving academically and more focused on school leadership activities than athletics—also identified as close with JahSun, especially Yaja. Additionally, JahSun had, over the years, garnered the respect and friendship of several younger students, most notably Hazeem, Kaliq, and Herc, juniors who were part of the group of friends still grieving the loss of freshman Tyhir a year and a half earlier.

Ms. Cain noticed that JahSun connected with classmates she would not have expected. He would go out of his way to support and uplift peers without nearly as much social cachet as he had. She remembered a moment when a student in her class had outed himself as gay. (An assumed-to-be-gay clique spanning multiple grades regularly hung out together, but very few were explicitly open with other peers about their sexuality.) Ms. Cain recalled that JahSun seemed to sense that this was a vulnerable moment in the all-boys classroom, and felt that as a popular, well-respected peer he could play a role in helping his classmate feel more comfortable. He was the first to speak up and acknowledge what the other student had said; though he did not share that identity, he told the class he could relate to the feeling of being different. Yaja echoed this memory of JahSun as a connector: he "touched everybody, he was . . . friends with the gay people, he was friends with the dorks."

Despite JahSun's diverse social ties, the circle of friends loosely formed around the football team continued to receive top billing in the hierarchy of grievers.[23] When school decisions had to be made, such as where to hang the scholar-athlete award JahSun had won posthumously or how to honor him at graduation, school leaders turned to this group. Yaja felt excluded:

They only called up those people, not even knowing that [JahSun] done had deep relationships with way more people than just, you know, them four to five. And there's no discredit to them, because I know they were super close to JahSun, but it was like, you know, to a certain extent, there was more people that could've spoke on that situation, spoke on that reality that actually felt it . . . So [there were] people that just didn't even get to actually feel any type of way because they felt like, you know, other people were gonna say something or do something. But I feel like that also played a part into why, you know, people had to move on quickly . . .

Specifically for me, I was not in JahSun's closest group of friends [so I felt like I couldn't] feel as hard as [them].

Being restricted and disenfranchised in his grief made Yaja, and others, feel like he couldn't process the loss as he would have wanted to, as if he wasn't entitled to his feelings and had to hide them. For him, it necessitated a specific, largely hidden form of emotional labor.

Not coincidentally, the students whose grief for JahSun went unrecognized were also excluded from the much-praised sense of brotherhood that had sprung up among the acknowledged mourners. To Yaja, only Monday—the shared experience, notably the vigil—had given him any semblance of "brotherhood." But already, in the logistical decisions concerning that day, a chasm was emerging in the school's eyes between the grievers and grieve-nots. As the year progressed, Yaja, while continuing to grieve in private, would become ever more disconnected from the social life of Boys' Prep.

Indeed, the resentment Yaja felt that a small group had become the "gatekeepers of who was close to JahSun" long persisted, as I later learned, into his early adulthood. In the years after graduating, it had become customary for JahSun's friends to assemble at his mother's invitation for memorial events or video calls. Sensing a possessiveness over the mourning of JahSun from some of his peers, Yaja would confess to feelings of self-consciousness when he attended, as if he had to explain his presence to prove he wasn't "a fake."

Yaja's experience reflects a larger pattern among both students and adults at Boys' Prep who failed to appreciate the unpredictable or unseen impacts of loss. Those who simply share a hallway, classroom, or school affiliation might still be profoundly impacted by the murder of a peer; and, within the complex social dynamics of a high school, it is hard to know the full extent of friendship connections. As Yaja explained, "even if you just walked past [JahSun] in the hallway, you felt that. Like even if you had one conversation with that man, you felt his death." But Boys' Prep's response mirrored the larger culture where recognition of grief is in limited supply and reserved for a small group of recognized friends. Continued supports closed in around this group, leaving others to fend for themselves.

Checking Out: Disengaging from School and Coping through Substances

Disenfranchisement of grief led some students like Yaja to check out of school. After JahSun's death, Yaja's senior year began to devolve. His grades kept slipping and he started isolating himself from peers, from teachers, and from me.[24] Having to defend his own friendship and legitimize his grief became debilitating. As a twenty-one-year-old, Yaja reflected, with insight conferred by distance, on the remainder of that year:

Nobody to me was like in tune with their emotions at that point, we all just kinda like carried on through the rest of the year. I remember there was one point in time where they said if we were skipping class, [we failed]. Like we had all just kinda, like, threw our shoulders up, like, "It is what it is at this point." . . . Because we were like, "Damn, we just took this big hit . . ." You can't come back from that in several days, several weeks or whatever . . . We crying for one day, [then] it was one day after that and ain't nobody dropped a tear, like, we just kinda kept going through the motions. So, you know, I just, I wish we had that at that time period, like just somebody there to tell us like, "Yo, take a minute to breathe, to understand you just lost something." Like, straight up, you know what I mean, "but you can do something different with it." Like it's that, it's that you can do something different with this experience.

Yaja described crying for one day and then just "going through the motions" because he didn't have adequate time to process the "hit" they all took. Teachers were on him. He was unable to focus. In response, he increased his marijuana habit, getting high every morning "just so I could make it through school." He described "teachers yelling at me and stuff like that, and then after the fact, I'm going to get high because I don't feel like thinking . . . I was just like completely checked out." In hindsight, Yaja wished someone had given him permission to fully feel what he was going through and some direction on how to "do something different with [his feelings]."

Even among students publicly recognized as part of JahSun's inner circle, lingering grief led to checking out. Though things at school were back to normal, many students still didn't feel anything close to that; their mourning remained present and proximate. Some found it easier to disengage through substances and distractions rather than continuously be reminded of the mismatch.

Ezekiel offers a poignant example. He'd had a rocky first three years of high school, developing a reputation among teachers and administrators as both an intelligent, promising student *and* a bit of an attention-seeking troublemaker who smoked more marijuana than he should. Senior year, though, things seemed to finally be clicking for Ezekiel. In Ms. Cain's philosophy class, which he shared with JahSun, Ezekiel often came alive. One day, he plopped down in the small circle designated for their regular Socratic seminars and declared with a winning grin, "I'm in a good mood, this discussion about to be good." He moved up to Honors English because the teacher of his "regular" English class thought he wasn't being challenged enough. And he was slowly reversing his troublemaker reputation. For instance, one day, in one of Ezekiel's classrooms, there was word of a theft. Mr. Pratt came in to check students' bags. When Ezekiel realized that the bag check was beginning at the end of the room farthest from him, he turned to me with a look of sincere surprise: "I usually would have gotten checked first." He took pride in the fact that one year earlier he would have been "checked, double checked, asked to take off his uniform . . . criminaliz[ed for his] false reputation," but perhaps a turnaround was brewing.

Then his best friend died, and everything shifted for Ezekiel.

As close as he and JahSun were, it happens that they had been quarreling over some inconsequential matter that Thanksgiving weekend. Though Ezekiel would never say so, other students theorized that their fight was part of the reason Ezekiel took the loss so hard. Whether or not this was so, Ezekiel attended the memorial service flanked by his mom and younger brother, planting himself in the back of the room, stone-faced and silent. He skipped many of his classes until winter break and was the ringleader of an intense bout of hallway horseplay that damaged school walls.

It was also during this period that Ezekiel began smoking marijuana more heavily—and his friends worried that he was doing harder drugs too. Even in the moment, the relationship between grief and his escalating habit was pretty clear to Ezekiel. He would frequently post on Instagram comments like "I can't believe my brother Jah died before the deal game, that's why sometimes I get high so I can't feel pain."[25]

After winter break, Ezekiel returned to Boys' Prep with the reality sinking in that high school was nearing its end—he would be moving to the next stage without JahSun. Though he resumed attending most of his classes and assured his teachers he wanted to improve his grades sufficiently to graduate, it was clear he was emotionally checked out. In the hallways between class periods, the roughhousing had abated, but Ezekiel launched a new set of games and verbal bullying, usually at the expense of younger students. Sometimes in class, he would cause disruptions that derailed the lesson, or would simply walk out to find his friends. Frequently during lunch or free periods, or when cutting class, Ezekiel would escape to Ms. Bloom's room, where he found comfort and could "feel the presence" of JahSun. As a result, by late winter, Ezekiel would be one of five seniors, all in JahSun's tight circle of friends, being considered for expulsion because of their disruptions in the building. While normal school life seemed to be moving on without them, the question now was whether Ezekiel and the others would pull themselves together in time to graduate.

Standing Still: Resisting Long-Term Planning

Another way that the boys responded to their losses and the disenfranchisement of their grief at school was to plant themselves firmly in the present—not dwelling too much on the past, but also not letting themselves dream too much about the future. Herc, for example, had been on a downhill trajectory since his suspension in November, telling Mr. Hopkins in his reinstatement hearing that he "wasn't thinking about the future." Many boys would echo the feeling that, facing so uncertain a future, it was hard to look ahead. Which left them at a standstill, unready or unwilling to make decisions with long-range consequences in mind.

Despite short bouts of inspiration or motivation, Herc's resistance to long-term planning hindered his school performance. He missed ninety-four class periods during the three-month winter trimester and generally appeared despondent. Later he reflected that experiencing so much loss put him in an "'I don't really give a fuck' . . . type of mood . . . like [he] didn't really care." He was mourning not only Tyhir and JahSun, but also several other friends outside the Boys' Prep community.

Herc's two closest friends, Jonquett and Latrell, the only people he really trusted, had left the school—one had failed freshman year twice and the other transferred to a less college-focused school. They still got to see each other at their McDonald's job, but at school, Herc spent much of his time alone. Gone were the lively lunch tables he'd enjoyed the previous two years. Now he'd quickly devour his meal while scrolling through social media or sneak out of the cafeteria to wander the hallways or sit in Ms. Bloom's classroom. In class, he went through the motions, finding little of interest in his schoolwork. Occasionally he would entertain his teachers or friends with a spurt of engaging enthusiasm, particularly in math class with Ms. Jordan. She had learned to live with his unpredictable ups and downs: "He's either in a really good mood or super down and tired, I never know what I'm gonna get from him . . . [it's like he] needs a pep talk every day." But even to attentive teachers, Herc never confided his grief to them.

Growing up surrounded by gun violence, the possibility of dying young had often occurred to Herc. He remembered as a young boy looking expectantly toward the future, dreaming of the day he would be a full-fledged grownup. Now, all that felt naive. How long, he wondered, did he really have? One day, he told me:

I've had people tell me they had a dream of me dying recently . . . getting killed . . . I mean I started thinking, like, if it's my time, it's my time . . . I mean I'm not going to make it my time unless I know it's my time. Like if I can prevent it . . . I'm going to do it . . . I just want a good sixtieth [birthday] or something . . . Yeah, I don't really care after sixty . . . ain't no point [if you] always got to be helped and stuff like that . . . One day I can see a couple of my grandkids so, I'm still cool . . . I just care about that.

Herc looked forward to meeting his grandkids, but imagined reaching sixty might be enough to feel he had lived a good life. And he had come to accept the idea that "his time" might come sooner.[26] With the future so uncertain, where did school fit, especially when it mostly involved boredom or failure?

After winter break, Herc's focus improved. Heart-to-hearts with his brothers, home from college, reminded him that getting through school would make it possible for him to avoid a life in the streets and having to "watch [his] back 24/7." But despite his proclamations of renewed commitment, he was having trouble making it stick. For those on a college trajectory, junior year is the big one: he had to improve his grades. Herc's teachers tried to make it as concrete as possible. In early March, as the third trimester was beginning—the final chance to reset and recover passing grades for the year—Herc met with his academic advisor, Ms. Estevez, a math teacher in her midtwenties and the only Latina teacher in the school. Herself very shaken by JahSun's death, she was generally understanding of the way her students were impacted, but there was no denying Herc's academic decline.

Ms. Estevez placed a sheet of paper between them. The worksheet listed his grades in each class from the first two trimesters and blank spaces for their goals for the final trimester. The two sat side-by-side in metal student desks at the front of the classroom. Ms. Estevez punched numbers into her laptop to calculate the minimum grade that Herc would need in each class to pass: "So the way it looks right now is Latin, here . . . to get a C- [for the year], you would need to get 114 points [this trimester]. But that's something you would need to talk to [the teacher] about, because if you get over an A+, that would make sure that you go into the final with a C-. So I would talk to her about extra credit, see what you can do."

Herc sat straight-faced and mostly silent. Perhaps he was begin-ning to script his conversation with his Latin teacher about extra-credit opportunities. Or perhaps, like me, he was in disbelief at the casual expectation that he might miraculously turn a second trimester grade of 46/100 into a 114 by the time finals rolled around. But Ms. Estevez continued, "Now, for my class . . . you need to aim to get a 78, which I feel like is feasible for you. If you get the 78, that'll make sure you go into my final with a C-. And at the end of the day, these two grades have cushion in them, like a range of a couple points, so that's still a feasible goal. Do you think you could do that? . . . Prob-ably, right? You can do that." Without waiting for a response, she continued to calculate his possibility of squeaking by in each class with a passing C- (Boys' Prep did not consider Ds passing). The cal-culations, accounting for his low grades during the previous two tri-mesters, were meant to show him how high this trimester's grades would have to be (e.g., "over an A+") for him to have even a chance of passing the full-year course (i.e., going into the final exam with an overall C- for the class).

Ms. Estevez reminded Herc that communication was key. "Nobody here is against you . . . the school wants you," she told him earnestly. For extra emphasis, banging the metal desk with each word, she re-iterated, "We. Want. You. Here." Herc remained silent. In closing, Ms. Estevez underlined the seventy-one tardies at the bottom of the page and offered to "blow up [his] phone in the morning" to make sure he was on time for school. Other teachers were ready to support him too. Ms. Bloom sought Herc out later in the day to set up a meeting to help him plan his next academic steps.

But making long-term plans continued to elude him.

In February, I witnessed a poignant example of this when Herc, Jonquett, and Latrell—the "three musketeers"—reunited at school for a posthumous birthday party for Tyhir that Ms. Bloom and another teacher had organized for the boys and Tyhir's family. After the gath-ering with pizza, birthday cake, and remembrances, the three boys left school to smoke together—and invited me to tag along. I hesitated momentarily before accepting.[27]

Once in their usual alley a few blocks from school, Herc hooked his bag to the fence and reached into his pants to pull out his stash, which he kept in a white cardboard jewelry box, wrapped in Saran Wrap and many layers of scented fabric-softener sheets. He said being high felt like he was "in love." Then he added, "I don't like myself when I'm not high." I joked with Herc that his storage method was so clever that I wondered what would happen if he put that much energy into—but before I could finish my sentence, Herc interrupted: "Don't say 'school'!" The other two laughed; I was pretty predictable to them by that point.

But they were serious. "School doesn't get me bread," Herc offered matter-of-factly. "I mean maybe in the long term—" and then Latrell completed the thought: "but we might not be here long term." They all nodded in somber agreement as they finished rolling their joints. Though their assembly was a kind of ritual of memorialization and healing, they did not discuss Tyhir or their other lost friends. The three boys seemed to savor being together like old times before Latrell and Jonquett had left school. They asked me to take some photos of them.

More than a year later, just before the three-year anniversary of Tyhir's death, Herc posted one of those pictures to Instagram, along with the modest wish "I just wanna see us get older 💯 🖤." Although counting on and planning for the future was hard, he still had dreams. Tragically, just two years after this post, Jonquett would become yet another victim of gun violence at age twenty.

Puffing Out: Asserting and Embodying Grief

So far, we have seen a turning inward on the part of many students in response to the school's decreased recognition of their grief, but others responded to the disenfranchisement of their grief by acting out in various ways. Take Hazeem, for example. A junior situated low on the popularity radar, he occupied a neglected corner of JahSun's social network, where in his view he was often policed for "grieving too much." (His own father had chastised him for posting so often on social media about the deaths of his friends.)

Perhaps in subconscious response to this criticism, Hazeem tried to push himself up the perceived grief hierarchy by questioning others' emotional legitimacy. Not long after JahSun's death, one of Hazeem's classmates, Sean, posted images to Instagram from the Monday evening vigil with the caption: "We missing you down here bro bro but your legacy def living on 💯 💪 🕊️ . . . Rest In Peace n Paradise Big Bro." Spotting the post for the first time while scrolling through Instagram during social studies class, Hazeem apparently turned to Sean and loudly asserted that Sean didn't know JahSun like that. By disenfranchising a peer's expression of mourning, Hazeem was propping himself up.[28] Sean shouted back. Their teacher, who relayed the story to me, worried things were getting so heated that it might come to blows. Feeling a violent urge well up in him, Sean left class to cool off. Hazeem stuck out the period, but then decided he did "not want to be around people right now" and got permission to spend the afternoon in the main office doing homework.

Of all the students I followed at Boys' Prep, Hazeem posted most frequently about his mourning of JahSun and Tyhir as well as his grandfather. In one example two weeks after JahSun's death, Hazeem posted a story to Instagram (fig. 5.2) that said, referring to JahSun, "💔 losing you I lost a part of me 💔," below which he listed three phrases he recalled as the last words JahSun had spoken to him, expressions of support and encouragement. The post can be seen as a form of puffing out, offering evidence of the depth and validity of his relationship to the deceased.

A few weeks later, Hazeem posted another digital memorialization: a picture of the program from JahSun's invitation-only funeral with a long caption detailing how his grief had been evolving. He wrote:

wassup bro I miss you my dawg 💜 ik you watching down on me mane . . . seeing me a couple months ago I was broken as shit my heart was shattered felt like the world stopped mane 😔 but listen bro ik you proud

Figure 5.2. Hazeem's Instagram story. Image of his feet with various captions, including the last words spoken to him by JahSun.

of me now knowing I'm doing better. I left them drugs alone like u always would tell me 💯 ik u see me out here tryna stop being violent towards n***as but bro it's too much anger, ima try though. I just miss you my dawg. me and Kaliq was just talking bout you and the shit you would tell us 🙏 we miss you mane. I'm still hurt but I'm tryna turn this pain into motivation. [. . .] 💪 just be w me every move I make 💯 #LLJ 💙 ✊ my dawg4life 🙏

Hazeem imagined that JahSun would be proud of the progress he had made in repairing his broken heart, finding motivation, and avoiding destructive activities like drugs and violence. He directed the message to JahSun, asking him to "be with [him] every move [he] make[s]." The post also demonstrated his continued grief to his online followers.

In addition to digital memorializations, the boys' physical embodiment of their bereaved status also functioned as public evidence of authentic grief in the increasingly grief-indifferent culture of school. Starting the first day back at school after JahSun's death, his friends talked about getting tattoos to honor him. By the end of the school year, a handful had followed through, mostly with JahSun's name and birth and death dates on their arms, though their tattoos would be hidden under school uniforms. Embodying grief by marking it on the flesh is a popular practice, particularly for marginalized grievers. A tattoo is a way of "carrying the dead with us" in a world where talking about death may not be socially acceptable and it "establish[es] the identity of the bereaved in a fixed and permanent way."[29] Many boys viewed it as a sign of respect and a way to ensure they would hold on to their friend's memory.

There were also less permanent markings. Nearly all the boys had t-shirts or sweatshirts commemorating fallen friends. The shirts, worn under uniforms or on evenings or weekends, were a way to "maintain proximity" to the deceased and "unify survivors," marking the wearer as part of the bereaved community.[30] Some boys talked about wearing specific colors they knew a deceased friend loved. During baseball season, Khalil put an RIP message inside his baseball cap and ordered new cleats with JahSun's name and jersey number inscribed on them.

Most of JahSun's friends also continued to wear the red rubber wrist-bands inscribed with his name that JahSun's mother had distributed at a December memorial service. Kaliq promised himself he would never take it off: "I [even] wash up with JahSun on." Theo had one he planned to keep around his wrist "til it fall off" and another on his dresser wrapped around a trophy.

Particularly during this period of disenfranchised and hidden grief at school, the boys found ways to assert their right to continue griev-ing. Sometimes they responded as if attention to grief was a scarce resource and accessing it required being seen as more legitimate or worthy than others. At other times, they embodied their grief through permanent or temporary markers that could serve as both a personal reminder and a public indication of connection to the deceased. These forms of *puffing out* also asserted that JahSun's life mattered by demon-strating the prolonged impact he had on his friends.

Checking In: Emotional Expression and Support Online

As is clear in the stories above, social media—and Instagram specifically—became a central site for the boys to process, share, and connect with each other around their grief, particularly once there was less space for it in school. Whereas conversations with friends around cafeteria tables or in school hallways largely omitted references to their collective loss, online the boys seemed to share their emotions more freely and connect with each other in their continued grief.

A study from around this time found that 33 percent of Black teens spend most of their waking hours glued to Instagram or other social media.[31] This tracks with the heavy use I observed at Boys' Prep. Even when phones were forbidden, the boys would sneak peeks throughout the day to scroll through their timelines, respond to messages, or even make a discreet video call. They would snap pictures of their desks, classrooms, their shoes on the floor, and post them with captions about their mood or activities.

Boys like Kaliq narrated their daily life online, particularly in the twenty-four-hour Instagram stories. Kaliq was known among his friends for having a good head on his shoulders and often functioned as a third parent for his siblings. His teachers praised him for regularly helping his peers in class. On weekends he worked alongside his uncle as a janitor at another high school. In the first few weeks of November 2017, before JahSun's death, Kaliq posted the following updates and philosophical musings on Instagram:

6:55AM. Going to be a great day, I'm going to school and I'm on time 😎

Allah please watch over the guys I came with 🙏 I need them all to be at the table when we all eating 💯 🔪 !

I'm really older than what I am 💯 feel like I shouldn't be in this generation

Wish I had another chance at everything 😵 !

Background of a street n***a with a mind of a Scholar 💯 🖤

Everyday that I wake up my undivided attention is going to getting my cake up & staying out them prisons 🙏 #Prayedup

[on Thanksgiving:] Y'all thankful for today, I'm thankful for everyday that I make back home 🙏 ! Rs

This sampling reflects the range of topics he covered, from the mundane to the deeply contemplative, from self-definition to future planning.

When JahSun died, Instagram was where Kaliq poured out his thoughts, his regrets, his hopes, his pain, his grief—as did many of his friends.[32] He immediately connected JahSun's death to all the other losses he'd already experienced and used his Instagram page to process:

I'm really a hurt n***a rn dawg. I lost Ty, I lost my old head big mike and
now my closest cousin 🧑 all in a matter of damn near 2 yrs. Sometimes
I be thinking this shit was meant for me 😢. These cold streets taking
everybody close to me away from me it's sad yo. Ty was like a brother.
Big mike was my old head, he always looked out, & jah was like my closest cousin but more like a brother 💯. I swear I need to distance myself
from the bullshit. I don't want no more of my n***as or sisters to leave
this earth. At least not rn yo 🧑 I'm really hurt and destroyed rn. RIP to all
my fallen soldiers 🙏 🧕

Kaliq scrolled back through his text history with JahSun and posted
screenshots of their conversations. Over the next few days, his Instagram remained active with narrations of in-the-moment intense
emotions like "I'm drained of strength, I'm broken in tiny pieces," or
"airplane mode" to signal that he was turning his phone off to messages and calls, as well as pleas for help (fig. 5.3).

As time went on, Kaliq's grief—like most grief—evolved, becoming less intense and visceral, but no less present in his life. Despite
frequently professing to be emotionally numb, Kaliq's Instagram told
a different story. He narrated his emotional ups and downs and the
strategies he used to cope with grief and pain. One day he might post
a picture of himself holding a bottle of liquor with the caption: "I need
a drink rn . . . I'm hurting." Another day, an image of his shadow on
an outdoor basketball court where he "leave[s] all [his] anger." Kaliq
pondered his future out loud online, perhaps hoping for feedback or
advice. Once, in the middle of the night, he ruminated: "Where the hell
Ima be in 5 years 🧑 at the rate I'm going, dead or wishing for money
on my commissary," referring to the choice between death or prison.

For Kaliq and his peers, grieving JahSun's loss online might be
prompted by any number of experiences or memories. Specific dates,
like birthdays and death anniversaries, would call for public acknowledgment of their loss, but seemingly random moments when they
poignantly remembered his absence might also inspire the desire to
share. In a post from Omari almost a year after JahSun's death, he
located himself at a local movie theater with the caption "I just saw

Figure 5.3. Kaliq's Instagram story. Text commentary about needing help.

Night School and just cried becuz I ain't graduate with my whole gang." For Omari, a lighthearted movie set in a high school with a pivotal graduation scene reminded him that JahSun never made it to high school graduation. Below the caption, Omari added a message directly to JahSun: "I miss you a whole lot gang 💔💯😣" (fig. 5.4).

The boys' online posts were markedly more frequent and, at the same time, more expressive of grief and emotional pain than any of their non-digital social interactions. They might even expose the discrepancy explicitly, acknowledging in their posts that they deliberately concealed their grief, sadness, or other vulnerabilities during in-person interactions, substituting studied smiles or performances of toughness. Kaliq created an Instagram story with a photo of himself assuming a serious expression, with a caption that read: "Im going thru da most shxt and I swear I never will show that I'm hurting 💯."

Others confided that their smiling expressions were hiding deeper feelings: Hazeem posted that he sometimes "smile[s] to hide the pain. I don't say much"; Herc shared a picture with a big smile and the caption "laughing to hide all dis pain"; and Kaliq paired a photo of his smiling face on a school bulletin board acknowledging an award he won with the caption "Still smile thru all the pain 🧑" (fig. 5.5). Omari frequently posted about ways he might disguise his true feelings, like one action shot of himself from a football game with the text "Hide The Pain Behind The Mask" and another post captioned "You Can See The Wounds But The Pain Is Invisible."

Online, boys also confessed to social or emotional missteps in the face of loss. At the end of his senior year, Rajae posted a picture of JahSun and several of their football teammates with the caption "Pushed a lot of people away when I lost you bro. Just wanna talk to you again 😣." A full two years after JahSun's death, Yaja shared online, "my anger has always been a reflection of how hurt I am, nobody understand that though." Social media functioned as a repository to explain unhealthy grief responses that the boys were able to reflect on in hindsight.

Unlike a private journal entry, Instagram allows for peer interaction with one another and as a group. When boys posted about

Figure 5.4. Omari's Instagram story. Image of his feet at a movie theater with a caption about missing JahSun.

Still smile thru all the pain

NOV 9, 2017

Figure 5.5. Kaliq's Instagram story. Image of Kaliq's smiling picture on a school bulletin board for an honor he received, his face covered by a caption.

grief or emotional struggles, they could expect to receive comments or private messages affirming their feelings or offering support. In the context of continued disenfranchisement of their grief at school, such acknowledgments were often very welcome. But even without direct responses, many boys reported that they found it helpful to have a public space to leave their thoughts and emotions, knowing that their feelings would register with others. Years later, Kaliq reflected on the role of Instagram in his processing of grief:

When I look at Instagram, I see it as a blank form of expression. No one's going to judge you or say anything. When I post stuff [about grief], nobody says anything. I'm just able to voice my thoughts and feelings . . . When I feel like I can't talk to nobody, like verbally, I use Instagram to express how I feel . . . After I do that, I feel better that I got that out.

Even without direct replies from his friends, Instagram filled a gap in Kaliq's social world, a space where he could express emotions freely.[33]

Instagram also opened a window on to others experiencing similar emotions, sometimes giving boys new language for their feelings. Particularly resonant posts would be copied and reshared. For instance, on the three-month anniversary of JahSun's death, several friends screenshot a post from one of them and reposted it on their own page, as if one person's post reminded others to acknowledge the date. Another time, Ramell wrote on Instagram: "All these close deaths got me thinking when my time gone come. I really live every day like it's my last, I'm not even 18 yet smh"; screenshots of his words were reposted by multiple friends over the following days, sometimes with a comment like "took the words right from my mind," as a community of young people grappled with the same questions. Kaliq often participated in these digital peer dialogues: he screenshot Hazeem's story with the simple text "got so used to this pain 😢" (fig. 5.6a) and then added his own commentary, "Seriously 🙍 shit can't even hurt me nomore" before sharing to his page (fig. 5.6b). When their grief was disenfranchised in in-person social contexts like school—and, at

Figure 5.6a. Hazeem's Instagram story. Text commentary about getting used to pain.

Figure 5.6b. Kaliq's Instagram story. A screenshot of Hazeem's original post, with additional text expressing agreement. The doubling of the camera icon and "Send message" box at the bottom and the user details at the top are an easy way to spot duplicated images.

least for some, at home—the boys fashioned a permanent *easy hard* state of accepted communal grief online among their peers.

Well after high school and into his early twenties, Kaliq continued to use social media to narrate his emotional ups and downs and share vulnerabilities he probably wouldn't say out loud, including reflections on his continued grief, life regrets, suicidal thoughts, pride about his own strength, and hopes for the future. More than a year and a half after JahSun's death, Kaliq posted his friend's picture with the caption "crying harder than ever. I swear you don't know how much I miss you dawg 💔." A few years after that, awaiting the birth of his first child, he shared a sonogram image and the words: "Ngl I need that unconditional love feeling so I'm waiting on you champ," referring to his unborn son. Instagram continued to be the space where he could check in with himself about his most vulnerable thoughts, both related and unrelated to grief, and share them with a public audience with whom he'd be unlikely to share in person.

The Hidden Hard at Scale

In sum, among the teens I came to know at Boys' Prep, I observed a range of responses to the disenfranchisement of their grief at school. Some *closed in*, drawing boundaries around a perceived group of legitimate grievers, while others *puffed out*, asserting their rightful place in the grief hierarchy. Many struggled to stay focused in school, *checking out* via substances or other distractions, or had a hard time moving forward with the future in mind, *standing still*. But unexpectedly and with steady intensity, nearly all the boys used social media to *check in* with each other and, perhaps more importantly, with themselves. For them, the digital world had become a space free(er) from emotional control, expected and imposed timelines for grief, and pressures to hide their feelings. Instagram offered the clearest view of their tremendous pain, their thoughtful memorializations, and their future wishes and worries, which were almost completely hidden at school.[34]

It is well documented that underfunded urban schools can be uncaring, punitive places for children—and even highly resourced institutions foster racial and class inequities that disproportionately harm students of color. Even within fundamentally warm environments like Boys' Prep, being a student can still involve misrecognition, unfair punishment, and humiliation.[35] In these contexts, it is rare that kids feel safe enough to bring their full selves to school. When their emotional complexity and their agency are not fully recognized by educators (or peers), it becomes more comfortable and less risky to keep some parts of themselves in hiding, including grief.

Given the paucity of what they could see and access, it is not surprising that Boys' Prep's adults developed mythologized ideas about students' resilience. A sense of brotherhood and the beautiful ways the boys came together after loss—all this they plainly saw. Less visible were the ways that institutional exclusion of grief generated a need to jockey for grieving status or left out many suffering students. And, while the adults witnessed behavioral outbursts or students seeming to check out of academic engagement ("chuck it," as the boys would say), their ongoing displays and expressions of grief, often heartbreakingly deep and real, all happened out of sight. With in-school grief pushed deep into the background, becoming merely wallpaper from most views, many school adults assumed students had moved on, further disenfranchising their grief.

I studied just a relatively small number of students (about seventy-five) at one school over the course of a few years. What would we find if we looked for this *hidden hard* across the entire school? The neighborhood? Across all of Philadelphia, or the country? Thousands of children and teenagers are killed each year, leaving thousands of schools to cope with loss and grief. How vast is this hidden hard? How many Black boys, and youth in general, are experiencing grief that is invisible to the adults in their schools, and perhaps in many other parts of their lives? Have we disenfranchised the grief of an entire generation?

This risk deepens when everyone—both students and adults—begins to normalize the premature deaths of Black boys, as we will see in the next chapter.

Chapter Six

Long-Term Social Injury?

THE REPEATED HARD

Late May, the night of the Senior Prom, I stand in a receiving line of teachers at the entrance to a hotel ballroom. We wait expectantly for "our boys" to arrive. To relish and share in their proud moment as the evening's stars, and to *ooh* and *ahh* at their transformation. We're used to seeing the students uniformed identically each day, but tonight we get to see them shine individually in patterned jackets, stone-embellished shoes, and colorful bow ties—and many with dates on their arms. A glittering window into their out-of-school selves.

For more than a century, Prom has been an exalted fixture of American high school life, a rite of passage for teenagers preparing to end one chapter of their lives and begin a new one. No exception at Boys' Prep. The evening is always the celebratory climax of senior year, all of high school even. Families host extravagant send-off parties with food, music, and big banners to take photographs in front of. And the boys themselves plan for months: stylish outfits, luxury rental cars, dates, after-parties.

This year, especially, everyone at Boys' Prep seemed acutely aware of how meaningful this night would be. A moment for the boys to exhale, enjoy themselves, be frivolous and excessive despite the really bad year. Beyond this day, the future was unknown and, for many of them, unsecured. But tonight, they would get to be kings. Dressed in their finest with all eyes on them.

As each boy enters, his teachers envelop him, clapping and yelling out his name. Some boys leave their dates standing awkwardly in the middle of the hallway to give their teachers hugs and fistbumps. Others stop mid-strut to pose for pictures, lapping up the cheers from their adoring fans. Omari shows off two large patches bearing JahSun's initials that he's had sewn into his suit jacket.

Quartell is among the last to arrive. With a matching blazer and loafers in red velvet, sunglasses, and a huge grin, he is hard to miss. Q, as everyone calls him, is about 5′6″ with a slim build, close-cropped hair, and the shadow of a mustache. He's normally reserved, describing himself as a "popular loner," so his gleeful entrance—practically dancing down the hallway—instantly draws a round of applause.

Inside the ballroom, red and black balloons fill the cavernous space lit by flashing colored lights. Tables covered in gold glitter encircle the dance floor. There is a dinner buffet that some students have started to dig into, while others congregate in groups on the outskirts of the dance floor.

A few minutes after relaxing into a chair at one of the teacher tables, I notice several school administrators huddling in a corner, whispering to each other, and then hurriedly leaving the room. Within moments, word spreads among the teachers that a shooting has taken place near the school. I slip out to the hotel lobby, where I learn that the shooting occurred at the send-off party at Q's house, where his family and friends went on celebrating after he left for the hotel. The victim was a young man who had briefly attended Boys' Prep some years ago. He was now in critical condition with a bullet lodged in his brain.

He was also, it turns out, Quartell's best friend.

When I return to the ballroom, Q has clearly just gotten the news. He is on the phone, talking to someone in hushed tones, his whole body rigid. Then he rushes out of the room, refusing eye contact with anyone. His date follows, looking confused and frightened. Ms. Wagner, his favorite teacher and special education aide, and I hurry after him, trying to keep up with Q's agitated stride.

We converge in the lobby. Q is distraught, balling his hands into fists, saying he needs to get home and "take care of this." Ms. Wagner doesn't think it is a good idea for him to leave just yet. After much back-and-forth between the two of them—Q and Ms. Wagner move outside into the parking lot, back into the lobby, back out again—Q agrees to let her drive him home.

It had been less than an hour since Q arrived at Prom grinning widely. And it would only be a few hours until his friend was pronounced dead in the hospital.

Back at the teachers' table, one teacher shakes her head. "They can't even have one night."

The Repeated Hard

This chapter concerns a new phase in the mourning experience of the boys we have been following, during which repeated gunfire injuries and death interrupted and disrupted the remaining months of the school year. While each terrible event would generate its own abbreviated reprise of the three stages I have so far described, in aggregate they form a new, momentously difficult stage of grief—the *repeated hard*. During it, as we'll see, Boys' Prep adults struggled to balance the often-competing dimensions of their role. Taken as a whole, the chapter illustrates how a school, despite its best intentions, can fail to understand its students, leaving them at risk for long-term social injuries.

The death of Quartell's best friend on Prom night illustrates yet another curse of gun violence in the lives of young people: namely, the way that it so often reshapes and poisons the rituals and pleasures of youth. During the two years I spent at Boys' Prep, and the several years since, I have come to see milestone upon milestone in the lives of Black boys contaminated by gunfire. Every rite, every event—almost every thought concerning the future—carries an inherent caveat.[1]

Too often violence infiltrates the most joyful, significant occasions, forever changing their meaning in the moment and in memory. Before Prom, the celebration of Thanksgiving was permanently marred by JahSun's murder; Easter would be when Bill, another Boys' Prep stu-

dent (whom you'll soon hear more about), would die. All school vacations and summer breaks contain the question of whether everyone
will return.

Violence also interrupts the most humdrum of the boys' daily activities, turning what otherwise would have been a normal, unremarkable day into one forever marked on a calendar in their hearts. A student might scroll through Instagram at lunch on a regular Tuesday
and read a friend's post that someone they knew had been shot. An
entirely ordinary walk home from school can pass a crime scene cordoning off the murder of a neighbor. And the typical markers of school
life—a hallway of lockers, metal desk chairs, classroom walls—hold
new meaning when they become memorial sites. The regularity and
repetition with which these boys experienced interruptions to both
the everyday and the extraordinary moments of their adolescence left
lingering wounds that Boys' Prep's approach to educating Black boys
was unable to alleviate.

Is This Normal?

To connect the regularity of death in the boys' lives and the challenges
inherent to the school's educational approach, I need to share a little
more of Quartell's story. At eighteen, Q's life was already steeped
in loss. I met him in the aftermath of JahSun's death; he was one of
the more reserved members of JahSun's close circle and on the football team. But it had taken me a while to really connect with him.
For months, the running joke between us was that Q never actually
attended classes, since I would always see him anywhere but there:
doing classwork at a solitary desk pulled into the hallway or going
back and forth to the special education office. Sometime in winter
I spent a lunch period at his cafeteria table. While the rest of the table
was caught up in a rousing game of Uno, Q taught me how to play
Pitty Pat, a classic Philly game, using the deck of cards he always
carried.

About a month before Prom, Q agreed to an interview. I learned that he lived directly across the street from the school, but didn't much like his neighborhood, describing it as "somewhere that's nowhere." When I turned the conversation to JahSun's death and other losses he'd experienced, he began to laugh. I'd grown accustomed to hearing nervous laughter from boys sharing about the grief they so rarely discussed in public, but his was both heartier and more casual. He unwrapped a stick of gum and popped it in his mouth. "I lose people all the time . . . every year . . . I don't really care about it anymore. I mean—I care," he corrected himself. "But I don't got no feelings toward it no more."

At my prompting, Q tried to enumerate the number of significant losses—counting up to seven on his fingers before giving up. He began with his grandmother, who died when he was eight years old:

I was sick about that. [Then] one of my friends died, another friend died, another friend died, another friend died. And everybody kept dying. Everybody still dying . . . Just gonna keep happening every month, every week, every day . . . I be asking, like, is it normal for, like, somebody my age to know so many people or seen so many people die before?

He played with a blue key-chain flashlight hanging from his waist, flicking it on and off, not knowing how soon it would be before he'd have to add another finger to the count.

I listened, as I would during every interview, trying to take in the meaning of his words while at the same time hovering more abstractly over the moment in order to prepare the next question. But in this moment, I wanted to respond directly to Quartell—and to everyone. I wanted to stand up and shout: *No, this isn't normal! This should not be normal!*

Quartell was struggling to finish his senior year and graduate. He was contemplating community college to study accounting. Some teachers considered it a miracle he'd gotten this far, given how many times he teetered on expulsion, and after having failed nearly every class freshman year, which he was forced to repeat. Others believed he had the potential to do far better if he were more focused and smoked less marijuana—which Q said helped him cope with his emotional pain.

"If nobody got killed at all, nobody died, nothing, my life would be totally different. Probably like ten times different," he told me. Then he added, with a deep sigh, "'Cause so many people died, like, it's just most of the reason why I am where I am now."

In the days following Prom, Q didn't answer messages from me or Ms. Wagner—though Mr. Pratt, a distant relative, was keeping tabs on him. When, the following Tuesday, Q failed to show up for his senior project presentation, the final requirement for graduation, it was rescheduled for Thursday. Thursday morning, I found Q posted at one of his favored locations: a desk pulled into the hallway, playing Meek Mill on his phone while finalizing his PowerPoint slides for his presentation about college sports and amateurism. A few minutes before go-time, he met with Ms. Wagner for a last-minute check of his script and slides (though she had already given him many rounds of feedback). Along with her pep talk, Ms. Wagner wondered aloud whether the *Friday* (the movie) t-shirt Q was wearing under his school uniform blazer really qualified as "professional attire."

But no matter. Q completed the presentation to the satisfaction of the faculty panel. His analysis was not particularly original or in-depth, but he had followed the directions and fulfilled the project requirements. Two days later, the repast for his friend following the funeral was hosted in the school cafeteria. Ten days after that, Quartell walked across the stage a high school graduate.

In addition to honoring the eighty-seven graduating seniors, the ceremony also conferred a diploma on JahSun, which was presented to his parents. When they stepped onstage, several of JahSun's friends—including Q—showered them with roses.

At the graduation ceremony the following year, the school would honor Tyhir following the same script, although by that time only a handful of his friends were also on the stage, since most had left Boys' Prep. And the year following that, another two ghosts would be recognized alongside the graduating seniors in what was becoming an annual memorializing ritual alongside the celebration.

You can see why Quartell would wonder whether it was normal for a kid his age to know so many other kids who had died. And though he had support from individual teachers, he never felt what he was learning in school helped him process or make sense of the string of shootings that punctuated his adolescence.

The Danger of a Decontextualized Education

The Boys' Prep curriculum was designed to provide a "classical" education for Black boys, shaping them into college-ready young men who could pursue professional careers and defy stereotypical expectations. The prep schools upon which Boys' Prep was modeled view "the classical curriculum [as] the cradle of high culture"—a possible entry point into the middle class or beyond.[2] Every day the boys recited a pledge (which by junior year, they would deliver from memory *in Latin*) proclaiming that education was their birthright, their pathway to success. The uniform also embodied the school's ambition and emphasis on personal responsibility. Though brotherhood and strong relationships with teachers were critical components of the model, the overwhelming sense was that students' responsibility was primarily to pursue *individual* success rather than prioritize commitments to a larger community.[3]

Perhaps the school's attempt to forge a separation from its neighborhood[4] was necessary since they were asking young people to imagine and prepare for futures they had few models for in their current realities or among the people they knew best. Most students did not have parents with college degrees or professional careers, though certainly some did. Immersing students in a different context eight hours a day, the thinking went, would provide them the tools to build new contexts for themselves: go to college, likely leaving behind their Philadelphia neighborhood with its attendant precarity and risks. The mostly white staff could provide academic training, motivation, and care, without necessarily having much culturally specific knowledge or competence related to the boys' race or class identities.[5]

In theory, this meant that at school, boys could take off the masks or fronts they might need to navigate their neighborhood.[6] Adults often held this up as one of the features of the school they appreciated most. Ms. Bloom told me she felt the school made it possible for boys to be silly. Dr. Stephens thought of his school as a place where Black boys could engage with different forms of masculinity than in other spaces. At an assembly early in the year, he offered, "Not all Black men have to just act in anger or respond to a situation by wanting to fight. That's weakness, that's stupidity. If you've fallen prey to that, I hope you're growing and learning." He fleshed out the contrast in a speech to prospective parents, sharing that Boys' Prep emphasized developing students' emotional intelligence alongside their budding masculinities so "they can proceed through adolescence without having to be overly macho." But, he added, "we recognize that the man we ask them to be [in school] may be different than on their walk home." The assumption was that with the private-school costume and the freedom to engage with new parts of themselves inside the school building, the boys would come to embody the dispositions and traits that school staff hoped to instill.[7]

However, like many other Black Male Academies—and schools serving minoritized populations generally—Boys' Prep's school practices often implicitly emphasized the ways that boys need to be reshaped or molded, rather than valuing the assets and culture they already possessed.[8] Despite the all-Black student body and a Black founder, little in the building marked it as "Decidedly Black" in the way other schools with all-Black student bodies might be.[9] A visiting counselor once recounted his surprise at seeing no Black faces on a bulletin board of famous mathematicians. Students made similar observations. One asked, somewhat rhetorically: "If you took all the students out, and left just the teachers and the classrooms, how do we know this is a Black school still?"

The uniform was a key area where students often felt their heritage was being erased. One senior vented: "We don't ever get to . . . embrace our culture . . . I don't see why I gotta dress like the Europeans told our ancestors to dress just to be successful. We should be able to wear dashikis or something if we want to." Another objected to the no-jewelry policy that prevented him from wearing a pendant of the African continent. Despite the school's core belief in the promise and potential of Black boys, students wondered how central their racial identity and cultural history were to the new kinds of men they were being asked to become.

Another element of this *decontextualized* educational approach was the school's promotion of student compliance over critical thinking. This was the source of some debate among teachers, especially since critical thinking was explicitly emphasized in the school's mission. Several staff members privately confided their worries that academic standards were too low or bemoaned the emphasis on behavior and assignment completion over authentic learning. A few were more vocal with their critiques. Ms. Thompson, a Black science teacher in her second year at the school, shared her view that "we value compliance of Black boys . . . Having someone's uniform in complete order is way more important [in this school] than their academic journey. And when I say academic, I mean cognitive ability. There are people in my AP class who cannot write." Ms. Thompson had been a fan of Boys' Prep since before she became a teacher, and when she was interviewing for teaching jobs, it was the only place she wanted to work. But, now, with two years under her belt, she saw that the school was not meeting its mandate. This put her in a moral bind: "I can't be a co-conspirator on the side of saying somebody has a good education and they don't."

Ms. Abadi, another young teacher of color, who resigned at the end of the year of JahSun's death, emailed the staff listserv to explain her decision. Among other critiques, she expressed concern about the school's level of academic rigor and the message this sent about Black students:

The first time I read the [school's] vision, I was completely bought in. It is invigorating, high-stakes, and rigorous. If fulfilled, it would set our students on a path to excellence. Yet while we espouse a vision of academic rigor and a college preparatory curriculum, in the past two years I have witnessed rampant low academic standards. I have seen students

receive As for below average work. I have seen students graded for completion and compliance rather than competency and correctness. I have
seen students tracked based on behavior, placed in honors classes and
rewarded for being silent and following the rules . . . When we send the
message to students that they can succeed by silently sitting at a desk
and submitting low-quality work, we are inevitably setting them up for
failure in academic spaces.

Ms. Abadi pointed to the need for students to not only be pushed
harder toward academic competency, but also rewarded for expressing a critical consciousness rather than simply following rules
and being silent.

Ms. Abadi's critique gets at the heart of one of the most enduring
tensions of education, particularly the education of low-income and
racially minoritized students: whether schools are preparing students
to reproduce the social position of their parents or whether (and how)
schools can support students toward upward social mobility.[10] In am-
bitiously and benevolently trying to shape boys' futures toward that
latter goal, Boys' Prep blocked out their present realities. And by placing a premium on obedience rather than inquiry, they may have also
been—paradoxically—limiting those futures.

Losing Bill

Spring break came about two months before Prom. Warmer weather
in Philadelphia, as in many cities, often brings a rise in shootings,[11] and
this year, Boys' Prep was not spared. Sixteen-year-old Bill, a sophomore, was shot midafternoon on Easter Sunday. He had been hanging
out with friends on a relatively busy downtown street when an argument broke out with another group of teenagers. One seventeen-
year-old pulled out a gun and, allegedly aiming for someone else, fired
four shots, hitting Bill once in the lower back.

Bill's social network at Boys' Prep was less diverse and more enclosed than JahSun's. Having attended the Boys' Prep middle school, Bill maintained close ties ever since with a small crew of friends, all of whom had, according to many of their teachers, collectively and successfully bought into the mission and culture of Boys' Prep. High achieving academically, Bill was also well rounded, having pursued and enjoyed several sports and hobbies, including boxing, football, and biking.

The initial reports from the hospital were that Bill would survive. "Bill's a lucky boy. He's going to be okay," one doctor told his family. A hopeful message went out to the Boys' Prep community. Adored by the friends and teachers who knew him best, Bill was described as "full of kindness," with "a magnetic spirit." Everyone was rooting for him.

But the bullet had hit a main artery, and late Tuesday night Bill's condition worsened. Unable to stop the bleeding, doctors went through at least six hundred bags of donated blood. His mother, Williesha, remembers in agonizing detail the reports from surgeons each time they came out of surgery to update her. As the family huddled in the waiting room discussing their options for next steps, Bill's heart stopped beating.

Word spread overnight on Instagram. Though Bill's closest circle was small, the reach of this news spanned all grades and social groups. Some students posted to share information, others about their own grief. Some boys, after they posted about Bill, reposted memorial messages to Tyhir (who would have been the grade above Bill) and/or JahSun.

It took Principal Donaldson the better part of the day to work up the courage to share the sad update with the school community. He was deeply shaken:

I had some dark moments with Bill where I was like, I can't do this. I was just praying so hard that he didn't pass away, and then when he did, I was just like, "I can't. How is this happening to me?" You get this focus on yourself. This is supposed to be my first year as principal. I can't do my job. Now, I've got all this. You get into this dark place, and then you

sort of like get some perspective in there. His mother just lost her kid.
This is not about you. Get your head out of the—Get back in the game
and figure this out.

Mr. Donaldson emailed the entire Boys' Prep network Wednesday
afternoon, followed by additional messages to school staff about
a memorial gathering at the school on Thursday and a faculty meeting
the following Monday before classes would resume.

It was becoming clear that JahSun's death was not a remarkable
and tragic exception; the more unusual fact was that, before JahSun,
Boys' Prep had been spared the loss of a current student while school
was in session. Bill's death now made it two in a single school year.
Just two months later, Quartell's friend joined a list of at least a dozen
other murdered young people in some way connected to the school
(see fig. 6.1).

Normalizing the Stages

Bill's death recapitulated the stages of institutionalized grief that followed JahSun's murder. Again, first came the *easy hard*: a brief emotional convergence between the generations brought on by communal grief. Following quickly was the *hard hard*, as tensions arose
between emotional support and academic pressures. Then, a new
strain emerged of the lingering *hidden hard*: covert grieving under
a guise of normalcy.

Certain lessons from November had been learned. More response
systems were in place; the staff appeared better prepared, with
a heightened sensitivity toward students. Yet the tempo of grief was
even more accelerated, the group of "legitimate" grievers smaller,
and the pressure to restore normalcy more intense. With the school
year drawing to a close, the *urgency to compensate*, this time not only for
schooling inequities but also for the lost time earlier in the school year,
seemed to be guiding the energy in the building. The ceremonies now
felt practiced, almost routine.

2016 2017 2018

JUL NOV APR

Tyhir | Primary data | Social media data | JahSun | Bill | Primary data
killed | collection begins | collection begins | killed | killed | collection ends

● Death of BP student, former student, or alumnus
● Death of outside-of-school friend or young family member of BP student(s)
▲ Non-fatal shooting of BP student, former student, or alumnus
▲ Non-fatal shooting of out-of-school friend or young family member of BP student(s)
■ Incarceration of BP student, former student, or alumnus
● Death of significant celebrity
■ Arrest, conviction, or incarceration of significant celebrity

Figure 6.1. Timeline of losses experienced by a selection of 75 Boys' Prep students. Data was collected primarily through social media observations and confirmed through interviews and informal conversations, but it is likely an underestimate of actual losses experienced within participants' social networks.

March 2016: Friend of several BP students dies of meningitis. **June 2016:** Friend of several BP students killed in Pulse Nightclub shooting. **July 2016:** Tyhir killed. **January 2017:** BP senior briefly incarcerated. **February 2017:** JahSun's friend killed; Latrell's friend killed. **March 2017:** Herc's cousin killed. **April 2017:** Kaliq's uncle killed. **May 2017:** JahSun's friend killed. **June 2017:** Herc's mentor/"old head" killed. **July 2017:** Yaja's friend killed; JahSun's friend killed. **August 2017:** Jonquett's friend killed; Hazeem's cousin killed; Herc's friend killed. **September 2017:** BP alumnus shot, survived; Hazeem's cousin shot, survived. **November 2017:** BP alumnus briefly incarcerated; JahSun killed; Philadelphia rapper Meek Mill incarcerated. **December 2017:** BP student's friend dies of asthma attack; BP student's uncle killed. **January 2018:** Hazeem's friend killed; Hazeem's friend shot, survived. **February 2018:** Friend of several BP students dies. **March 2018:** Kaliq's friend stabbed, survived; Herc's friend killed; former BP student killed. **April 2018:** Bill killed; Owen's friend killed; Philadelphia native Bill Cosby convicted and incarcerated. **May 2018:** Denzel's friend killed; Khalil's mentor/"old head" killed; Quartell's cousin killed; BP student's friend killed; Herc's friend killed; friend of several BP students shot, survived; former BP student and Quartell's best friend killed on prom night. **June 2018:** Kaliq's cousin shot, survived; Herc's friend shot, survived; female friend of several BP students killed; rapper XXXTentacion killed. **July 2018:** Larry's friend killed; friend of several BP students killed. **August 2018:** Herc's friend killed; friend of several BP students killed; former BP student arrested for that murder. **September 2018:** Kaliq's friend killed; rapper Mac Miller dies of drug overdose. **November 2018:** Ezekiel arrested and briefly incarcerated while in college; Larry's friend killed; Latrell's friend killed. **December 2018:** Ezekiel's friend killed.

The Thursday of spring break, a day after word of Bill's death hit students' social feeds, Boys' Prep opened its doors for an informal gathering of mourning and community: pizza and writing supplies and a warm atmosphere for the sixty or so students who showed up, along with about a dozen teachers. There was an eerie feeling of déjà vu, as some of the same students who had participated in JahSun's memorial events just a few months prior also took part.

On Monday, school resumed, and just as after JahSun's death, the faculty gathered for an early morning meeting to prepare for another challenging day. But this time the feeling in the room was a little different from the fall. Although again a handful of teachers were noticeably distressed, the tone of the discussion was more matter-of-fact. After relaying logistical updates and facilitating a group brainstorm about Bill's closest friends, Mr. Donaldson concluded by encouraging teachers to "be present with each other as well as focused on our students . . . It's not going to be an easy day, week, school-year conclusion for any of us." Sensitivity was there, but also a sense of hopeless resignation at the tragic, unalterable reality of their situation.

Across the school, teachers translated the message of latitude and support into concrete behaviors, offering students a break from academic expectations and the freedom to deal with their grief in any way they needed to. Mr. Donaldson had written a script for Bill's teachers that they could choose to read to their class; at least one teacher did so. It read, in part: "Let's allow each other the freedom to process in a way that feels true for each of us." Another teacher offered each of his classes four options for using their time with him: write a reflection, do regular classwork, "take a personal day," or finish a project. Knowing her sophomore students would be most affected, Ms. Finn kept the overhead lights off in her room and made tea for her students. Student volunteers refilled the kettle in the bathroom several times to heat enough water for the whole class.

Where offerings of support had been largely spontaneous and improvised in November, this time it seemed to me that they were carried out with more planning. Some teachers picked up "best practices" or tinkered to improve the strategies they or others had tried in the fall.

Ms. Kallum reflected that she had learned from the last time how to respond best to students: "I think I was a little bit more in tune to things that they might be experiencing. So I talked to guys individually and asked them if they knew [Bill] and then how they were feeling and stuff." Ms. Finn borrowed the strategy her friend and colleague, Ms. Cain, had used in November: creating a short survey for her classes to get a sense of what each student was feeling and what he might need from her in the coming days. Mr. Marker, Bill's English teacher, copied Ms. Kallum's idea from the fall and created a space in his classroom for students to write notes to Bill and deposit them inside a pair of boxing gloves to represent his favorite sport.

In the hallways, once again, the *easy hard* moment of shared grief meant a temporary lifting of the usual demands on students' behavioral and dress-code compliance. Generally, the first day back from spring break marked a uniform change, as students were allowed to swap their blazer and tie for a school-branded polo shirt. But instead of a day dedicated to smoothing out the kinks in the new uniform— the untucked shirts, the wrong socks, and so on—this Monday, clothing irregularities were overlooked. Likewise, no penalties for defacing school property were imposed on students who wrote messages in Sharpie on Bill's locker door. No one hollered at or wrote up the students who skipped classes to seek the company of their friends in the hallway.

Even so, many students were having a difficult time, particularly in the classrooms where Bill had been. In homeroom, his classmates were glassy-eyed as they stood for a moment of silence. In computer class, one of Bill's close friends sat in the back row. Ignoring class instructions from his teacher, he found a piece of blank printer paper and began writing. With the teacher still talking at the front of the room, he walked up the aisle of computers and lay the paper across the keyboard at Bill's empty seat. His message included several hashtags referring to his friend's death as well as "Love you Bill." In art class, Denzel sat across from Bill's chair, headphones in his ears, staring into space. "We all hide our emotions," he confessed to me. "It wouldn't be good to show them in this environment."

As before, some students felt territorial about their grief and possessive of the memory of their fallen friend. Freshman Trayvon, a close friend of Bill's, was frustrated that some of his peers were using social media to express grief he felt was unearned, given their relationship with Bill. He said, angrily, "I'm just sick of all these guys pretending they knew my mans, posting about him, looking all sad . . . All these n***as posting like they knew my mans . . . They posting 'RIP I love you.' But did you ever tell him you love him when he was around?" This echoed a sentiment he had expressed earlier on social media. Sunday night, as Trayvon prepared to sit in classrooms and at lunch tables that no longer included Bill, he'd posted on Instagram: "Just cause y'all met my homie once or twice don't mean y'all tight. where was y'all at when we was walking home in cold weather to the L [train] everyday after school or sunny days getting water ice and pretzels or them L rides after detention. y'all can't relate to our pain 💯." While students like Trayvon were suspicious of others' grief and felt compelled to assert their own standing in a cryptic grief hierarchy, other groups of boys leaned on each other and seemed to appreciate not having to go through their mourning alone.

This time, the designated counseling room received considerably more use. In addition to an external grief counselor visiting for the day, the Boys' Prep middle school social worker also spent the day at the high school, about a mile from her usual building. As a familiar face, she was a magnet for Bill's closest friends. Throughout the day, the energy in the room vacillated between lively and somber. In the middle of an energetic group conversation, one student would pull back from the circle and burst into tears or curl over with his head in his lap; within seconds, a peer or adult would go over to rub his back or engage him in sympathetic conversation. Despite the profound challenges of being back in school without Bill, the structural and relational processes in place at Boys' Prep eased the pain of the day. As before, after JahSun's death, the *easy hard* day was filled with many poignant and affirmative moments of communal support.

Also, as before, it was over in a flash.

Having deviated more smoothly from the standard protocols on

Monday, the Tuesday pivot back to normalcy in school routines also seemed more streamlined. And a *hard hard* stage was thus ushered in: varying student needs, mixed messages about discipline and academic expectations, along with institutional and peer policing of grief. This time, by Tuesday, even Bill's closest friends were expected back in class, while in the hallways renewed disciplinary attention to the uniform and student behavior could be felt and heard.

And yet, across the school, adults seemed more aware of the difficulty of a rapid return to business as usual. For instance, Mr. Gilbert, a white English teacher in his seventh year at Boys' Prep, wondered: "What do our boys do when they go home and everyone's getting back to normal and they're like, 'Well, why are you acting like this? . . . Are you still upset about this, seriously?' . . . So I don't know that there's that safe space . . . to work through what they're going through." Mr. Gilbert imagined that students might be getting messages from people in their life beyond the school building that it was time to move on before they were ready. Without continued supportive spaces inside the school, these students might be left without anywhere for their grief to land.

In his classroom, Mr. Gilbert debated starting *Lord of the Flies*, as planned, or swapping reading selections to avoid an untimely discussion of young boys killing each other. Ultimately, he chose to stay on schedule, reasoning that, given the nature of an English classroom, he would be able to monitor the impact of sensitive topics on bereaved students through class discussions and their writing.

In Mr. Khan's elective class on Race and Ethnicity, he tried to use Bill's murder to discuss the concept of racist stereotypes. Mr. Khan, one of only a handful of men of color on the faculty, projected on the pull-down screen a collage of headlines and excerpts from newspaper articles on the shooting. The characterization of Bill by the police department as having "no priors" and coming "from a good family" generated controversy. One student thought it was "good to mention that." Another hedged: "It's a double-edged sword." A third student called out, "It's never fair, [but] it's just natural." And another shared his belief that if a white kid had been killed, the articles would have focused on the victim's psychological and emotional status, not his police record. While some students seemed ready to probe deeper political and sociological questions, others were clearly uninterested in participating. Sybrii leaned back in his chair, pulling at his eyelids. Next to him, sitting quietly with arms crossed and eyes closed, was Kaliq. Later, he put his head on the desk and fell asleep. Unsure of the best way to move forward, Mr. Khan decided to return to his regular curriculum the following day.

Without a clear curricular model that would give students the tools for analyzing and making sense of their social reality—with its regular occurrences of violence and loss—teachers were left on their own to decide whether and how to bring the students' emotional struggles into the classroom. And yet, as before, the *hard hard* period included inconsistency across the school about whose bereavement behaviors warranted support, concern, redirection, or punishment and how much to continue talking about their shared loss.

A Permanent Hidden Hard

Just like in the winter following JahSun's death, public displays of grief and mourning after Bill's murder gradually lessened in intensity. With the end of the school year approaching, the entire school community seemed caught up in an accelerating tempo of anticipations, distractions, and deliverables, especially for the seniors: final exams, capstone projects and internships, year-end celebrations. As overt expressions of grief receded, a new wave of covert grief—another *hidden hard*—set in.

The grief this time was perhaps somewhat less hidden, but no less hard—especially for seniors grappling with both peers' deaths and, in some cases, struggling to meet final graduation requirements. Major school milestones were bittersweet because they conjured up thoughts of what should have been. Perhaps more experienced at managing grief themselves, school staff seemed better attuned to the potential for pain that might surface on particularly meaningful days. For example, in an email to the faculty listserv on the day seniors cleaned out their lockers, Ms. Neal encouraged sensitivity from her colleagues under the subject line "Senior emotions heads up": "Please be aware that this is an emotional day for many guys, especially JahSun's friends. As they look at his locker, they see a stark reminder that he is not moving on with them. Thanks for your understanding as they are spending some time in the hallways reminiscing." Despite such thoughtful acknowledgments, there was far greater complexity and nuance to many boys' emotional experience than most of their teachers could access.

Again and again, I was struck by the cumulative effect of multiple schoolmate deaths, even for those who didn't know the victims well. Struggling to put such immense and terrifying feelings into words, Eric, a senior who had been friendly with JahSun and had barely known Bill, reflected on how the school losing a second student made him think about Black men's longevity:

JahSun, his death made me mad and sad. But I felt like Bill's death, it made me more mad than sad. I didn't know Bill very well. He was two grades below me, but it was a sense of hopelessness. Why we gotta keep dying? That's how I felt. Why? Why can't we just . . . get that 80 years, that ripe old age. But we don't even have the privilege for that, because of where we live, and how we live, stuff like that. It just seems hopeless at times. There are some good times to brighten it up, but sometimes the reality, it hits you. Yeah. It's just bad . . . No one is exempt from death. But I feel like as Black men, we're already prone to death and then to kill each other, it's counterintuitive . . . I fear the presence of [death], how close it is to me.

Eric, who became the salutatorian for the senior class and went on to attend a prestigious HBCU, echoed some of these sentiments in his graduation speech to the Boys' Prep community. For him, and surely for others, the "closeness of death" wasn't directly dependent on having had close relationships with his murdered peers.[12]

One Saturday in early April the reality of multiple premature deaths happening within the school community hit home for everyone, when Bill's funeral happened to fall on JahSun's birthday. JahSun's mother, Maxayn, had scheduled an afternoon football game in his honor followed by an evening bowling fundraiser for a scholarship she had established in JahSun's name. When she learned about the funeral, she was conflicted but decided to reschedule the football game but continue with the fundraiser as planned. Within the span of a few hours, students went from a somber funeral for one friend to a memorial bowling party for another. Some changed from t-shirts with one friend's image to another's.

Multiple losses and the crowding of loss-related events heightened a sense of the increased presence of death in and around the school. Irell, a senior, reflected: "Death is in the air here . . . It's like a feeling that right now the school is attracting death towards it. Not to say, like . . . just because you go to Boys' Prep people are targeting you on the street, but JahSun died. Bill died. I have personal friends that died. It's just, I don't know, every time I come here, [I'm] reminded." Irell pointed to the painted mural in the hallway of one of Boys' Prep's late founding teachers, which—coincidentally—he had been partly responsible for damaging in a recent tussle. To him, even this school wall gave him a palpable feeling of absence and death and was a "reminder [that] you're not really here."

The experience of multiple losses could be seen in the boys' activity online. When posting about the death of a friend, many boys took a roll call approach, following the most recent loss with a list of all their other significant losses. Herc, for example, returned from spring break with more than just Bill's death on his mind. The day Bill finally succumbed to his gunshot wounds was Herc's seventeenth birthday, and the following day, one of his non-school friends was killed. Reflecting on his junior year, what Herc remembered most was the way deaths started to accumulate, each one seeming to build on the previous one in its effect: "I started losing people back-to-back. I lost my man, Kyle, in August. He from my hood. Then we lost JahSun like two months later after that. Then I lost Bill, then Murak like the next day. I lost Bill on my birthday, and I lost Murak like the day after my birthday." After losing a second friend in two days, Herc shared an Instagram story with the caption "R.i.p. to da guys 🖤 🕊," referring to eight fallen friends, including the two most recently added to his tally (fig. 6.2).

Other boys used their Instagram bios to acknowledge multiple deceased loved ones. This format provides space for only the user's Instagram handle, name, and a few lines of text. A roll call of "RIP" and "Long Live" hashtags as long as Herc's would occupy most of the available space. In these bios and their posts, the boys' memorial lists tracked and quantified loss over time, serving as one way they narrated their own identities to peers online. As grief constantly simmered in the background of their on- and offline lives, the *hidden hard* became a permanent state for many students.

Making and Faking It to the Finish Line

With a group of juniors and seniors still shattered in the aftermath of JahSun's death and another cohort of sophomores coping with Bill's loss, any aspirations at Boys' Prep to reach for a higher goal than completion and compliance were dashed to pieces. School staff now mostly aimed to quell the chaos and make it to the end of the year. In parallel, many students now simply hoped to reach the finish line with as little effort as possible. As senior Yaja recalled, rather than school being about learning, "It became more about passing . . . for all of us who were completely struggling."

Both students and staff had an interest in seniors graduating. Some students required steadfast personalized efforts from their teachers or extreme hand-holding, like the support Ms. Wagner provided Quartell in putting together his senior project presentation and making sure he was ready on the big day. Ms. Kallum similarly delivered vital one-on-one support to Rajae all year. As he described it, she became a second mom, making sure he got his work in and was able to graduate on time. Special relationships between teachers and students facilitated the comprehensive one-on-one assistance that some students required to reach the finish line of the school year.

In other cases, some administrative sleight of hand seemed to be

Figure 6.2. Herc's Instagram story. Memorial to eight deceased friends and family members, including Tyhir, JahSun, and Bill (other names removed).

involved to nudge a student to the next grade level or onto the graduation stage. After Yaja's devastating senior year, Dr. Stephens told him it would really hurt his heart not to see him graduate. The CEO asked all of Yaja's teachers to create additional assignments for him so he could boost his grades to passing. Yaja remembers one teacher, whose class he wasn't even enrolled in, developing and assisting him with various assignments to bring up his Latin grade in the final stretch.

Herc also needed help to pass his junior year. You may recall his meeting with Ms. Estevez and the nearly impossible A++s it was calculated he would need to pass each of his classes. Indeed, he did perform better in the third trimester and earned praise on his report card for showing improvement, and yet he still only passed two of seven classes. Herc enrolled in a full load of summer-school courses and made a heroic push, but finished the summer still *one* credit short of qualifying for twelfth grade. However, he negotiated a compromise with the administration: he would take both eleventh- and twelfth-grade English at the same time, leaving him with no free periods and no room for error. Only by passing every course senior year would he be able to graduate on time.

With a high school diploma squarely in his sights perhaps for the first time, Herc began senior year feeling more motivated. Things were a little more stable at home and, with most of his closest friends having left Boys' Prep, he had fewer distractions. He had also been learning to share more with his teachers about what was going on in his personal life and what he needed to be successful in class, and he had several teachers who regularly checked up on him. It began to pay off. Herc was more focused, coming to school more regularly, earning the highest grades he had throughout high school (see fig. 6.3). Despite two years of average grades well below passing and continued suspensions for excessive lateness, Herc's senior-year recovery efforts were enough to earn him a diploma. As he walked across the graduation stage, he thought about all the times he could have gotten kicked out of school and felt grateful for all the "people in [his] corner . . . motivating [him] to keep pushing beyond." In an Instagram post he made commemorating his 2019 graduation (fig. 6.4), Herc acknowledged

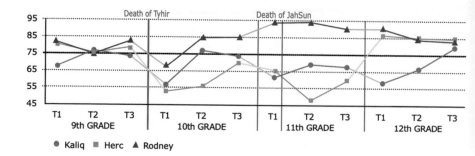

Figure 6.3. Academic trajectories following peer loss(es) for Herc, Kaliq, and Rodney.
Each marker represents the average grade for all classes (chart does not include
summer school or Kaliq's additional year). All boys experienced a drop in their average grades after Tyhir's death, but only Herc and Kaliq did after JahSun's (Rodney
did not consider JahSun a close friend). The three showed different trends and
timelines for bouncing back, and Kaliq did not complete enough credits to graduate
from Boys' Prep.

Note: The Boys' Prep school year is divided into three trimesters (T1, T2, T3), and
only grades of 75 and above are considered passing.

his losses and struggles and the "support system" that helped coun-
terbalance them.

Others, like Kaliq and Hazeem, were never really able to make
Boys' Prep work for them. Hazeem transferred out in the middle of
junior year. He started cyber school, then bounced around, and would
eventually receive his diploma from an alternative high school. Kaliq
kept having bursts of motivation to improve his school performance,
then flaming out. He never had an adult in the building who consistently stayed on him.[13] By the end of senior year, he was two credits shy
of graduation and had to come back the following year to take science
and Latin (see fig. 6.3). By the end of that fifth year, Kaliq still hadn't
passed Latin. Without the language credit, he couldn't get a diploma
from the school district until he completed an additional six-month
program—basically "gym class," as he described it. Kaliq eventually
received his diploma two years after his peers.

Still, there were others who found ways, while at Boys' Prep, to
make steady academic progress despite major setbacks. Teachers

Liked by ██████████ and **95 others**

.herc. These past 4 years i done been thru it all, I'm still in shock i made it this far.. losing homies left and right, going broke, in Nd out of trouble, Nd etc. Buhh i kept going even at my lowest points, I still stand tall and when i wanted to give up my amazing support system kept me in it! I will nvr lose 🖤 🏆 #Freedaguys #Longlivedaguys herc out 😎

View all 25 comments

hazeem_23 Congrats brodie 🖤 💯

.herc. hazeem_23 gl ski 💯

Figure 6.4. Herc's Instagram grid post about his 2019 high school graduation. He holds a phone in his right hand and poses with his diploma and a stack of money to his left. In the caption, Herc summarizes his high school experience and accomplishments. The image is cropped for anonymity.

and peers often pointed to Rodney as a prime example of a student who had turned devastation at the death of his best friend, Tyhir, into "motivation to improve in every single [way]," as Ms. Bloom put it.[14] Rodney's academic achievements were certainly a testament to this: though his average grades took a dip upon returning to school following Tyhir's death, he recovered quickly and was able to maintain a stable high level of achievement (see fig. 6.3). Rodney echoed this in relation to athletic successes as well: "It motivated me better because, like, when it happened, I had a lot of anger and stuff. Now, I just take it all out on the [basketball] court . . . I don't think I would have ever done some of the stuff that I did if I wouldn't have lost people. Like, that shit helped me strive and go harder for them people that passed."[15] Rodney was able to forge a sustained memorial-based motivation, a self-driven commitment linked directly to the memory of a lost friend. After graduating with Herc in 2019, Rodney was one of the few students from these social circles to go directly to a private university, where he played on the varsity basketball team and graduated in 2024. Even years later, when he discussed his college achievements, Rodney still references the loss of Tyhir as a source of his motivation.

Yet, Rodney was largely an exception. Despite their best efforts, most boys only managed to follow through on inspiration from their losses in fits and starts. Yaja attributed most of his peers' quick drop-off from initial feelings of motivation to the acceptance of the "reality" that their losses are "not something that's gonna stop today."

As the end of the school year approached, it became clearer and clearer to me that the problem was not just that our deeply flawed educational system meant that many students arrived at Boys' Prep unprepared for high-school-level work,[16] but that Boys' Prep itself was unprepared for the fullness and nuances of students' lives. The decontextualized approach to educating Black boys navigating poverty, mortality threats, and grief missed the mark, making classroom learning and aspirations for college feel largely irrelevant to students given their repeated losses. By intentionally prioritizing the contexts they wanted students to be prepared for, school staff limited the range of responses they could mobilize when the ravages of the inequality and oppression their students come from entered school life.[17] And they had no tools at the ready to help their Black male students feel empowered to engage in efforts toward civic participation or positive change in their communities.

Beyond reading and math skills and historical facts, Boys' Prep offered little to help students contextualize their losses in ways that might facilitate them finding a sense of purpose. This left many students, even those who made it across the graduation stage on time, with feelings of hopelessness, both about the violence in their city and about their own prospects of social mobility.

Students' Long-Term Social Injury

For so many Boys' Prep students, and their peers across the city and country, prolonged yet unrecognized grief without a constructive outlet grew into social injury.[18] Not a transient emotion prompting a repertoire of time-limited behaviors, their grief etched a long-term, even permanent, scar on their individual and collective trajectories. A reshaping of the boys' synapses of possibility.

I use the phrase *social injury* to highlight grief as a collective experience shared by Black boys. For this group, the deaths of peers expose a very specific identity-based vulnerability; immediate closeness with the deceased was not necessary to experience this injury. Repeated experiences of proximate loss and resulting grief only deepened the sense of threat and vulnerability.

The injuries are also social because of the ways they impact the boys' understanding of their place in the world at large. As I saw it, the most damaging effect of repeated losses was on the boys' imagination of the future and sense of possibility. Other scholars have described the effects of community violence on youth as "leveling expectations," changing the standards by which they might measure success.[19] Particularly as repeated losses intersect with the precarity of poverty, many struggle to meet previously held long-range future goals.

This was certainly true among JahSun's friends. Rajae, for instance, was all set to apply to the same colleges as JahSun; they planned to be roommates. Rajae was hoping to pursue a career as a teacher. It's impossible to know what would have happened had they attended college together, but in JahSun's absence, Rajae was barely able to submit his applications. "Him dying was probably the reason I didn't go to college [right away]," Rajae reflected years later. Though he ultimately completed three semesters of community college, he decided his time was better spent working full-time as a home health aide. Rajae's sense of what was possible and desirable for himself seemed to have been fundamentally altered by the death of his best friend.

Others reported similar shifts in focus spurred by loss. Herc, who had been pretty serious about basketball in middle and early high school, stopped enjoying the sport after his friend Tyhir died. He gradually began replacing practice sessions with smoking to help him relax, and eventually quit the school team. His ambitions of being a journalist also faded as his grades dipped in the wake of JahSun's death. As he neared the end of high school, he had taken college—and therefore his planned career path—off the table: "Have you seen my grades? I'm not getting no scholarships," he told me matter-of-factly at one point.

The social injuries of grief constrained possibilities for so many of the boys. In place of any visions of justice or social change, many students' longer-term responses to loss manifested in feelings of numbness and the normalization of peer deaths; hypervigilance about avoiding danger or worries about their own death; and hopelessness about continued violence in their neighborhoods—all of which served to narrow their own aspirations.[20]

Teachers' Moral Distress

Losing two students in one school year took a toll on teachers too. For some, like their students, these added to an already-too-long list of losses. Bill was Ms. Woo's fourth student in five years of teaching to become a victim of gun violence. "After the first one, I was a wreck. Now I think I'm desensitized. I'm starting to understand what the kids feel," she reflected. Simply as a rank-and-file member of an underpaid, undervalued profession, any teacher can become demoralized. Striving to discharge a college prep mission in a savagely unequal school system adds even more demoralizing fuel; then to cope repeatedly with the murder of one's students can drive even the most dedicated of teachers to quit. Recently, Ms. Woo's mother had suggested she leave teaching to avoid the stress and pain.

Indeed, many Boys' Prep teachers described constant feelings of moral distress, a sense of being unable to fulfill their personal moral commitments to do the right thing because of institutional and structural constraints. "Moral distress"—or "moral stress," as it is sometimes called—has typically been used to describe the experiences of nurses and other health professionals working in contexts where resource deprivation or institutional bureaucracy force them to perform professional duties that conflict with their own conscience.[21] For teachers, seeing students unable to fulfill obvious potential or stalled in their development, and feeling ill equipped or lacking the resources to help, is similarly devastating. How do you meet the educational needs of a student entering high school at a second-grade reading level? And how do you then support that student while also challenging the one next to him who may be ready for advanced work beyond his grade level? The difficulty of simply providing appropriate instruction to a classroom of diverse learners tests the foundational moral instincts that bring most teachers into the profession.

JahSun's and Bill's deaths intensified this moral distress. Mr. Marker, Bill's sophomore English teacher, articulated this clearly when he explained that his "mantra" as a teacher was instilling in his students "that they have a future, that there is stuff that comes after this." Even though he did not share a racial or class background with his students, Mr. Marker believed that age and life experience gave him a place from which to guide the boys and help them build connective tissue from this moment in their life to the next one. He remembered vividly what it was like to be a teenager and to feel the immense weight of every moment and the difficulty of looking far ahead.

Bill's death was Mr. Marker's first student loss, and it "shattered" the foundation of his approach: "It is really difficult to think that this idea of the future being guaranteed is not always true. So it's been obviously emotionally devastating, but also philosophically challenging for, like, what it is that I'm trying to do every moment in the classroom. It's made me reconsider whether or not I can have that sort of patience [for the future]." Premature death not only challenged Mr. Marker's teaching philosophy, but left him with a fundamental dilemma about how to pursue equity: "Sometimes I think it's unjust for me to ask a student experiencing trauma . . . to do [schoolwork]. And it is also an injustice that . . . the students they are competing against [for college and jobs] grew up like I did [and] did not have those experiences [of peer loss]." He wondered whether, by giving his students a break to grieve, he was perpetuating a cycle of inequality that left his students further behind their more privileged peers.

Ms. Gallo, one of the college counselors, worried that she and other colleagues were beginning to lose some of the indignation Mr. Marker expressed. In a conversation the week after Bill's death with several colleagues, there was general agreement that the experience of losing Bill felt different from losing JahSun. They were disturbed at the thought that they were starting to feel numb to the deaths of children. It was as if their students' normalization of early death as a survival mechanism was rubbing off on the adults. Paradoxically, while their sadness after Bill's death was less intense than JahSun's because it was not the first, they were more overwhelmed by the number of students they wanted to care for and the depths of their needs. How could they respond properly while also fulfilling their professional obligations in this college preparatory environment?

The experience of moral distress hit Ms. Bloom hard as well. Soon after Bill's murder, she told me she thought she was becoming "desensitized" to all the death. She didn't feel that much anymore: "After Ty, I was barely functional. With Jah, I think I was in survival mode—just for the guys. Now, I don't know . . ." Her voice trailed off. Although she never taught Bill and hadn't know him well, she was connected to many of his friends and felt a responsibility to support them. But she was starting to realize that her efforts were not sustainable:

I just feel like this year I haven't had a minute to breathe. I've taught more classes than I ever had with a [freshman] class that's been the most challenging class I've ever taught. On top of it, I have a lot of kids who lean on me. I feel like I haven't really had a minute to process everything or take care of myself. And there's so many of them. I leave sometimes, with guilt. [One student] is in my class today just sitting there. Maybe he needed to talk to me and I just was so busy that I just walked out. It's just a lot.

Ms. Bloom's classroom had become a space of both joy and mourning since Tyhir's death nearly two years earlier, and she was the go-to person for so many students when they were struggling. But now she worried about herself.

Ms. Bloom's experience hints at the systemic nature of the problem. The heroic efforts of lone teachers cannot meet the emotional needs of a school full of students, even under less extreme circumstances. Nor can schools retain high-quality, committed teachers when the day-to-day work in the building is so acutely demanding and draining. In fact, Boys' Prep saw a mass exodus of teachers toward the end of the following year. It included several longtime teachers who had been vital to the life of the school and to the informal support systems of many students—among them, Ms. Bloom, Ms. Cain, Ms. Finn, Mr. Khan, and Mr. Marker. A full third of the school's thirty-six teachers departed after the 2018–2019 school year—hemorrhaging, as one teacher calculated, sixty-four years of Boys' Prep teaching experience.

For the teachers involved, there was great sadness, even guilt, at finding themselves part of the mass migration, which felt like desertion. With his first child on the way, Mr. Marker reluctantly decided to leave teaching, at least temporarily, to be a full-time dad. Others, like Ms. Bloom and Ms. Finn, were trying to salvage a waning commitment to the profession by moving—again, maybe just for now—to suburban schools where they expected to be less overwhelmed by students' experiences of trauma or the effects of neighborhood gun violence.

Of course, the story is more complicated. High faculty turnover is endemic to low-income schools; and, at the same time, many well-loved and talented teachers chose to remain at Boys' Prep. But the unusually high number of faculty departures during the same period when the Boys' Prep community suffered so much loss suggests that teachers' moral distress may be heightened by youth violence. If a sense of collegiality and solidarity among the faculty is central to a thriving school environment, then the disintegration of its teacher core is perhaps another debilitating aftershock of neighborhood gun violence. Mr. Gilbert presciently predicted as much the year before when he said, "There's been a lot of changes [at the school] that have been difficult, but I think if we all stay here, we win. We'll work that out. There's no choice in the matter. But if people start leaving, then it becomes an 'I'm not sure' [situation]."

A Repeating Cycle for the Brothers in Grief

This study briefly opened a window on to the inner lives of a group of boys whose experiences converged at Boys' Prep, as well as the school adults with whom they interacted during one academic year. It is at best a snapshot of a moment in what I hope will be, for each of these boys, a thick album of a long and complex life. A life filled with accomplishments and triumphs, personal growth and insight, and re-lationships that bring meaning, connection, and joy.

Sadly, as time marches forward, these Black boys seem to be stuck inside a gruesome infinity mirror: a kid wearing a memorial t-shirt for his dead friend ends up in a memorial photo on another t-shirt or posted to a friend's Instagram page. And the cycle repeats.

*

In October 2019 when Boys' Prep suffered the loss of yet another student by gun violence, students and alumni expressed a sense of res-ignation that such tragedies had now happened enough to be almost commonplace at the school. It was not unusual to hear comments from students like "This happens every year," "BP can never catch a break," or "too many funerals." On Instagram, more than a dozen students and alumni shared the phrase "this school is cursed." The original im-age, white text on a black background, become more and more pix-elated as it was copied and reposted over and over (fig. 6.5).

There was also, around that time, a flurry of offers of support and brotherhood. Deron, generally a bit of a loner not known for his school spirit, made an unexpected public offer to his classmates online: "For all my brothers I just wanna say y'all know I care deeply about my bonds rs 💯. Y'all know who I'm talking to and if y'all ever need me

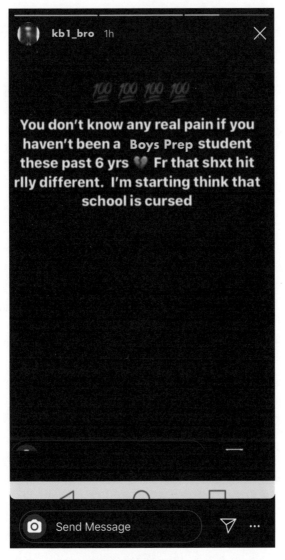

Figure 6.5. Keith's Instagram story in late 2019. The white text was taken as a screenshot from another peer (notice the doubled formatting at the bottom). Keith added the 💯s, indicating his agreement with his peer's statement. This image was reshared by multiple students. Note that Keith's own thumbnail picture was a picture of his friend Bill, a year and a half after that loss.

I'm there for all you no matter what it may be cuz y'all like blood to me
🎱 ✏️ 🔒 💪. Stay strong and be safe out here. I love you all. ❤️ " Similarly, a Boys' Prep alum who had graduated two years earlier shared
on Instagram that he was available if any student "need[ed] someone
to talk to." The shared experience of being part of a school community that was suffering so much seemed to create reflexive bonds and
feelings of responsibility.

Though by this time I was no longer at the school to observe daily
life, numerous accounts from both faculty and students suggested
that the three-stage cycle of institutional and student grief repeated
itself. An abbreviated moment of collective grief quickly gave way to
periods of institutional tension and unrecognized mourning. A kind of
schoolwide numbness also seemed to have taken hold. My impression
is that as the gun deaths of students became normalized, the school's
commitment to the collective healing process waned, while, at the
same time, the pressures to maintain a focus on academic goalposts
and compliant behavior intensified. The school had noble hopes for a
student body that it didn't fully understand and that it wasn't prepared to fully serve. And students continued to respond in a range of
ways, including closing in and drawing sharp social boundaries, puffing out to assert their right to grieve, checking out of school commitments and standing still in terms of future planning, and also checking
in with peers through emotional disclosures and brotherly support
online.

JahSun's little brother, Bashir, by then a high school junior, was
struggling to figure out how to deal with his new and continued grief.
In a private message through Instagram, he told me, "I don't want to
be sad but last time I tried [hiding my sadness,] it just was not good at
all." He was determined to figure out another way to grieve besides
masking it.

In the next chapter, inspired by the creativity and conviction of
youth and communities dealing with tremendous grief in other contexts of gun violence, I offer insight into another way forward, both
for boys like Bashir and for his school.

Chapter Seven

From Grief to Grievance

In the early afternoon of Valentine's Day 2018—three months after JahSun's death and two months before Bill's—a nineteen-year-old entered his former school, Marjory Stoneman Douglas High School in Parkland, Florida, armed with an AR-15-style rifle. The gunman shot into classrooms, hallways, and stairwells. In just six minutes he would kill fourteen students and three staff members and physically wound another seventeen people. It was the worst high school shooting in history and came on the heels of several other high-profile mass killings in the preceding months.

The Stoneman Douglas massacre occurred at a time when the country seemed to have grown numb to the gun violence epidemic, with even the most notorious events staying in the headlines for an average of only four days.[1] The vigils, memorials, and "thoughts and prayers" of a national *easy hard* would quickly give way to the local community or school's more enduring *hard hard* and *hidden hard*. Like the demoralized children at Boys' Prep, the country itself seemed mired in a shared sense of malaise, hopelessness, and powerlessness when it came to ending the carnage. It was a moment when, to quote Dave Cullen, a reporter who had been covering mass shooting events since Columbine decades earlier, "America had hit rock bottom."[2]

But this time history would unfold a little differently. Already during the three-and-a-half hours the Florida teens were barricaded in classrooms and crouched behind desks, unsure if they were waiting for death or rescue, they were able to pull themselves out of the national numbness and realize not only that something had to be done, but that they could be the ones to do it. Trapped with just each other and their phones for those terrifying hours, fear and anger compelled some of the Parkland students to take immediate action. By that evening, teenage survivors and friends of victims stood before masses of cameras and microphones—or going viral online—calling defiantly on their nation's leaders to do something. As the country fell into its practiced shock and mourning, there was also a new strain of outrage, energy, and courage articulated by an eloquent, publicly grieving group of teens—and it produced a sense of hope that the country and its leaders would be roused toward substantive change to protect children from gun violence.

That fresh sense of hope did not penetrate the walls of Boys' Prep. It happened that the day after Parkland, three Black Philadelphia teenagers were shot on their way home after picking up takeout dinner. All three were known to Hazeem, who alerted me to the event and told me he was feeling "a little off" because he didn't yet have an update on their injuries.[3] In the days that followed, little was said about either event, but to the extent that gun violence came up in conversation at Boys' Prep, it was the Philly "mass" shooting, not the Parkland one, that preoccupied the boys.[4]

Even so, on a national level, Parkland triggered an avalanche of protest.[5] Within a week, the outlines of an anti–gun violence youth movement had taken shape. A busload of Stoneman Douglas students rode to the Florida state capital to lobby elected officials. By March, they were hosting one of the largest demonstrations in the history of Washington, DC. Even while coping with their immense grief, the teens tirelessly and methodically went about changing gun policy in America.[6]

To the students in my study, all the attention on Parkland felt like a slap in the face—another indication of how little people cared about the insidious, daily gunfire visiting their Black communities. Empirically, they had a point: during the 2017–2018 school year, September to June, 138 people were killed in mass shootings across the country;

during that same period, in Philadelphia alone, there were 243 homicides.[7] Where was the national uproar over that? The Boys' Prep students knew their friends' deaths occupied a different place in the country's consciousness. Unlike the Parkland dead, their murdered friends were rarely viewed as innocent victims, their lives somehow more "lose-able" and the grief their losses activated less "legible."[8] It is a cruel irony that by deeming the Parkland deaths worthy of national sympathy and outrage, the public conversation was further diminishing the loss and grief experienced at Boys' Prep.

A Contextualized Education

In the months that followed, I became aware of yet another significant difference between the school I was studying and Marjory Stoneman Douglas High School. While the Boys' Prep students contended with an education that was largely decontextualized from their lives, long before the shooting the students at Stoneman Douglas had been equipped with a range of tools and resources that prepared them to contextualize, analyze, and ultimately develop forward-looking responses to the tragic injustices that came their way.

Through a series of curricular and extracurricular programs already in place before the Valentine's Day massacre, Parkland students had gained valuable skills both to process what had happened to them individually and, in the same breath, to see the bigger picture. Perhaps surprisingly, Florida *at the time* had one of the most comprehensive statewide curricula for civic knowledge and engagement, a result of the 2010 Sandra Day O'Connor Civic Education Act. Middle school evidence-based civics courses were mandated across the state, and students were required to pass a civics test before moving on to high school.[9] In an attempt to make civics classes more engaging, the state promoted "teacher-led discussions of current events and controversial issues [and] extracurricular activities—particularly those requiring teamwork and collaboration; student participation in school governance; and, simulations of democratic processes such as mock trials."[10] Further, at Stoneman Douglas, and across Broward County, a robust debate program had, just that fall, explored issues of gun control. And in AP US Government and Politics, a course many of the survivors who rose to national prominence had taken, they had been discussing special-interest groups, including the NRA.[11] The Parkland teens had the tools to choose "a story of hope" and, if they wished, a path that centered their own agency and role in making public change as they also healed themselves and each other.[12]

In contrast, as we've seen, the *hidden hard*, the *hard hard*, and even the *easy hard* at Boys' Prep failed to provide a backdrop either for meaningful efforts toward social change or for long-term communal healing. In this chapter, I consider what might have been possible at Boys' Prep had students had other outlets for their grief, and had the school been able to adopt an orientation toward students that acknowledged and developed their critical consciousness and sense of agency in relation to their broader community.

Limited Hope and Half-Hearted Political Responses at Boys' Prep

Hoping to capitalize on the national sympathy for young people facing gun murders spurred by the Parkland shooting, a local Philadelphia politician organized a press conference on the front steps of Boys' Prep two weeks after the mass shooting. The politician's team brought signs proclaiming "Peace," "Love," "We Count Too," and images of crossed-out AK-47s. While the news crews set up outside for what would be the first of a three-stop media tour of Philadelphia schools, Boys' Prep seniors were ushered from their classes into the cafeteria to make additional signs. Some covered neon poster paper with hashtags memorializing their dead friends; others wrote slogans like "We don't want to die," "Books not bullets," or "Black Lives Matter."

The students filtered out of the building and lined the steps of the school, marveling at the big cameras and the possibility of being on

TV. Their signs and school uniforms framed the local lawmaker—the same politician who spoke at JahSun's memorial in the school cafeteria back in December—as he offered remarks on the deepening gun violence crisis in Philadelphia.

Four students had been selected to join him at the podium to share their stories. Theo spoke about JahSun, his football teammate and friend, as well as multiple family members who had been killed in recent years: "When something like this happens, the world seems to come to a stop." Sophomore Sybrii talked about how Tyhir's death a year earlier had impacted his life. He reported the sad lessons he'd learned, including that he could no longer trust everyone and had to watch his back. Kaliq offered a message to his peers that it was okay to walk away from a fight. He ended his speech early because he got too emotional—although for years he would claim that it was just that the sun in his eyes had thrown him off. Yaja spoke last: "The worst part of this reality is that it never stops and it never changes. We just keep adapting to it and becoming null to death around us." And then, breaking from the script he had carefully written out: "I stand firm with ending gun violence. We matter."

Years later when Yaja reflected on his senior year at Boys' Prep, including the rally on the school steps, he would own up to an inner conflict. At times he would recollect the warmth of his school community as they came together to support each other after JahSun died and for the remainder of the school year. He recalled the vigil on the football field, certain classrooms where teachers gave him and his peers the space to feel their feelings, and the social worker's office where he and another friend would spend many periods when they just couldn't bear to be in class.[13] But with some distance from high school and after a host of new life experiences, Yaja also realized how much more could have been done to help him and his friends heal during that awful year when two of their classmates died, along with so many others from the neighborhood. He didn't blame his teachers—he knew they were struggling too—but he didn't think the adults really got how much more their students needed. To him, the post-Parkland rally and speeches were a poignant example of exactly these missed opportunities.

Even at the time, Yaja and his friends were cynical about the politician's motives, assuming he was principally focused on self-promotion. And they felt their own role was mainly performative. Only two speeches included anything close to a call to action, and they were vague at best. The sad truth was that none of them really believed anything could be done to slow or stop the killings. Yaja remembered the discouragement he and his peers felt:

The day we went out there to do that [press conference], we hated it . . . we hated every second of it. Kaliq was standing right behind me, Omari standing behind . . . We didn't even want to be there. . . . We all knew, in the back of our minds, or we talked to each other about it, that somebody else was going to die . . . That was a conversation [among] all of us: Who was going to be the next person, you know? So you deal with it in school, you deal with it outta school. How do you find purpose in that?

Even as they held up protest signs in front of camera crews at a moment of genuine national attention directed at this issue and at youth, the boys felt hopeless about the possibility of change. They did not see a clear role they could play in shifting the conversation or preventing future violence, nor were they inspired to seek one out. They were too terrified by the question of who they would be grieving next.

Dr. Stephens, in his speech at the rally, seemed aware of the mismatch between his students and the moment:

They have to have an understanding of the building blocks that it takes to succeed, but they also have to have a vision, a vision of the big picture. They have to understand what is destined to them, they have to feel empowered, they have to be strong. James Baldwin, he said, "Your crown has been bought and paid for, all you have to do is put it on, all you have to do is wear it." But I have to be honest, it's hard to feel like they can have that long-range plan. It's hard sometimes to feel in control of one's own destiny when life and love can be snatched from them, from us, so quickly.

Dr. Stephens's words reflect one of the central tensions of a future-oriented school curriculum in a context of high mortality and vulnerability to violence.

Two weeks later, on the one-month anniversary of the Parkland shooting, a contingent of Boys' Prep students participated in a school walkout, organized nationally by March for Our Lives teens. The school's participation in the walkout, like the rally, demonstrated the administration's intuition that their students needed opportunities to envision social change and to partake in collective action. But whereas at other Philadelphia schools students marched with banners and chants to City Hall with specific policy demands they had been discussing in classrooms, the Boys' Prep event felt perfunctory and merely symbolic. The group circled the block around the school and then gathered on the steps for a moment of silence. Some students weren't even sure what they were marching for, confessing they participated only to get out of class.

As efforts toward change, activism, or consciousness-raising, these events felt half-hearted and inadequate. The most palpable feeling following gatherings like the rally and walkout was defeat: Quartell wondering aloud if all this death was normal, or Kaliq saying he was so "used to losing people" that he had become "numb to it."[14] Without exposure to models of youth empowerment and community engagement—or a sustained connection to larger social justice movements aiming to disrupt the systemic causes of gun violence—students' instincts of hopelessness and powerlessness remained largely intact.

Finding Shared Grievances for Gun Violence Prevention

Though it wasn't apparent at Boys' Prep, elsewhere in the country young people had begun to draw connections between mass shootings such as Parkland and the decades-long ravages of gun violence in poor Black neighborhoods. Growing in political power, Parkland survivors linked their movement to other groups of youth who had long been committed to tackling gun violence in all its forms. Young speakers at the March 24 March for Our Lives rally in Washington, DC, represented groups from at least eight different cities and a multitude of experiences of gun violence.[15] Two standouts were seventeen-year-old Alex King and eighteen-year-old D'Angelo McDade, seniors at North Lawndale College Prep, the majority-Black charter school on the West Side of Chicago, where I taught from 2008 to 2010.[16]

Alex and D'Angelo had both been touched by gun violence in ways similar to the Boys' Prep students and without the limelight of a nationally covered mass shooting. Alex lost a teenage nephew; D'Angelo himself had been shot while sitting on his front porch. Both teens had also experienced countless other gun deaths within their peer and neighborhood networks. But unlike most Boys' Prep students I came to know, they had discovered a way to do something about it that was helping them pull themselves out of their own dark thoughts. The Chicago teens had found comfort and purpose in the philosophy of Kingian nonviolence, which was operationalized in their school through the Peace Warriors, peer nonviolence leaders. The extensive Peace Warrior training, drawing on Martin Luther King Jr.'s "Six Principles of Nonviolence," teaches students to break up fights in school, mediate altercations between classmates through "peace circles," and offer emotional support to peers who have experienced loss.[17] The Peace Warriors aim to be proactive, rather than reactive, in aggressively promoting nonviolence in their school and the wider community. Since the group's inception in 2009, it has had measurable impacts on in-school violence and student suspensions and on students' feelings of hopefulness and emotional healing.[18]

D'Angelo agreed with King's Principles of Nonviolence that he learned about through the Peace Warriors, particularly the fourth principle: to "accept suffering without retaliation for the sake of the cause to achieve the goal." He felt that suffering could educate and transform and that, indeed, he and his peers were transformed through this work. And they hoped to promote that change in others. But D'Angelo also knew that anti-Black racism meant that his stories of gun violence would never get the same national coverage or public sympathy as when the problem hit the wealthy white suburbs—and that what attention his community did get risked ignoring the root causes of violence. In his speech to the March for Our Lives crowd of 800,000 and the millions more tuning in on television, D'Angelo highlighted the many layers of his kind of "survivor" experience:

For we are survivors not only of gun violence, but of silence. For we are survivors of the erratic productions of poverty. But not only that, we are the survivors of unjust policies and practices upheld by our Senate. We are survivors of lack of resources within our schools. We are survivors of social, emotional, and physical harm.

In essence, D'Angelo was proclaiming that the losses he and his peers experienced were not just personal, but political, because they were produced in a context "shaped by collective injustice."[19]

For his part, Alex sought to acknowledge the connections across the crowd, even across divergent experiences: "Our pain makes us family. Us hurting together brings us closer together to fight for something better."

Indeed, the Parkland and Chicago students had connected with each other in the earliest days of the ballooning movement. Six Chicago youth traveled to Florida, and later the Florida crew made a visit to Chicago.[20] They became friends. They shared their stories of trauma. Both groups were grieving friends lost violently, prematurely, and unjustly. They saw their issues and goals as intertwined, though they acknowledged the differences. Both groups were also surrounded by adults who supported their efforts, and both had accessed school-based programs and curricula that helped them develop civic awareness and skills. And both groups also understood their own agency and power, and felt a responsibility to their communities and country to act. However different their backgrounds, each of these teens had discovered that their grief might find some solace and healing in the development of what could be called *grievance*.

A grievance is a complaint or protest arising from a feeling of being wronged. It is a way to see and say what is not right in the world and what it could be.[21] Linguistically, grief and grievance are "cousins,"

both originating from the French term *grever*, meaning to harm; together, these words "document the turning of the burden of loss into
an appeal; the burden comes to assume a voice, an appeal for intervention, adjudication, judgement."[22] Looked at in this way, grievance
is a powerful and empowering transformation of grief, helping those
who have been silenced move "from suffering injury to speaking out
against that injury."[23] Grievances in this form are often collective,
making private grief shared, and forward looking—even hopeful.

Of course, there are wise and legitimate critiques of the suggestion
that young people—and especially Black young people—ought to
be generating protest from their grief. Political scientist Juliet Hooker
warns against "romanticizing" or "instrumentalizing" Black grief with
the expectation that it be used as a "democratic resource."[24] This is,
so often, what has happened in the aftermath of racist police-involved
killings of Black people, where the costs to activists, as Hooker details,
can be both physically and morally grave.[25] But as the youth movement that emerged out of Parkland illustrates, the chance to articulate
and share grievances in the face of loss offers the potential not only for
social change, but for young people to develop a deeper understanding of their environments, their histories, and their possibilities. Grievance in this case, among youth, isn't so much an instrumentalization
of grief, but an inoculation against generational despair.

What Might Have Been at Boys' Prep

In the aftermath of the tragedies that befell it, Boys' Prep offered students few opportunities for grievance. No sustained invitations for students to develop a historical or critical perspective on the social issues
that most directly impacted them. No occasions to understand their
grief and anger in collective terms, let alone channel it toward civic
participation or social change. Yaja, for example, could easily have
stood on the bandshell stage alongside Alex and D'Angelo, X González
and David Hogg from Parkland, and all the others in DC. He was

an exceptional leader and orator, but he didn't have the same feeling of being part of something bigger—nor the hope that the gun violence in his community could ever really be quelled. Instead, his school prioritized moving forward, and motivating students to escape the conditions that led to their grief, rather than being part of efforts to transform those conditions.

Looking back on that catastrophic year, Kaliq also felt something was lacking in the school's response. He wished that Boys' Prep had "had things to make us feel more powerful." He wanted the tools to become part of something bigger than himself and his own pain. Had Boys' Prep's approach been more attuned to this dimension of recovery, Yaja, Kaliq, and others might have experienced their social injuries differently.

At first blush, a school may seem neither suitable nor qualified to teach youth how to productively channel grief into grievance. After all, schools are standardizing institutions, tasked (among far too many other things) with instilling conventional civic behavior, not civil disobedience or protest. And yet, a long and rich history of educators and scholars have argued just the opposite: that schools are, in fact, *uniquely* suited to develop students into active citizens, able to critically assess their social environments and intervene in injustices.[26] And that schools ought to be responsive to their student communities—their cultural specificity, their needs and challenges, and their assets.[27]

Education scholars Scott Seider and Daren Graves make this point, starting with the premise that schools can and should be spaces of consciousness-raising, and arguing that developing a curriculum that instills a critical outlook is all the more important for youth marginalized by race and class.[28] They cite James Baldwin's 1963 essay, "A Talk to Teachers," in which Baldwin encourages educators of Black children to "try to make each child know that [his environment is] the result of a criminal conspiracy to destroy him [and] that if he intends to get to be a man, he must at once decide that he is stronger than this conspiracy, and he must never make his peace with it." For Baldwin, and the education scholars who draw from him, schools have a responsibility to guide students toward developing a *critical consciousness*. That is, the skills to understand the (racial) injustices of the world, "resist [their] negative effects[,] and challenge [their] root causes."[29]

The term "critical consciousness," or *conscientização*, was originally coined by Brazilian educator and philosopher Paulo Freire to encompass both reflection and action as necessary components of the kind of social transformation that could be taught in educational settings.[30] In Freire's formulation, as in the ways it has been taken up more recently, the development of a critical consciousness about one's social circumstances not only allows one to imagine and work for a better future, but is itself also a form of humanization within a society that too often dehumanizes those with less power, including racial minorities, the poor, and children.

An essential element of critical consciousness is *radical* or *critical* hope—specifically, hope that recognizes both the barriers to its achievement, but also the "cracks in the concrete" where collective action can break through.[31] Hope is itself a form of resistance, as education scholar Shawn Ginwright has written, "reaffirm[ing] what is possible, and worth fighting for." Hope framed collectively is even more powerful as a counter to numbness, the normalization of loss, or the tolerance of continued injustice and as a shared vision and commitment for a better future.[32] In this sense, developing young people who feel hopeful about the future and prepared to take on its inevitable challenges is one of the most important roles of a school.

One lesson I take from successful youth social justice movements is that emotional recovery is aided both by hope and by feeling needed by a larger public. Both the Parkland and Peace Warriors teenagers, to cite just two examples, felt they had a role to play—that perhaps *only* they could play, despite their trauma and grief. The issue needed them; their community needed them. Their grievances gave them a sense of purpose and a feeling that people were listening and, therefore, that change might be possible. This form of active hope and action is all the more important during adolescence, a critical period of identity and worldview development, since peer loss during this time can destabilize secure conceptions of the future.[33]

In the wake of the deaths of their friends, where could the students of Boys' Prep find hope? Where could they find a sense of purpose? The structural and ideological strengths of Boys' Prep—its small size, its emphasis on strong, individualized student-teacher relationships, its lack of district-level oversight, its interest in developing students' emotional capacities—positioned it to respond well to the immediate challenges after the shooting deaths of students. The initial collectivization of grief—the *easy hard*—at Boys' Prep was genuine, generous, and imaginative. Administrators could nimbly shift the school schedule and contract for local, if temporary, resources without bureaucratic constraints. Teachers could change up classroom plans and follow up directly with struggling students (even via text message) to offer support and warm consolation.

But after that? Feeling at all times the tremendous burden of compensating for an unequal education system that had already left their students far behind, the school leadership at Boys' Prep rushed anxiously to get back to the "classical" curriculum and the business of a college-preparatory education. Almost compulsively, they doubled down on their idealistic embrace of respectability politics, particularly in the school's fixation on the student uniform, effectively deporting students' sorrow and grief to the online world, and to individual relationships between students and a handful of highly sensitive, overwhelmed teachers.[34] At the curricular level, without a schoolwide orientation toward social change or issues of racial justice, teachers had few tools to draw on to help students interpret their grief or contextualize it into a fuller understanding of their lives. Lost was any opportunity to generate positive feedback loops between personal experience, deep analysis, and constructive grievances. Instead, the adolescent boys faced the double curse of experiencing the deaths of peers as a *normal* event in their young lives and multiple incentives to suppress their strongest emotions as a means of coping, leaving them to fall into the state of numbness they widely reported.

Boys' Prep is unusual in many ways, but in lacking a commitment to civic education or a contextualized analysis of racial injustice and the potential for community transformation, it is not. This is a common story, particularly for schools that see their mission as remedying the academic achievement gap or promoting equal educational opportunity against the odds. In an increasingly market-driven educational system, test scores (or college-admissions statistics) are king; many schools serving poor and racially minoritized students prioritize students' *individual* academic achievement over any other metric. Too often, these schools see "character education"—grit, resilience, self-control, respectability—as the key to meeting these goals, rather than civic education or empowerment.[35]

Sociologist Joanne Golann argues that this approach to schooling, with its attendant emphasis on compliance with behavioral standards, leads to the development of "worker-learners—children who monitor themselves, hold back their opinions, and defer to authority—rather than lifelong learners."[36] Strict forms of control around interaction and expression limit the opportunity for students to develop the social skills essential to full democratic participation.[37] Being intent on keeping students out of trouble precludes encouraging them to get into the kinds of "good [and] necessary trouble" that civil rights icon John Lewis maintained our country needs.

When bigger structural change feels too daunting, the understandable fallback is to focus on incremental change: individual students' academic advancement or escape from the neighborhood. In schools like Boys' Prep, collective hope is often deferred in favor of more attainable individual wins.

Without an eye toward collective social participation, students may fail to understand their own experiences in the context of larger struggles. On top of losing their closest friends, our youngest citizens are at risk of losing a sense of purpose, a belief that change for the better is possible, and a hopeful outlook on their future—and ours. I am left to wonder whether the boys' overwhelming responses of emotional numbness and disempowerment would have been different if Boys' Prep had a cultural and curricular focus on civic or critical engagement with societal issues beyond the walls of the school.

Teaching Critical Consciousness and Collective Hope

Just like the Parkland and Chicago students, the Boys' Prep boys had the instincts to weigh in on big problems. I saw this in the letters students wrote that first Monday back at school after JahSun's death. Even students who didn't know JahSun talked about what more they could have done to prevent his murder or how they hoped their classmates would come together to make a change. Problem-solving instincts were also evident in Yaja's efforts, a year earlier, to launch Freedom to Speak, a school club designed to give boys space to talk openly about their experiences and emotions with each other.[38] Forged by, as Bettina Love has put it, the "civics project [of] simply being a dark person,"[39] the boys already had the raw materials; they just needed tools and training to put them to work toward social change.

What would it look like to support the teenagers at Boys' Prep, and at other schools where students regularly experience the deaths of friends, in developing a more reflective orientation toward the anguish of loss? How could an institution tasked with educating young people also hold sacred their tender emotions of grief, while simultaneously helping them voice warranted grievances about their unrelenting losses and the larger culture of injustice within which their lives are embedded? Would such a reorientation help young, vulnerable boys heal?

Turning from despair to hope requires "transformative teaching," teaching that pushes back against ideas of individual grit and resilience, and instead "connect[s] the moral outrage of young people to actions that relieve the undeserved suffering in their communities."[40] The classroom, as bell hooks reminds us, can be "a location of possibility" where learners and teachers "face reality even as [they] collectively imagine" alternatives.[41] This approach to teaching, which takes into account youth's social conditions and context, reframes Black youth not as "civic problems" but as "civic problem solvers," and their grievances as political, not personal.[42]

Examples of transformative teaching for critical consciousness development are associated with many positive outcomes, particularly for marginalized youth, including "resilience, mental health, self-esteem, academic achievement, high professional aspirations, and civic and political engagement."[43] There is also evidence that critical consciousness gives youth feelings of increased control or agency over their lives and their surroundings, a sense of membership in a collective with a common purpose, a critical—rather than false—hope for the future, and a pathway to "radical healing."[44]

A range of models already exists for developing students' critical consciousness. Explicitly promoting and training youth in activism and political engagement is just one, and certainly not the only, approach. Curricular strategies, such as courses on social engagement, civics, sociology, or African American history, help students understand the social and historical context of their lives as well as find blueprints in past movements for change. Internship programs, service-learning and youth-led philanthropic endeavors, youth participatory action research projects, and collaborative arts-based activities allow students to engage directly with their communities and connect their burgeoning skills and interests with real-world concerns. Approaches outside the classroom, like the Peace Warriors program, community meetings, culture circles, and restorative justice programs, can help shift the culture of a school.

Most adolescents will never have the national audience that the Parkland teens received, but even without the news crews and trending Tweets, a school can signal to its students that their critical perspectives and intellectual contributions matter. School leaders can offer students formal invitations to suggest school policy changes and support student-led initiatives like peer tutoring, counseling, and mediation.[45] Black boys can be empowered to think about ways to change the systems, organizations, and people who impact their lives.[46]

To be in a position to support students' grief and underlying grievances when death comes to the community, schools like Boys' Prep need to cultivate and value their students' emerging agency. Making space for transformative teaching practices and critical consciousness-raising—while also centering students' collective healing and wellness after a loss[47]—requires a school to embrace a different stance toward its students. It necessitates balancing attention to students' individual academic advancement with a schoolwide commitment to social responsibility and justice. I know this is a lot to ask of institutions already tasked with so much and encumbered by so many obstacles. But how much more do we ask of children when we expect them to remain committed to their education as their friends are dying?

Collective Grief and Grievance beyond School Walls

Despite the missed opportunities at Boys' Prep, there was one unexpected place where I witnessed collective grief and grievance activities unfolding in the wake of students' deaths. Let's return to the scene of the anti–gun violence rally on the steps of Boys' Prep two weeks after the Parkland shooting, where in attendance beside the students and staff was JahSun's mother, Maxayn. In a short speech at the podium, she announced her plans to establish a scholarship fund in her son's honor. (Later she would also launch a mentoring program to provide life coaching and mental health support to Boys' Prep students.)

Flanked on both sides by the senior class her son had been a part of, Maxayn explained to the cameras: "It's my way of giving back . . . [and] coping with this pain . . . And also to show other parents that we have to use this pain for a purpose, we have to—we can't sit in it, we can't grieve in it. It's time to get angry and it's time to do something about it." As she saw it, she had a role to play in helping young men learn to love themselves enough that they would never think of taking another's life.

Also around this same time, Maxayn created a memorial Instagram account for JahSun where she would post baby photos, treasured memories, and information about the events and initiatives she was sponsoring. Using the account to interact with her, JahSun's friends would often refer to Maxayn as "Mom." Some even saved her phone number under a version of that title. On Maxayn's birthday, Khalil posted a picture of the two of them together with the caption "Happy birthday to one of the most strongest women I know on this planet. You know I will help keep Jah name alive. But enjoy your day and love you mom 🖤🖤🖤🖤🖤🖤🖤🖤." In return, Maxayn frequently wrote messages on social media referring to JahSun's friends as her "sons" or "extended children" and with comments like "y'all stuck with me now." In one post, she theorized that "Jah knew what he was doing when he brought us all together."

For a long stretch of the winter and spring following his death, JahSun's crew of close friends made regular trips to Maxayn's house on Sundays. Ms. Bloom and Ms. Woo would drive them and order pizza for the group. Sometimes the boys hung out with Maxayn in the living room, chatting and eating and looking through JahSun's things; other times, they would venture off to JahSun's room. The close connections that formed between the boys and Maxayn provided a needed service to all. It has long been understood that Black women often become "play mothers" or "othermothers" to young people in their extended non-biological networks, doing additional emotional and care labor beyond raising their own children.[48] But in addition to Maxayn's "othermothering" of JahSun's friends, the group of boys did what I call "othersoning" work for Maxayn, perhaps filling some very small part of the void left by JahSun's absence. This form of "restorative kinship" affirmed the value of JahSun's life and the persistence of his memory.[49] JahSun's friends were committed to making sure that Maxayn was going to be okay. Khalil explained, "We all talked to his mom, seeing her happy [was important]. After that, I just like, I became more comfortable, because I knew that she's happy . . . so it basically forced me to be stronger."

As the years have passed, many of the boys have continued to reach out to Maxayn on JahSun's birthday and death anniversary, as well as Mother's Day. And she honors many of them with birthday wishes and congratulatory messages when they reach important milestones. Maxayn's own life trajectory has been forever altered by the death of her son. In addition to the mentoring and scholarship programs she has developed on the side, she has also rerouted her own career to focus on violence prevention and victim support services. Maxayn has plans to write both a memoir and a book to bring together the stories of other grievers. She doesn't always feel sure she "grieved properly" and periodically makes plans to take a leave from work to focus on herself. She also hopes to eventually move to the suburbs and then perhaps out of Philadelphia altogether, to give herself and her now-teenage daughter more space to heal and an escape from the continued gun violence risks in Philadelphia.

Bill's mother, Williesha, and Tyhir's mother, Tanisha, have also found ways to stay connected to their sons' memories through community gatherings and forms of continued relationship with their sons' friends. Williesha has partnered with local anti–gun violence organizations, raising funds and sponsoring Philadelphia youth to write about their experiences with violence. She also recently opened up a candy store named for her son. She spends most afternoons there greeting kids who attend school across the street and selling them sweets. She hopes to eventually employ a young person from the neighborhood in the store. Though Williesha felt tremendous guilt that she had not been more committed to these kinds of community efforts before she was personally impacted, she now sees herself playing an important role in supporting other youth in the community, including Bill's friends. She still invites them on her annual family trip to celebrate Bill's birthday, and sometimes they reach out to her to invite her to join them on a visit to the cemetery.

Tanisha's efforts primarily take place on social media, where she took over her son's Instagram account and uses it to share memorializations and family updates, and through an annual basketball tournament. Each July, around the anniversary of Tyhir's death, Tanisha gathers with his friends from school and the neighborhood to share the sport he loved on the very basketball court now painted with his face and birth and death dates.

The efforts of Maxayn, Williesha, and Tanisha, and so many parents like them, offer a window into what is possible for community-driven activism, healing, and change. In their grief, these Black mothers' actions have reflected an inherent understanding of the collectivity of suffering.[50] To varying degrees, they were each able to find a sense of personal purpose in their pain, use their grief as a resource for the community, and develop and share collective grievances. In staying connected to their sons' social worlds and continuing to publicly memorialize their lost boys, they also—perhaps unknowingly—gave a sense of purpose to their sons' friends and classmates. In these unexpected and spontaneous relationships, mothers and friends found something they needed in each other and formed relationships that perhaps filled some tiny piece of the gaping hole they still faced.

In becoming *othersons* to their friends' mothers, boys took on a new role that was meaningful and communal. They were able to continue to grieve in collective ways, while feeling needed and valuable. Though these relationships may not be forever—they seem to be hard, on both sides, to sustain over time—they offer a hint of the healing that is possible when grief is faced collectively and when people find authentic roles to play in each other's lives.

The Reaches of Injury

This book chronicles the aftermath of a violent incident, which was both all too terrible, yet all too normal. Similarly, the task of assessing its impact is both impossible, yet of the greatest urgency. Which is why we must try.

Typically, historians and journalists use two gruesome numbers to calculate the damage of the violent acts and events that fill history books and headlines—from battlefields and bombings to mass shootings and street crime. They are the number of dead, and the number of wounded.

During my years at Boys' Prep, just the number of students who died by gunfire is itself so huge and horrific that already the losses suffered defy comprehension. I did not know Tyhir and I only distantly crossed paths with Bill, but both, as I have come to know them in death, were beautiful, special boys with much to look forward to and much we could have expected from them in the years to come. JahSun I knew: he was both exceptional and ordinary. Exceptional in his capacity for deep thinking, his kindness and openness toward many circles of peers, and his range of musical and athletic talents; yet ordinary in that he was like all teenagers—with an array of gifts and flaws and the right to look forward to a long life ahead. For those stolen boys, there is no more catastrophic or final fate; no school effort, no personal memorial, no piece of writing can change their ending.

But the impacts of their deaths reverberate outward, wounding so many others. For the mothers of each of these boys, their sons' murders have left deep scars in their hearts, their daily lives, and their families. Though time has made the pain less acute and overpowering, it will never be far from their thoughts.[51]

Also for the teachers and school leaders, the parade of student deaths represented a philosophical and existential shattering of their personal and professional missions. It might be easier to make sense of the story on these pages if there were an obvious villain, if we could imagine Boys' Prep as a toxic school or its staff as ill intentioned. If we could ignore their pain too. But this was an institution full of dedicated and empathic adults doing their best to support struggling young people through an impossible year, and also struggling themselves to fulfill the educational mandates of their jobs.

Now to this tally of the injured, we must add another tier of suffering, never fully recognized and too soon dismissed. Another deep and destabilizing vein of grief, where damage can fester and grow. We must acknowledge the young friends of the dead who are haunted by ghosts as they simply try to grow up. As they sit in classrooms with memorials on the walls, looking to their left and right and wondering which chair might be empty when they return from school vacation. As they scroll through social media questioning whether a flurry of pictures of a friend is a birthday celebration or a death notice. As they long to share an inside joke or get a pep talk from a trusted friend now gone. For these young boys, perpetual losses become enduring injuries that are collective and shared across their generation and their communities, and yet too often the institutional erasure of these wounds pushes them underground to be nursed privately and silently.

As long as young people are murdered in terrible numbers, there will be thousands more of their friends and classmates who will be injured, sometimes permanently, by these losses. Children to whom attention, consideration, and care are owed. We must recognize their grief and help them make sense of it, encourage them to act as positive resources to their communities, lest their futures be haunted.

Looking Ahead

Until all children in this country are safe on the street and at school, it is reasonable to ask what the losses at Boys' Prep may teach us, beyond a fuller appreciation of their ravages. Are there ways to curtail, contain, or mitigate some of the harmful effects that untimely death can cause to a victim's friends and classmates?

While concrete fixes and policy directives are beyond my scope and the scope of this book, there are some tangible takeaways from my accounting of Boys' Prep. First, schools need the resources to invest more into the holistic care of their students. Schools like Boys' Prep require permanent mental health staff who can be available, one-on-one, to students consistently, not only during known emergencies—and who understand the nuance of their students' social context. The student-to-counselor ratio has been improving nationally, but it still falls well below recommended levels and there has also been a concerning trend of cops replacing counselors, particularly in schools serving students of color.[52]

Additionally, there are many promising approaches to developing trauma-informed (or trauma-sensitive or -responsive) institutions, teachers, and pedagogies that can make school a place where students won't be punished for their grief and can find healing and support.[53]

Teachers, who inevitably become first responders to students' grief, need the flexibility of time and autonomy to be available to students in crisis, and the training and resources to take on that role as needed.[54] Retaining effective and empathic teachers who can support students both in and out of the classroom will require that those teachers feel valued (emotionally and financially) and not overburdened.

The response to school tragedies cannot be to rely on the heroism of select teachers going above and beyond their duties—and then, too often, burning out.

Finally, since, as we've seen, lofty school mandates—even ostensibly benevolent ones—can sometimes blind administrators and teachers to their students' emotional difficulties, careful attention must be paid to the impact of a school's core values on healthy child development. Among such core values, an explicit commitment to student agency may protect children from the paralyzing sense of powerlessness in the face of peer loss. As discussed, one approach to enhancing young people's sense of personal and generational efficacy is to help them find authentic roles in movements for and toward change.

Of course, equipping a school to support grieving students should never imply a passive acceptance of the violent status quo. Nor can we leave the larger political struggles to the students to wage. The escalating epidemic of gun violence—and the racial inequities of its impacts even during periods of relative peace and stability—is the anteceding problem to be solved, and the burden of fixing that falls on us all.[55]

*

In December 2021, a few years after completing the research for this book, I met up with Kaliq in a coffee shop in Philadelphia. We talked about his life, his memories of Boys' Prep, JahSun, and this study. At one point, Kaliq teared up and I wondered if I'd ever seen him cry before. Despite all the times we had discussed death and grief, he was always the one who declared numbness, that it didn't really affect him anymore. But now he could admit that this was never really true; he just hadn't felt safe as a teenager to share the extent of his pain and sorrow. "Now I'm starting to grow and understand, [but] back then I just wanted to show that I was strong," he reflected. He worried that bottling up his feelings had been more harmful than if he had dealt with them at the time.

That afternoon I wished I could stay and talk longer, but I had packed my schedule for my short visit to Philly. I had another person to meet on the other side of the Schuylkill River and Kaliq offered to give me a ride, a role reversal of the times I would drive him to the train after school. In the car, I asked about the music he'd been listening to lately. He pulled up the artist YoungBoy Never Broke Again on his phone and connected it to the car stereo. The rapper also known as NBA YoungBoy is roughly the same age as Kaliq and has led a pretty troubled life.

Something compelled me to record our conversation in the car. It was one of those rare moments in both research and human relationships that felt significant even as I was in it. As Kaliq pushed play on "Lonely Child," he told me that parts of the song "just catch me all the time." I've since listened to this song many times, and to the recording I made of Kaliq narrating it and singing along. Each time the chorus plays, it feels like it's cracking open a window into the inner thoughts of all the boys I came to know and just how deeply and silently their grief resonates:

> I'm just a lonely child
> Who wants someone to help him out, oh, oh, ah, ah
> Take this pain away, this pain away
> Because my head been runnin' wild, wild

Epilogue

History doesn't come to a stop when a study ends, or pause while it evolves into a publication. Significant changes with a bearing on this book have occurred since 2017–2018, the school year it documents—in the world at large, in Philadelphia, at Boys' Prep, and most importantly in the lives of the teachers and students.

The COVID-19 pandemic brought not only death, disease, and profound disruptions to millions of people's schooling and professional trajectories, but also a staggering increase in gun violence across the United States. The year 2020 was the worst on record since the early 1990s, and then 2021 was even worse. Gun deaths among children and teens increased 50 percent in just two years.[1] And, at the same time as the country was undergoing a supposed "racial reckoning," the racial disparities in violent victimization that have long existed have grown starker: Black children under eighteen are now 100 times more likely to be shot than white children.[2] Philadelphia experienced some of the worst of this, tallying the highest homicide rate among the top ten largest US cities in 2021.[3]

Both COVID-19 and the increasing gun violence epidemic have, thankfully, led to more attention to grief as both a shared and an unequally distributed burden. Grief counseling and support services for youth have expanded in Philadelphia and elsewhere, as have community violence interruption programs. But there is still much work to be done.

Boys' Prep has also seen its fair share of change. Though the school's charter was ultimately renewed, multiple administrative transitions—including the departure of Dr. Stephens, Principal Donaldson, and Vice Principal Hopkins within a few years of this study—and tremendous faculty turnover have made the school unrecognizable in certain ways. And yet, it appears that the same underlying values of compensation, preparation, and protection still guide the school. The institution remains popular and respected among neighborhood families, many of whom believe there are few "good schools" available for their sons. And the school still struggles each year to meet all of their students' needs, to get them to college as their mission dictates, and to maintain the disciplinary order and behavioral respectability they see as their core.

As for the teaching staff, by 2023, five years after the year documented in this book, only Mr. Pratt, Ms. Kallum, and three other classroom teachers from that time remained at Boys' Prep. After the mass exodus of teachers in 2019 and the difficult COVID-marred school year that followed, summer 2020 brought another slew of departures, including Ms. Estevez, Ms. Gallo, Mr. Gilbert, Mr. Leonard, Ms. Neal, Ms. Wagner, and Ms. Woo. Some moved to other schools, but several left teaching altogether in search of new careers through which they could direct more attention to broader-scale change or to caring for students as whole people beyond the classroom. One teacher became a social worker; another wanted to focus his energies on his YouTube channel with tips for other teachers. Ms. Woo left teaching to pursue doctoral studies focused on healing-centered education. Even two years into graduate school, she still kept a collage of all of her murdered students as her phone's lock screen—a constant reminder of her "why" and a source of motivation for her. She had to update the image several times: at last count, it included eight pictures.

Ms. Redmond, who had been at the school since its founding, also continued to keep a running list of Boys' Prep students and alumni who had died. She worried that if she didn't keep this record (saved as a digital Post-it note on the desktop of her computer), no one else would. In 2022, after sixteen years at Boys' Prep, Ms. Redmond left too. At first, she wasn't sure if she wanted out of teaching to pursue her chaplaincy work full-time, but she landed a job teaching middle school Latin in the suburbs and decided to give that a try. She also, somewhat reluctantly, moved out of Philadelphia into the suburbs.

And Ms. Bloom, after nearly four years away from Boys' Prep, began to wonder whether to return there or to a similar school in the city. At the suburban private school where she had been teaching, she didn't feel very needed and found the job too "easy."

And the young men—no longer boys—have, of course, moved on from high school. Most have continued to shoulder losses, but also have found ways to push through and find some avenues for hope. Their grief, alongside the arduous management of the other risks and impacts of gun violence, continues to shape their lives and their relationships even as they pursue professional trajectories, partnerships, and parenthood. I was able to catch up with some of them between 2021 and 2024.

Like so many of his peers, Kaliq never made it to college. His winding road since leaving Boys' Prep involved a string of different jobs, a bad car accident, temporary incarceration for a DUI (he says he failed the walking sobriety test because he was tired) and the suspension of his driver's license limiting his employment options, getting kicked out of his house after a fight with his mother, and a lot of lonely pondering about his purpose in life. Kaliq has also experienced a lot of joy, most notably the birth of his son, the satisfaction of growing to better understand himself, and the encouragement he's found to improve his life from music and inspirational quotes on Instagram. He is determined to break the cycle of emotional suppression. He has been trying to show his younger brother how to "open up" and talk about his feelings and plans to teach his son to be more vulnerable with his emotions. Though Kaliq knows he has more healing to do himself, he has a dream of starting a men's group to "inspire other young Black men [to] really understand the feelings you have and thoughts you can have." He recently moved down south to do carpentry and construction work with his grandfather and has been feeling more free and relaxed away from the drama of Philadelphia.

Herc pursued certification as a sterile processing technician soon after graduating and has been keeping up relatively steady work in hospitals. He is devoted to his young son, a brand new baby, and his niece. But he has had impossibly bad luck, losing three very close loved ones the year after graduating from Boys' Prep. Two friends, including the boy called Jonquett in this book, were killed in quick succession in late 2020. And just a few months later, Herc's older brother accidentally shot himself in his bedroom while cleaning his gun. Herc was down the hall and rushed into the room to hold his dying brother. Herc's profile picture on Instagram is a collage of his four most impactful losses—those three, plus Tyhir, his first significant loss, back when he was fifteen. Despite the deep impact on Herc of the deaths of JahSun and Bill, as documented in this book, it is striking that he has four other losses that he holds even more central to his identity. Barely into his midtwenties, Herc can now count nearly twenty close friends and loved ones who have been killed by guns.

Yaja is finally finding a bit of peace after several traumatic years since high school. After just squeezing by to graduate in 2018, he felt deserted by the school that had previously been a home to him. The teachers who had claimed to be "like family" stopped reaching out. Yaja was attending a community college "in the boonies," as he described it, and working at the camp he had attended for many summers. But he was slowly unraveling and has confessed to trying to end his life twice during the two years after high school. He didn't feel like anyone really understood him or cared about him. Luckily, something finally clicked. Yaja began to recognize the importance of the work he was doing at the camp, mentoring youth, and often dreamed about how he might use his advancing professional position to help other kids growing up in poverty. He also started living with his girlfriend, now wife, and building a sense of home together. But he continues to battle demons related to unresolved grief, conflict with family, and how to make use of his exceptional mind.

Hazeem has been slowly coming into his own passions. He was working for his family's business driving sick and elderly people to their doctors' appointments. But more recently he took a job at a middle school as a "climate specialist," where he provides discipline and encouragement to the young students. Hazeem seems to like the position, and it makes him feel like he's helping the next generation avoid the mistakes of his peers. He also has been trying to build a career as a self-taught photographer. Hazeem launched a project he calls "PTSD" for Photography Through Society's Deaths; he wants to collect stories of people impacted by gun violence and photograph them in hopes that the images and stories will help young people coming up see another way besides turning to violence.

During high school, Bashir was perhaps the most academically ambitious of them all. Even as a freshman—a new "little brother" to JahSun's older friends—it was clear that he was on a track toward college. But, while managing to maintain his grades, Bashir continued to struggle to keep focus after JahSun's murder. It was hard for him to turn eighteen and surpass the age of his brother when he was killed. Still harder was his actual graduation from Boys' Prep. Already in his cap and gown, as he prepared to enter the auditorium, Bashir broke down, feeling, as he later explained, that he was disrespecting JahSun by walking across the stage that his brother had never gotten to.

So far, family and financial struggles have kept Bashir from a clear college trajectory; he's bounced between community and private colleges and, in the meantime, pursued work as a volunteer EMT and firefighter. He still hopes to be able to return to college full-time to pursue his dream of becoming a neuroscience researcher or medical doctor. He wants to make his brother proud.

Acknowledgments

I have been waiting years to be able to put in print my deep gratitude to so many people who have been both at the center and on the cheering lines of this project.

My deepest thanks go to the boys in this book for sharing your vulnerable moments with me and showing me your joy even during the toughest times. It was the honor of a lifetime to come to know you and that you trusted me with your stories.

To the administrators, faculty, staff, and parents at "Boys' Prep," thank you for welcoming me into your community and spaces of work and for sharing so openly your day-to-day triumphs, challenges, and hopes. It has been a pleasure to learn from and with so many of you, and I look forward to continuing to think and work together to support youth in these most tender times.

I am especially grateful to the mothers and other family members of JahSun, Tyhir, and Bill for allowing me to tell their stories. I am in awe of each of you for your strength, resilience, and commitment to using your experiences to help others. To Maxayn, especially, this book and our other collaborations would not have been possible without your selfless care for other young people.

And to the boys snatched from us too soon, who will never get to read this book. You are loved and missed, and you have left an indelible mark on so many. May your memories be a blessing.

*

The North Lawndale College Prep community, and the Project 55 Program that placed me there, will always be my launching point and source of inspiration. Thanks to everyone who nurtured my personal and professional growth during that time. I will always remember precious AJ, Jimmy, and Melvin and everyone who loved them.

Research for this book began while I was a student at the University of Pennsylvania. Guidance from my Penn teachers and mentors helped me through the planning, research, and early writing. Kathy Hall, you have been a steadfast source of support, encouragement, and understanding from the day we met, and I learned so much from your careful reads of my early papers. Camille Charles, thank you for your candor, your frank advice, and for introducing me to Elizabeth! John Jackson, I've deeply valued your mentorship and our collaborations, and I have tremendous appreciation for your eternal positivity and optimism. Numerous other Penn faculty supported my intellectual development over the years, including Amit Das, Dave Grazian, Emily Hannum, Grace Sanders Johnson, Peter Kuriloff, Annette Lareau, Robin Leidner, Brian Peterson, Sharon Ravitch, Michael Reichert, Dorothy Roberts, Elaine Simon, Howard Stevenson, Krystal Strong, and Deborah Thomas.

Getting through graduate school and the early years after would not have been possible without peers and colleagues with whom I tested ideas, collaborated, vented, and shared many a coffee shop table or bar counter. Thanks especially to Sarah Adeyinka-Skold, Mercy Agyepong, OreOluwa Badaki, Irteza Binte-Farid, Tara Casebolt, Lisette Enumah China, Amanda Cox, Nina Daoud, Charles H. F. Davis III, Jeylan Erman, Arlene Fernandez, Kalen Flynn, Janay Garrett, Lauren Harris, Peter Harvey, Rita Harvey, Amber Henry, Jasmine Blanks Jones, Kelsey Jones, Christiana Kallon Kelly, David Kirui, José Loya, Julie McWilliams, Bethany Monea, Demetri Morgan, Michelle Munyikwa, Briana Nichols (my forever academic wife!), Vena Offen, Jessica Peng, Meaghan Petersack-Cannon, Cleveland Pickett, Russ Powell, Aliya Rao, Nora Reikosky, Atenea Rosado-Viurques, Edward

Smith, Cristin Stephens, Rachael Stephens, Treva Tam, Jenna Tonn, Tom Wooten, Robin Wright, Calvin Zimmermann, and Tali Ziv. When friends become writing collaborators, there is nothing sweeter; thanks for being both, Ellen Bryer, Katie Clonan-Roy, Charlotte Jacobs, Ina Kelleher, Michael Kokozos, Cassie Lo, Pavithra Nagarajan, and Veena Vasudevan.

Beyond Penn, I have been lucky to find mentorship and support for this project from a range of scholars, most especially Joseph Nelson and Nikki Jones. Other senior scholars who have offered critical advice over the years through conversations at conferences or phone calls and Zooms include Sofya Aptekar, Jamie Fader, Michelle Fine, E. Patrick Johnson, Jocelyn Smith Lee, Desmond Patton, Victor Rios, Patrick Sharkey, Forrest Stuart, and Debra Umberson. And during my three years at Boston College, I found so many colleagues to be generous with their time and support, especially Kathleen Flinton, Lisa Goodman, Régine Jean-Charles, Andrew Jorgenson, Margaret Laurence, Becca Lowenhept, Neil McCullagh, C. Shawn McGuffey, Robert Motley Jr., Geoff Sanzenbacher, Juliet Schor, Scott Seider, and Stanton Wortham.

Critical financial support during the early years of this project at Penn came from the Graduate School of Education; the Urban Studies Program; the Center for Experimental Ethnography; and the Harry Frank Guggenheim Foundation, as well as smaller grants from the Gertrude and Otto Pollak Summer Research Fellowship; the Center for the Study of Race and Equity in Education; the Center for the Study of Ethnicity, Race and Immigration; the School of Arts and Sciences; the GSE Student Government; the Graduate and Professional Student Assembly; the Sachs Program for Arts Innovation; and the Center for Africana Studies. My time at Boston College made the writing of this book possible in terms of both the time and resources it afforded me; many thanks to the Core Curriculum, the Institute for the Liberal Arts, and especially to Brian Gareau and Elizabeth Shlala.

And thanks to Barnard College for the financial resources and time flexibility during my first year on faculty to reach the finish line. (An extra-special shoutout to my newest writing group and Barnard first-year faculty crew: Amelia Frank-Vitale, Amelia Simone Herbert, Maricarmen Hernandez, and Lisa Jahn.)

As the project moved decisively into book form, there were so many readers whose insights and critiques shaped my decisions about structure, storytelling, tone, and argument. I had a book workshop dream team in Freeden Blume Oeur, Debbie Carr, and Natasha Warikoo alongside four fantastic graduate students: Babatunde Alford, Brianna Diaz, Emily Redfern, and Danielle Walker. Tom Wooten and his Harvard ethnography class offered valuable feedback and questions at just the right moment. Jeanne Heifetz's masterful cutting of tens of thousands of words got me within my contracted word count. I am especially grateful to my anonymous reviewers at the Press as well as the reviewers of my related article at the *Journal of Contemporary Ethnography* for their incisive, supportive, and motivating feedback. Audience members and co-panelists at ASA, SSSP, ESS, and AERA and at talks I gave at Penn and BC over the years have offered useful provocations and suggestions. Thanks also to Mark Masyga for your initial work on the figures and tables.

This work has been enriched by so many incredible undergraduates I've been lucky to work with. Unbeknownst to them, my students have shaped my thinking immensely—particularly my *Grief and Resistance* and *Encountering Confinement* courses at Boston College. I've also received excellent research assistance from an unparalleled team of interns over the years: Ana Blanco, Ajibola Bodunrin, Kim Craig, Mary Devellis, Amelia Galbraith, Faith Iloka, Sarah Ix, Kassidi Jones, Kate Lewis, Rekha Marar (while still in high school!), Amari Mitchell, Angelica Qin, Alex Pereira, and Beth Verghese. And best of all, my Boston College undergraduate book development workshop crew, who may have read my manuscript more carefully than any other set of readers: Samuel Brown, Joya Cullinan, Claire Ehrig, Jarvis Goosby, Kevin Lopez, Isabella Lora, Jane Paulson, and Layla Saenz. My Barnard research assistants, Isabella Hernandez, Nori Leybengrub, and Lauren Seeger, helped me with final polishes to the text and images. Thanks to all of you for your hours of careful work and your attention to the sensitivity and confidentiality of the material entrusted to you.

I could not have asked for a better editor to work with on my first solo book. Elizabeth Branch Dyson, your belief in this book from the first time we met has helped me stay the course even when finishing this project felt daunting and scary. It has been a joy to get to know you over these years we've worked together, and I'm so grateful to have had you leading the team. Thanks also to Mollie McFee and everyone else at the Press for shepherding the book through.

★

My and my participants' words in this book are complemented and enhanced by the work of others. Thanks to the following artists who generously allowed me to reproduce their words:

"Lonely Child": Words and Music by Kentrell Gaulden, Tahj Vaughn, Thomas Horton and David K. Mcdowell. Copyright © 2019 Big Thirty Eight Music, Artist Publishing Global, Tahj Money Publishing, WC Music Corp., Dmac Publishing, TNTXD Publishing (ASCAP), and Copyright Control. All Rights for Big Thirty Eight Music and Artist Publishing Global Administered by Kobalt Music Services America, Inc. All Rights for Tahj Money Publishing Administered by Sony Music Publishing (US) LLC, 424 Church Street, Suite 1200, Nashville, TN 37219. All Rights for Dmac Publishing Administered by Lush Music LLC. All Rights on Behalf of TNTXD Publishing administered by WC Music Corp. All Rights Reserved. Used by Permission. *Reprinted by Permission of Hal Leonard LLC and Alfred Music and Lush Music LLC*

"Without You": Words and Music by Quavious Keyate Marshall, Javon Hollins Tavoris, Ryan Vojtesak, Cedric Benjamin Leutwyler, Anh Tran, Shane Lindstrom, Michael Dean, Xavier Dotson p/k/a "Zaytoven", Elias Sticken, Marco Granata, Andre Kraut, Eugene Tsai. Copyright © 2022 Shane Lindstrom Publishing Designee, Papa George Music, WC Music Corp. and Copyright Control. Copyright © 2023 Universal Music Corp., Quality Control

★

Finally, my family. I applied to PhD programs in 2012 at my mom's encouragement even though I wasn't sure I was ready. As with everything, her unconditional love and confidence in me also came with concrete support—reading application drafts, driving me places, reminding me to make doctor appointments. The same day I was accepted to Penn, we learned she was terminally ill with a brain tumor. Designing, carrying out, and writing up this project while my mother was dying was challenging, to say the least. It was also, at times, cathartic and healing. I think about my mom, Ruth Nass, all the time and how proud she would be, but I'm also so sad for how much she missed out on in seeing my professional (and personal) life develop. Despite her physical absence, her care for me and the way it lives on in my memory have made the completion of this project possible.

In almost every way, this book would not be here without my dad, Teddy Gross, who was my earliest teacher, my most steadfast and reliable editor, and my loudest and most loving cheerleader. Thank you for reading hundreds of pages, some many times, and listening to me present my research more times than either of us can count. Though I may not have always shown it in the moment, I'm grateful for the times you pushed me to develop more precise language and to rethink titles. There are more than a few words, phrases, and entire paragraphs in this book inspired by (or revised because of) our conversations or your meticulous editing. I am probably only just beginning to appreciate all the writing—and life—lessons you have passed on to me through your unending dedication to my development as a writer and person.

Randy, one could say that our relationship developed alongside this book, since we met just as I was beginning to write up my dissertation. I negotiated the book contract at your kitchen table in Hanover and wrote the first draft during our first year living together. I submitted the near final draft just days before our baby was born, polished off the final draft during his first weeks of daycare, and reviewed the proofs the same week we became homeowners together. Your wells of support and encouragement are bottomless, as is your ability to bring humor and calm to the toughest moments. I will forever treasure the memories of you diligently marking up my manuscript draft (printed at one-quarter size to save paper!) and then sharing your feedback while feeding our baby. Thanks for doing the night shifts and taking such good care of our family. I love you.

My son, Philando, was born as I reached the final writing stages of this book. (My deepest gratitude to Mama Loida for your loving and skillful baby care, which allowed me to return to this work without worry.) Philando, your name holds our family's desire to honor and remember the beautiful souls who have been stolen by violence and racial injustice. Your existence has given this work new meaning for me and even more urgency. I sincerely hope that by the time you can read this book, we are living in a world where gun violence is not a viable threat for you and your peers.

Author's Note

Besides the acknowledgments, the author's note has always been my favorite part of an ethnography. As a graduate student, I found the backstories behind polished texts incredibly useful for imagining my own future research and in reassuring me that every ethnographer struggles. None of us has it all figured out. And yet, behind each methodological decision was a lot of thought. I hope what I offer here contributes to this important behind-the-scenes genre.

But first, I want to address what may feel like the elephant in the room for some readers: namely, my whiteness.

Who Am I to Write This Book?

Conducting long-term research embedded in people's daily lives is always a fraught endeavor. Even with the best of intentions, there are so many ways to misstep, to exploit, to harm, to misrepresent. In the last decade, urban ethnographers—code for those who conduct ethnography with people living in urban poverty, often people of color—and their critics have brought these issues to the forefront. Some questions now being debated touch on the very morality of doing this work: Should white people ever research Black life, or Black death? Other questions lie deeper in the weeds: Should we name our field sites so studies can be verified or repeated?[1]

I am grateful that these questions have sparked many thoughtful, nuanced, sometimes contentious conversations about research ethics, researcher positionality, and representation. Some participants in these conversations would question whether I, an upper-middle-class white woman, should have done this project at all. When studying communities of color, and urban Black contexts specifically, white ethnographers have a long tradition of sensationalizing urban violence or the struggles of poverty, exploiting the communities they've researched, or claiming to *discover* phenomena that are utterly obvious to the people represented in the text.[2]

Knowing this history and these debates, I've had many second thoughts over the past eight years. These feelings were strongest when I attended memorial services, met with mothers who had lost their sons, or conducted interviews with young people in the aftermath of a death. I wondered whether the good this book might eventually do was worth the intrusion of an outsider into people's most wrenching moments. My worries were perhaps most intense during the months I sat in my comfortable, quiet apartment devoting myself to writing while periodically texting or video chatting with the guys whose lives were rarely comfortable or quiet and who continued to be burdened by precarity and loss.

During that time, Langston Hughes's poignant 1938 poem, "Kids Who Die," was pinned to a bulletin board above my desk. Here are a few lines:

> Of course, the wise and the learned
> Who pen editorials in the papers,
> And the gentlemen with Dr. in front of their names
> White and black,
> Who make surveys and write books
> Will live on weaving words to smother the kids who die

I would certainly fall under Hughes's critique, but does drawing attention to the pain and suffering of people largely stripped of power in our society necessarily smother them, or can it spur needed conversation and change? This tension is unavoidable in most academic scholarship dealing with, as we sociologists say, "social problems" like poverty, oppression, and violence. And yet, I have to believe this work—if done well—can contribute in meaningful ways, not only to our understanding of the scope and scale of gunfire's toll on Black children and their futures, but also to ongoing efforts to protect and support previously unrecognized victims of our national violence epidemic. I believe I was well positioned (though certainly not uniquely so) to make a contribution in this arena.

I will no doubt remain conflicted long after this book has been published. But I try to listen to my participants here as well. JahSun's, Tyhir's, and Bill's mothers thank me for keeping their sons' names alive (I discuss the decision to use their real names later in this chapter). The surviving boys—now definitely young men—have expressed over the years that our "interviews" during their high school days gave them a space they didn't know they needed to process what was going on in their lives. Some of them have been proactive about staying in touch, reaching out with updates about their lives or requests of some kind; others communicate more passively with me via social media likes; several have read and approved drafts of this text. Though I surely made some missteps along the way, those who can still consent continue to trust me with their stories.

Identity and Positionality as a Researcher

In the preface, I shared that this project emerged from my past experience as a teacher. So it is not surprising that I was drawn to a school somewhat similar to the one where I had taught: a college-oriented charter high school considered a gem in its working-class Black neighborhood. The two schools also shared the strange contradiction of having almost exclusively Black students, yet not really feeling like Black spaces, since a range of white cultural norms and white people held power and authority throughout the building.

Unlike white and other non-Black ethnographers who have

studied Black men and boys in public or family life,[3] my decision to
position myself and the research inside one of these schools meant that
my presence rarely felt like a white intrusion into a protected or private
Black space. Nearly half of Boys' Prep teachers were white women
in their twenties, thirties, or forties. Indeed, the students with whom
I spent time all identified at least one white female teacher among
their list of favorites. And, despite my primary research focus on the
students, I felt a sense of fellowship with many of the teachers: I had
strong memories of being in their position, and I had deep respect for
the fact that many of them had stuck with this most taxing job far
longer than I had.[4]

Even though a young-ish white woman in the Boys' Prep school
building was not an anomaly, in my interactions with students, I experienced many moments of outsiderness. On almost every core social
identity category—race, gender, class, age, religion—I differed from
the Black teenage boys in my study. When students made cultural
references or shared race- or gender-specific experiences I could not
fully comprehend, if appropriate, I asked lots of questions, sometimes
in joking or self-deprecating ways. But often, if it was not central to my
research questions or the conversation at hand, I did not interrupt and
followed up later, after some investigation on my own. Despite these
challenges and the larger power imbalances present in the work, I believe, as Philippe Bourgois writes, that "ultimately . . . the research was
feasible because all humans everywhere respond well to respectful
interaction. We all appreciate having our life stories taken seriously.
The urge to convey meaning transcends the barriers of institutionalized social inequality."[5] I believe that more than my outward social
identities, the boys responded most strongly to my interest in learning
about their lives and the genuine attention I gave them.

Interestingly, my perceived age was the identity marker students
seemed most curious about. Though I started the research at age
thirty, most students guessed I was between nineteen and twenty-four
and a college student, despite my attempts to explain doctoral-level
study. When I would reveal my age, some boys asked for proof; they
couldn't believe I was *so old*. While never dishonest, I capitalized on

my age ambiguity to differentiate myself from the teachers and seem approachable, while avoiding suggesting that I was a peer (and therefore a potential romantic prospect[6]). I aimed to present what has been described as a "least-adult" and "least-gendered" identity.[7] I am a straight, feminine-presenting woman, and while I did not intentionally play down my own femininity, I rarely wore dresses or heels (except to the school's graduation, Prom, and other special events). Instead, I erred on the simple and casual side of business casual, adding funky earrings or sneakers to represent my style and sometimes serve as conversation starters.[8]

It has been suggested that female researchers may be aided by "common cultural stereotypes" in gaining the trust and openness of participants, since women are often assumed to be nurturers and good listeners.[9] I certainly found that many students and adults came to see me as an unthreatening and trustworthy confidante. A handful of students let me know that I had become one of the few, if not the only, adult with whom they shared certain experiences, thoughts, or feelings. Students might text or call me outside school hours if they had a problem, or send a note of thanks if I had been helpful to them earlier that day. I suspect that my gender informed my ability to play this role for participants.

Overall, I found that the identity differences with my participants actually allowed me to probe deeper than I otherwise might have, since the boys did not assume we had shared experiences they could reference in shorthand. Black researchers who interview Black youth have also observed this phenomenon, as have both male and female scholars who study adolescent boys, though they were not crossing as many identity boundaries.[10] When boys would offer only the CliffsNotes of an experience followed by "You know what I mean?," I would often respond, "No, tell me more," because I could not personally relate to their experience.

I should note here, in relation to my identity and positionality, that personal blind spots may have played a role in my observations and interpretations too. Specifically, religion is a dimension of the boys' lives I was not always closely attuned to, since it is not central to my own worldview. My own religious background—Jewish, but secular and agnostic—does not give me much foundational personal knowledge about the experiences of the boys in my study who primarily identified as Christian or Muslim, many quite observant. Throughout this work I have done my best to mitigate gaps like this in my understanding through engagement with prior literature, conversations with knowledgeable colleagues, and "member checks" with participants themselves,[11] but certainly the religious and spiritual dimensions of the boys' grief are underexplored in this text and worthy of further attention.

It also goes without saying, I hope, that one research study can only do so much, and this book's focus is specifically on the boys' lives at school—supplemented by their activities on social media. More can and should be learned about how boys grieve and make sense of the violent deaths of friends through an examination of their out-of-school time, including family life, sports teams and other activities, community and religious engagements, and social interactions with neighborhood peers and/or romantic partners.

Recruiting Participants

I arrived at Boys' Prep about six weeks into the school year in 2016, a few months after the gun murder of freshman Tyhir, which had occurred mid-summer. My plan was to find a handful of school spaces and activities—both formal and informal—where I could begin to acclimate to the culture of the school and get to know students organically, while simultaneously pursuing a targeted recruitment strategy for students who might be experiencing acute grief. I aimed to spend two to three days per week at the school for observations and, eventually, one-on-one interviews.

With the help of a few teachers, the school social worker assembled a list of nineteen students who were, in their view, most affected by Tyhir's death. I met briefly with these students in groups of two or three in the social worker's office to introduce myself, explain my research and what it might entail, and gather contact information. I was heartened that, with the exception of one student who declined to participate and two who wanted to think it over, the remainder expressed immediate interest in taking part. I began setting up short meetings without the social worker to lay out the research process in greater detail and discuss the consent documents I would ask them and their parents to sign, which included the option for them to let me observe them on social media.[12] I also showed them a selection of published ethnographies to preview what this inquiry process might result in (though perhaps none of us quite realized how far away that stage would be!). The books helped illustrate ethnographic research— including the use of pseudonyms and the reason for audio-recording interviews.

Students expressed excitement about the attention they would get as part of this project or eventually being a character in a book. Some seemed eager for any opportunity to shake up the day-to-day and perhaps occasionally get exempted from class. Others were anxious about whether they would have to change their behavior to participate. Herc, a sophomore who brought two of his friends to our first meeting, asked, "When you shadow us, like, I curse a lot. Is that okay?" I nodded, "It's fine. I've heard it all before." He added, "And I talk about girls in a disrespectful way sometimes." I said, "I don't want you to change how you would normally act just because I'm around." Herc continued, drawing laughter from his friends, "Like, I'm not stupid, but sometimes I act stupid."

As the signed forms trickled in, I began setting up initial semi-structured interviews.[13] Herc, Hazeem, Kaliq, Latrell, and Jonquett were among the first boys I interviewed. All had been close with Tyhir the prior school year. I began regular observation at the lunch table the five of them shared, and this group quickly became my first focal participants.

After I attended three events connected to Tyhir's birthday in early February, I met additional boys who said they had been close with Tyhir but had not been included on the adult-generated list. The more students I got to know, the more open the initially hesitant boys became. About three months into my fieldwork, one student vouched for me to another student, saying, "She's cool people. You should talk to her." Another, when I met him for the first time, said that he had seen me hanging out with his friend Ezekiel. "Any friend of Zeek's is cool—he's the in, the gatekeeper." Students who fully grasped my research would text me with information about gun violence events that might have impacted Boys' Prep students or go out of their way to introduce me to peers with relevant experiences.

While it is likely there was sampling bias in who was initially most willing to talk to me, this was at least partially overcome with time.[14] As I demonstrated a consistent presence at the school, while moving through the building in ways a teacher wouldn't (like sitting in the cafeteria during lunch or using a student locker to store my belongings), students started to understand my role and potential value to them. I was eventually able to onboard nearly all the boys from the social worker's initial list as well as several others referred to me by friends and teachers. By the end of the first year of research, I estimate that I had built close research relationships with about thirty-five students.

The Second Year of Research and Role Shifts

As my first year of research concluded, students' grief about losing Tyhir was receding into the background at school—the *hidden hard*, as I have described it. While still very present in their thoughts (which they shared with me in one-on-one interviews) and in their posts on social media, their experiences of loss were no longer part of their day-to-day school life in a way that I felt could sustain another year of ethnographic investigation. I began reimagining my research questions to expand my conceptualization of "loss." I wondered how the multiple kinds and dimensions of loss in the boys' lives intersected. I thought about moments when they experienced loss of dignity, like in losing a fight or a sports game; loss of social status as well as the loss of time, like being required to repeat a grade of school; and the loss of loved ones to fates other than death, like incarceration.

I began the 2017–2018 school year with revised research questions and the goal of getting to know new groups of students who could help me answer them. A new principal, vice principal, and approach to school discipline provided much to observe and unpack. I was eager to try to understand how Tyhir's death might have long-term implications for his friends' experience of school, and also to contextualize their grief within a more holistic understanding of loss.

JahSun's murder in November changed everything, including my very role and identity at the school. Broadening my research with new questions no longer made sense. Deeply shaken myself, I returned to my original research focus and began a concerted effort to map and reach the social circles of which JahSun had been a part.

In the weeks following JahSun's death, I followed his daily class schedule, observing in the specific classrooms and other school spaces where he had spent time. A teacher drew up a list of his closest friends so other school adults would know which students they should keep their eyes on. I drew on this list as an initial resource for identifying students with whom to connect. Rather than having official meetings with them about my research, in the days and weeks following JahSun's murder, I began introducing myself to them one-on-one or in small, naturally occurring group settings in the hallways or cafeteria. If the initial introduction went well, I would follow up the next time I saw them with more details about the research process and consent documents for them to review. I began with the students I already knew from observing their classes, and slowly worked my way to the perimeter of the social circle. Most of the boys agreed to be interviewed and observed, and I began spending more time with them. During the winter and spring, I also focused more on the senior class, who were collectively impacted by the loss of their classmate at a critical moment in their college transition process.

JahSun's death also changed my role in the school community and made me a more visible adult in the building in ways I did not anticipate. The morning after we learned of JahSun's death, Dr. Stephens, the school's CEO, texted to ask if I could come into school throughout that week to be available to students who might want to talk. At faculty meetings, Principal Donaldson reminded teachers that I was around and suggested that if students needed to leave class because they were upset, I was one of the people to whom they could go for support. He once told a group of students that I "knew the science behind" grief. Despite my repeated attempts to clarify my expertise, I became a de facto grief counselor—a role for which I was neither trained nor qualified in any technical sense. The fact that, in a moment of crisis, I was called on to "help" students in a semi-official way underscores the vast gap in resources at Boys' Prep to serve students' social and emotional needs.

My relationships with school adults also evolved now that we shared the experience of losing a young person we adored and in whom we saw so much promise. Among teachers I had not previously been close to, there was a shift, as if they felt we were now on the same side, trying to support the kids through this difficult stretch. Teachers started to notice which students were my focus and would intentionally seek me out to give me updates on them. Adults would sometimes ask my advice on how to handle a particular situation related to a memorial object in the building or a specific struggling student. The evolving trust enabled me to broaden my focus to include the adults in the building, as I tried to observe and understand how the school, both as an organization and a set of people, was responding to the students' tragic loss.

In April of that year, Boys' Prep was rocked by the murder of yet another student: sophomore Bill. Once again, I spent the following weeks in triage mode, suspending my planned research activities to be as present and as useful as possible. It was all-hands-on-deck at the school, and as a caring adult without formal responsibilities, I was able to be nimble, checking in on students who were particularly hard hit or helping adults pass messages throughout the building.

At times I felt hyper-visible and quite uncomfortable with the thought that I had come to the school to study the aftermath of one tragic event, which, catastrophically, then kept recurring. A few days after Bill died, when students and teachers gathered in the cafeteria to find solace together, one teacher offered sympathetically, "This is more than you ever wanted for your research, right?"

In terms of my research focus, I now had a choice to make. I had not known Bill, or many of his friends. Should I also try to integrate myself into *his* peer group? Or should I remain focused on Tyhir's friends (now mostly juniors), JahSun's friends (mostly seniors), and the other students I had already come to know as they made sense of this new loss? Given the proximity to the end of the school year, I decided on the latter course. I also aimed to give more attention to the adults in the building who were trying to manage, for the second time in one year, the combination of their own grief, their students' grief, and their professional responsibilities.

Developing Research Relationships

Ethnographers invariably encounter a variety of gatekeepers throughout a study. In my initial school visits or when I would meet a new student, boys would express curiosity (sometimes wariness) about what it meant that I was a researcher. Many students initially assumed I was a reporter, counselor, or student teacher—roles with which they were more familiar. In one early interaction, I got a probing question from Yaja, a junior at the time, who asked me—with skepticism and a little suspicion—why I had picked *this* school for my project. I answered honestly about my research interests combined with the challenges and serendipity involved in gaining research access. He was satisfied with the answer but continued to keep me at arm's length. Then, after an impromptu hour-long conversation stretched out on the floor of the hallway one afternoon, Yaja told me I had passed his proverbial test. He texted me that evening, "The community recognizes you." Over the following year, Yaja served as an important research node, connecting me to and vouching for me with a range of other students, including JahSun.[15]

At the school, I occupied a somewhat liminal space between stu-

dent and teacher: a key I was entrusted with gave me access to all
the classrooms and offices, but I had no space of my own and kept
my jacket in a student locker with a combination lock. I had no formal, pedagogical, or disciplinary obligations and was rarely asked to
fill in for an adult staff member or to report to administrators.[16] Many
teachers allowed me to visit their classrooms without advance notice.
I often sat in the back so as not to distract the students and to see
as much as possible, but in a few classes I was a regular participant
and sometimes helped students with assignments when they were
working independently. I had an understanding with both staff and
students that I would not enforce school rules, punish students, or report misbehaviors; yet sometimes I found myself chastising students
for roughhousing or encouraging a student who was cutting class to
consider returning.

In my research relationships, particularly with young people,
I aimed to center care, respect, and reciprocity.[17] I did my best to treat
my interactions with participants not as efforts to "build rapport" in
order to gain access or collect better data, but as sincere human connection.[18] The relationships I built inevitably involved the periodic dis-
comforts and conflicts of all complex human relationships, but also
humor, affection, and even love. Especially resonant for me is scholar
Crystal Laura's description of the role of (non-romantic) love in ethnographic research. "Taking love seriously in social research," she
writes, "means that the process and product of scholarship has real
consequences for the lives of three-dimensional human beings, the researcher him- or herself included, not for imagined 'others' somewhere
out there."[19] My conversations with students and my presence in their
lives surely impacted them; it would be dishonest and even dangerous
to claim otherwise. I did everything I could to ensure that those impacts
were not negative, and when they appeared to be positive, to document them carefully since that would also constitute valuable data.

My care and curiosity were often reciprocated. Students made a
point of checking up on me, sometimes wishing me a good weekend
or asking how I fared in a bad snowstorm. They asked me questions
about growing up in New York, my college experience, my love life,

my ambitions of becoming a professor—and I tried to be genuine and open in my responses. The boys also often noticed if I was wearing a new pair of shoes or got a new phone. Through social media, participants came to know more about my life than they otherwise would, which may have created a sense of familiarity, and perhaps even some balance, in the research relationship.[20]

When to Intervene

As a researcher embarking on my first major ethnographic project, I know I was not alone in entering the field without anticipating every potential methodological or ethical dilemma that might arise.[21] Throughout the period of research, I had to make a number of decisions about whether and how to intervene in the boys' lives. I therefore found myself developing protocols as situations required and will share here two representative stories of the higher-stakes decisions I had to make.

One of the clearest commitments I made to my participants was confidentiality. This felt especially important in the context of their school lives, which involved much surveillance and little privacy. However, this promise was tested very early on. Just a week or two into getting to know Hazeem, he texted to ask if we could meet the following day. He was very upset and described a lifelong history of fighting, ending in the casual admission that a group of kids from another school were coming to Boys' Prep that afternoon to fight him. Not knowing him or the context very well yet, I was unsure how serious the situation might be or whether I should alert a staff member, even though Hazeem had specifically asked me not to tell anyone.

I debated this for several hours, weighing the sense of responsibility I felt to prevent violence if I was in a position to do so, yet also wanting to honor the confidentiality I had promised Hazeem in the research consent form he'd recently signed. Eventually, I came to what felt like a middle ground: I reached out to Kaliq, one of Hazeem's friends, who was apparently also going to be involved in the fight, to get his read on the situation. This was a break in confidentiality, but not the kind Hazeem most worried about. Already in my short time of knowing him, Kaliq struck me as the most rational and savvy of the boys I had met. He assuaged my worry: "It's going be cool. I doubt anyone will show up. People are just social media thugs." I therefore decided not to break Hazeem's trust further by telling any school staff.

In the end, Kaliq was right: the fight never happened. However, this initial test of my trustworthiness signaled the need for a better plan. A few weeks later, I explained my dilemma (without naming names) to Mr. Pratt, the head disciplinarian, who had taken me under his wing and let me come along with him on his drives through the neighborhood during the let-out period after school—what he called "safety corridors." He agreed that if I learned something that might put students in danger, I could give him a vague heads-up—like "After school today, put some extra people outside"—and he would not ask for more details or names. This plan seemed like a good compromise, though thankfully I never needed to use it.

Another kind of methodological—and ethical—dilemma confronted me more than once when students would plead with me to vouch for them to authority figures. Usually it was to avoid a minor infraction, like walking a late student to class and explaining to his teacher that I was responsible for holding him up. But a much bigger ask came just a few months into my fieldwork, when Herc was caught with marijuana in his backpack for the second time. He spent several hours in the main office with school administrators. When his mother arrived to pick him up, I introduced myself and we ended up having a long conversation while she waited for the principal. After their meeting, Herc and his mother found me to explain that he would have to appear at a school board hearing since he was being considered for expulsion. Could I, they asked, write a letter on his behalf to the board? (Herc would also ask two of his teachers for support letters.)

I was unsure what to do. In my role as researcher, shouldn't I be letting things play out as they would if I wasn't there? Yet, an expulsion would have enormous detrimental consequences for Herc; moreover, I possessed information about him that few other people in the school knew—that less than two months earlier, he had attempted to take his own life. Selfishly, I also realized that if he left Boys' Prep, I would be unable to continue observing him for my study.

Against the advice of an advisor, I wrote the letter.[22] A few days later, I learned that the board allowed Herc to return to school. Though my letter was surely just one of many pieces of information and factors in the conversation, I did learn that certain phrases from my letter were brought up during the hearing.

There were also smaller, day-to-day decisions I was required to make, such as when students would ask me for money or rides, or when I observed escalations of play fighting or bullying in the hallways. The rule of thumb I developed over time was to provide small gifts and acts of service when I could and avoid intervening on disciplinary matters unless someone was in physical danger. In hindsight, though, anticipating the kinds of scenarios I might face would have allowed me to respond to requests and in-the-moment dilemmas in a more consistent manner.

My Own Grief

Over the years, people with whom I have discussed this project have often responded with some version of "Wow, your research sounds so intense/sad/hard. How do you deal with it? How do you take care of yourself during the work?" I find it hard to focus on such questions, given how negligible my experience of grief has been compared to what the boys, and their teachers, consistently go through.[23]

Even so, I would be remiss not to acknowledge the role my own grief played in this project. My own feelings of loss, sadness, and anger about so much early death sometimes felt in conflict with my role as a researcher.[24] It would happen most acutely during the ritual and memorial events for JahSun, whom (unlike Tyhir and Bill) I had known personally. Before his death, JahSun had consulted with his father before signing my consent form and then told his mother how much he enjoyed being interviewed by me. The feelings had been mutual. In fact, I was in the process of scheduling a follow-up interview with him when he died.

I remember well the dread I felt as the date for JahSun's memorial service at the school drew near. Although I had derived some strength and solace from the earlier gatherings and during the school days of the previous two weeks, the moment I pulled into the school parking lot, I began to feel extremely conflicted and uncomfortable. I was still an outsider in most ways in the school and, although deeply saddened by his death, I did not feel fully a part of this grieving community. I concluded my field notes that day with the only word I could come up with that captured the conflict between being a mourner and a researcher: "weird"—which, although not adequate, reminded me how often it was the students' go-to-word to describe a complex emotional response.

I felt *weird* walking in and not being sure where to sit: Should I sit with the teachers (adults, mostly white people) in the back rows? Should I try to sit with students, since my research questions pertained most to how they were experiencing this period? Should I sit alone in a far back corner to have a view of everything? Should I be floating like the photographer so I could see different parts of the event and the behind-the-scenes?

In the end, there were only a few open seats and I made a game-time decision. Once I was seated, in a back row squeezed between a teacher and a sophomore I did not know well, a new conflict emerged: Should I apologize to my neighbors on either side for taking notes on my phone? I did not want them to think I was being disrespectful by using my phone, but I also did not want to draw attention to my role as researcher in that moment. As the service continued, I became more aware of my own grief and wished that I were sitting with people to whom I felt more personally connected, for support or just camaraderie in silence. When the service ended, I watched students and adults find each other for warm hugs and words of condolence. I felt a longing to really be *of* this community, so that my own grief would have a little more space.

Four months later, when Bill died, I felt a very different kind of internal dissonance. I had not known him. For days after his death, I racked my brain for a memory of Bill in the hallways or cafeteria. I looked up his schedule and compared it to my field notes to see if I had been in any of his classrooms. After all I had been through that year *with* everyone at the school, I felt like a fraud that I was not personally sharing their grief over Bill's death. As I have come to know and befriend Bill's mother, Williesha, over the years, I have continued to feel a profound loss that Bill was someone I never got the chance to know.[25]

There is yet one more important aspect of my personal relationship to grief that informs this project. During the years leading up to my research, during the study itself, and for most of the initial writing period, I was experiencing what I now have learned is called *anticipatory grief* for my mother.[26] For six years, she suffered from an inoperable brain tumor. Though she outlived her initial prognosis by more than four years, she was bedridden and not herself for most of that time, during which I often traveled on weekends from Philadelphia to my childhood home in New York City to visit her and my dad. Over those years, I grieved the parts of her I was losing along the way and was already in deeper mourning, anticipating her death long before it happened.

In March 2019, my mother died. I posted about her death on social media, where many of the boys from this study still followed me. Several reached out with comments of sympathy or support. I will never forget one message from Keith, one of the first students I met during his freshman year as he was mourning Tyhir. He wrote: "I've got your back because you had mine when I was down."

In a strange way, my prolonged experience of anticipatory grief provided me some small sense of a parallel experience with boys who believed the deaths of more of their friends were inevitable and imminent.

Leaving the "Field"

For many months I fretfully anticipated the formal conclusion of my in-person data collection, what ethnographers call *leaving the field*. I

had come to care deeply about many of my participants and genuinely enjoyed their company. I was also nervous about the next steps
of having to take stock of all that had happened and make sense of it
through coding, analysis, and writing—tasks that, at the time, seemed
like they would feel so disconnected from the day-to-day experience
of sharing space with people. And I worried that my departure might
be another addition to a long list of losses for some students who had
come to rely on my regular presence at school.

The natural schedule of the school year made some of this easier. As I prepared to leave at the end of the 2017–2018 school year,
I was not the only one saying goodbye. Because it had been such a
challenging year, everyone's goodbyes—including graduating seniors and teachers moving on—felt more poignant. The transition
was eased by my periodic visits to Boys' Prep and to related events in
the neighborhood for another two years. These drop-ins helped me
test theories I was developing through my writing and allowed me to
continue to provide support to participants as a listening ear.

But, of course, no longer is the "field" only a physical site; and, in
that sense, the conclusion of my research period has had a slippery
timeline. Social media (as well as text and direct messaging) has allowed for continued connection, communication, and updates from
participants. I regularly collected screenshots from Instagram for
three years after the conclusion of the in-person research and still
sometimes catch myself analyzing a post as I scroll.

Over time, the number of participants I remain in purposeful contact with (and who seem to intentionally stay in touch with me) has
shrunk to just a handful—especially since moving out of Philadelphia
in 2020. However, those relationships have deepened in meaningful
ways. JahSun's mother and I have worked together on several projects,
reciprocally enriching my scholarship and her activism. One young
man from the study accepted my invitation to speak at a public event
at Boston College, after which we spent a couple days touring the
city. I was able to help another find a therapist when he reached out
to confess suicidal thoughts, and I wrote a recommendation letter for
another who hoped to attend a four-year college after several years

attending community college. Another allowed me to hire him as my wedding reception photographer.

Over the course of the year before this book was published, I reconnected with as many of the central participants as I could—both former students and adults—and shared sections of the book for their reactions and approval. Though some, understandably, found it quite painful to revisit the memories of this period, most expressed gratitude that this story was being told.

Writing and Naming Decisions

Ethnography, particularly within the discipline of sociology, is experiencing a moment of reckoning around naming versus anonymizing research sites and participants. Given the compelling arguments on all sides of this debate, I made choices about naming practices that I believe simultaneously provide information and context to my readers *and* protect my participants responsibly and ethically. These were difficult decisions; I am not convinced I have made them perfectly, but I have taken them seriously and done the best I could.

First, I have chosen to name Philadelphia as the city where my research was conducted because I see this context as vital to understanding the extent and impacts of neighborhood gun violence during the years of my study. During a moment when violent crime was lessening nationally, Philadelphia's epidemic of gun violence was soaring.[27] At the time of this study, Philadelphia was also, notably, the poorest of the most populous cities in the country.[28] Philadelphia has been one of the lowest-ranked school districts nationally for the high school graduation rates for Black males.[29] The experiences of the boys at Boys' Prep could not be fully understood without this context. Further, naming the city allows my work to gain from and contribute to the historical context offered by decades of influential ethnographies about Philadelphia (Black) life.[30]

Within the city of Philadelphia, however, I do not disclose the neighborhood and I disguise the name of the school. Though neighborhoods across Philadelphia differ in meaningful ways even when they share similar demographics, the specificity of the neighborhood is secondary to the school context itself, the primary focus of my investigation. And, while the possibility of revisits by future researchers if I revealed more details is intriguing,[31] I find the prospect of risk to the school more credible. It is impossible to predict how this work could be taken up to harm the school's reputation or future activities. As sociologists Allison Pugh and Sarah Mosseri argue, "Informants (and researchers) do not know how a book's portrayal will be received (either by themselves or by other readers); that common uncertainty means unmasking practices incur very real risks, particularly in an era of trolling, doxing and other threats incurred by the unveiled. These risks are borne largely, but not solely, by participants, who are much more vulnerable than researchers."[32] The survival of a school like Boys' Prep relies on both public and private funding as well as family enrollment, and I would not want to take the risk of jeopardizing that.

I realize that the unique features of Boys' Prep will make it easily recognizable to some readers; however, I subscribe to Victoria Reyes's perspective that there is value in *plausible deniability*, which "allows for the people who are studied to disavow knowledge or participation in the research."[33] Though you may *think* you know, you can never be sure—a fact I believe offers participants some continued protection. And my analyses will not haunt the school—or its staff and students—for years in online searches.

With the exceptions described below, the names of all people in this book have been replaced with pseudonyms, which are a mix of names participants selected for themselves and names I chose. For example, Herc comes from "Hercules," the name he initially requested I use. Other names, I selected from the list of teenagers murdered by guns in Philadelphia in 2017 to pay homage to their memories.[34] In all cases, I did my best to select a name for each boy that conveyed similar class, racial, and/or religious markers as his original name while also disguising them as best as possible.[35] I took a similar approach to masking the names of the adults who became central to my analysis.[36]

The one set of names I did not anonymize belongs to the three beautiful boys whose untimely deaths form the foundation of this investigation and analysis—Tyhir, JahSun, and Bill—as well as some of their family members who expressed their preference to be named.[37]

The possibility of using the real names of murdered children did not occur to me when I began this study or wrote up consent documents. The idea that it might be preferable *not* to change their names first emerged a few months into my fieldwork. When I met with Tyhir's mother, Tanisha, for the second time, I gently raised the idea that I would have to change Tyhir's name in anything I wrote—which I assumed would be required by the Institutional Review Board. I suggested she begin to think about a pseudonym she would be comfortable with. She sat for several minutes in deep thought, then said that she really could not think of any other name and wondered aloud about the necessity of a pseudonym. She said that if I was going to write about her son, she would want readers to know who he was and to honor his memory with the name she had given him. A year later, I had a similar conversation with Maxayn, JahSun's mother. I began to dismantle my assumption that a pseudonym was the only possibility, but I also felt conflicted.

The conflict was particularly acute when thinking about JahSun, since he had previously been a consented participant in my study. Less than a year before his death, I had discussed the concept of anonymization with him; he had even suggested a possible pseudonym for himself. After his death, facing the question of whether to use his real name, I revisited the consent form he had signed. I wondered what responsibility I had to the JahSun I had known in life who had signed the form, and how, now that he was dead, to weigh our formal understanding against his mother's preference that I use his real name. Looking for advice, I met with a representative from the UPenn IRB, who told me, with a cold frankness I was not expecting, that "the dead are not human subjects." Though I did not necessarily agree, I was no longer legally or institutionally bound by JahSun's signed consent form.[38] Further conversations with Tanisha and Maxayn, and with Bill's mother, Williesha, convinced me that insofar as this study would preserve their memory, Tyhir, JahSun, and Bill should keep their real names.[39]

In the final stages of the production of this book, a new question about anonymity and visibility emerged around the cover design. When the image of JahSun's decorated locker (see fig. 2.1) was selected for the cover, his face was blurred in all of the photographs. Though this is what I had initially decided was appropriate for the version of this image included inside the book as a documentary artifact, it no longer felt right as a book cover, which would be so much more visible. We have been conditioned by the media to associate blurred faces of Black boys with crime, but more importantly, it seemed potentially more in keeping with the decision to use JahSun's real name to also show his face.[40] JahSun's parents had the same reaction to the draft I showed them and together we decided to unblur the pictures of JahSun (though his friends, who are still living and who were minors at the time of these photographs, remain obscured). However, at JahSun's parents' request, one change that was made to the original image for its use on the cover was to replace one of the photographs his friends had taped to the locker with a more flattering picture.

A final challenge in the writing of this book was how to tell the story of a phenomenon (grief) that is both deeply personal and private *and* also communal and shared; both invisible and immeasurable *and* at a human scale so immense. Over the course of just two years at Boys' Prep, there were dozens of shootings that took the lives of members of students' social networks (see fig. 6.1 for one kind of accounting of this). Each loss and its aftermath cries out for recognition and could be the subject of its own book. The decision to focus primarily on JahSun's death and tell the story chronologically over the course of a single school year reflected my desire to make the collective experience of loss and grief at the school tangible and immersive for the reader. And yet, I hope that the specificity of this ethnographic account does not lull us into imagining that this was merely one sad year at one unlucky school, rather than a raging epidemic that has produced an entire generation wounded by grief.

Appendix A

Glossary of Social Media Abbreviations, Slang, and Emojis

Table A.1. Social media abbreviations and shorthand

ABBREVIATION	CONTEXTUAL MEANING
ashit	as shit
da	the
gvng	gang, but generally just referring to a friend
gl	good looks/good looking out, thanks; good luck
idk	I don't know
ik	I know
ima	I'm going to
LL	Long Live (similar to RIP)
nbs	no bullshit
ngl	not gonna lie
nun	nothing
rn	right now
rs	real shit, usually referring to a statement that is both factual and serious
shxt	shit (avoids online auto-censors for curse words)
ski	broski abbreviation; friend, usually male
smh	shaking my head
wtf	what the fuck

Table A.2. Local idioms and slang

WORD/PHRASE	CONTEXTUAL MEANING
bid/bidding	play or make fun of; playing around
the bid	a funny time or experience
bread or cake	money
brodie	close friend, brother
dap me up	a greeting via fistbump, tapping, or hitting hands
dawg	close friend, brother
drawn	acting out of character or out of line
flex	show off, brag
mane	man, close friend, brother

Table A.3. Emojis

EMOJI	CONTEXTUAL MEANING
😢😭	tears falling, sad
😩	grief; tired
😥	wiping away tears, sniffling; trying to play it off, hide feelings
😤	angry, frustrated
😎	cool, chilling
🤦🤦	facepalm, shaking my head, annoyed; terrible situation
👼	deceased (young) person; angel
💪💪	strong, staying strong
🙏	praying, begging, hoping
🤞	fingers crossed/hoping for; how close you are with somebody
🤙	cool
🏃	running, moving forward; chasing
⛓	close or deeply connected to someone; locked up, in jail
🔒	close or deeply connected to someone; locked up, in jail
💉	blood, as in family
🕊	dove, often symbolizing the deceased's journey
❗	extra emphasis
💯	being honest, "keeping it 100"; agreement, yes
💔	broken heart, grief
❤️	love, heart
🖤	strong love; love between men/male friends

Participant Details

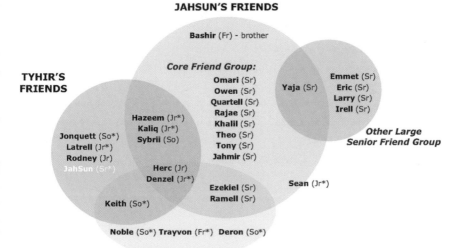

JAHSUN'S FRIENDS

Bashir (Fr) - brother

Core Friend Group:

**TYHIR'S
FRIENDS**

Hazeem (Jr*)
Kaliq (Jr*)
Sybrii (So)

Omari (Sr)
Owen (Sr)
Quartell (Sr)
Rajae (Sr)
Khalil (Sr)
Theo (Sr)
Tony (Sr)
Jahmir (Sr)

Yaja (Sr)

Emmet (Sr)
Eric (Sr)
Larry (Sr)
Irell (Sr)

*Other Large
Senior Friend Group*

Jonquett (So*)
Latrell (Jr*)
Rodney (Jr)
JahSun (Sr*)

Herc (Jr)
Denzel (Jr*)

Ezekiel (Sr)
Ramell (Sr)

Sean (Jr*)

Keith (So*)

Noble (So*) **Trayvon** (Fr*) **Deron** (So*)

BILL'S FRIENDS

Figure B.1. Overlapping student friendship circles at Boys' Prep. Names are followed
by students' grade level; asterisks mark students who did not graduate from Boys'
Prep. Note that this image only includes individuals who are discussed in this book,
though each of these circles of peers had many more members.

Table B.1. Details about adult participants

NAME	RACE AND GENDER / AGE	TENURE AT SCHOOL (AS OF 2017−2018)	ROLE AT SCHOOL OR SUBJECT TAUGHT / GRADE LEVELS TAUGHT
Ms. Abadi	Middle Eastern woman / early 20s	Second year	Science teacher / multiple grades
Mr. Adams	Black man / late 30s	Third year	Disciplinarian Athletics coach
Ms. Bloom	White woman / mid-20s	Fifth year	Science and math teacher / freshmen
Ms. Cain	White woman / mid-30s	Seventh year	Social studies and philosophy teacher / juniors and seniors Department chair
Mr. Donaldson	White man / late 30s	Eighth year (first year as principal)	Principal Basketball coach (previously math teacher)
Ms. Estevez	Latina woman / mid-20s	Third year	Math teacher / multiple grades
Ms. Finn	White woman / mid-30s	Fifth year	Social studies teacher / sophomores
Ms. Gallo	White woman / late 20s	Third year	College counselor
Mr. Gilbert	White man / late 30s	Seventh year	English teacher / freshmen
Mr. Hopkins	White man / mid-40s	First year	Vice principal
Ms. Jordan	White woman / mid-30s	First year	Math teacher / juniors and seniors
Ms. Kallum	White woman / mid-30s	Seventh year	Latin teacher / seniors
Mr. Khan	Asian American man / early 30s	Fifth year	English teacher / freshmen Athletics coach
Mr. Leonard	White man / late 20s	First year	English teacher / multiple grades Athletics coach
Mr. Marker	White man / early 30s	Third year	English teacher / sophomores
Ms. Neal	White woman / early 30s	Fourth year	English teacher / seniors Department chair
Mr. Pratt	Black man / early 40s	Eighth year	Head disciplinarian
Ms. Redmond	White woman / mid-30s	Twelfth year	Latin teacher / multiple grades Department chair and alumni coordinator

NAME	RACE AND GENDER / AGE	TENURE AT SCHOOL (AS OF 2017–2018)	ROLE AT SCHOOL OR SUBJECT TAUGHT / GRADE LEVELS TAUGHT
Ms. Rivera	Latina woman / early 40s	Third year	Social worker
Dr. Stephens	Black, biracial man / early 40s	Seventh year (first year as CEO)	CEO of Boys' Prep middle and high school (previously principal of HS)
Ms. Thompson	Black woman / late 20s	Second year	Science teacher / sophomores
Ms. Wagner	White woman / late 20s	Fourth year	Special Education teacher Department chair
Ms. Woo	Asian American woman / mid-20s	Fourth year	Science teacher / multiple grades

Notes

Preface

1. Gramlich 2023.

Chapter One

1. Rankine 2015. The role of death and mourning in Black life has been poignantly explored by many poets as well as by scholars, including Ellis 2011; Ewing 2018; Grinage 2019; Hartman 2008; Holloway 2003; Sharpe 2016. Christina Sharpe, for example, argues that many young people live and are "produced by . . . the contemporary conditions of Black life as it is lived near death" (7). Aimé Ellis describes the way popular culture has produced "a modern-day black male subject that asserts that to be black, poor, and male is to live with the sense that one is at once bound for and yet strangely emanating out of death" (1).
2. For example, Glass 2013; Peña 2022; Rojas 2021.
3. While I have shared some limited details of the circumstances of JahSun's and others' deaths, I encourage my readers not to dwell here. As far as I am aware, none of the murders discussed in this book were incidents of "gang violence"; however, I find that preoccupations with this label can often serve as cover for racist distinctions between supposed *deserving* versus *undeserving* victims.
4. Cox 2021; Currie 2020; Goldstick, Cunningham, and Carter 2022; Hemenway and Nelson 2020. For a discussion of the causes and consequences of the earlier crime decline, see Sharkey 2018. For a report on the gun violence surge of 2020, see Everytown for Gun Safety 2021.
5. For example, Abt 2019; Beard et al. 2019; Beckett and Clayton 2022; Knopov, Siegel, and Pahn 2017; Sharkey 2018; Wintemute 2015.

6. For research on collective years of life lost, see Currie 2020; Philadelphia Department of Public Health and Mayor's Office of Public Engagement 2019; Szymkowiak and Mallya 2015. For calculations of "missing Black men," see Wolfers, Leonhardt, and Quealy 2015.

7. Abt 2019; Krivo et al. 2018; Sharkey and Marsteller 2022.

8. Harding 2009, 772. David Ansell (2017) put it succinctly: "Where you live dictates when you die . . . Inequality itself is a cause of death" (xiv, xix).

9. See, for example, Ayers 2014; Cann 2014; Jimerson 2014; Kubrin 2005; Lohmon 2006; Patton et al. 2018; Woodbine 2016. It must also be noted that the number of gun violence survivors far outweighs the number of fatalities. For research on survivors' experiences and subsequent roles in their communities, see Jacoby et al. 2018; Lee 2012; Rich 2011; Richardson et al. 2016.

10. Kotlowitz 2020, 21.

11. Beeghley 2003; Spungen 1997.

12. Balk, Zaengle, and Corr 2011; Sklar and Hartley 1990. Surprisingly, exposure to gun violence is not included on the list of Adverse Childhood Experiences around which much social policy to support children has been framed, though there is an effort to change this (see Rajan et al. 2019).

13. There are decades of research substantiating the physical, psychological, and neurological impact of violence and trauma exposure on children (for example, see Bell and Jenkins 1993; Wright et al. 2016). Exposure to recent violent crime on a child's block can lower vocabulary and reading scores, reducing passing rates for Black students by as much as 3 percent (Sharkey 2010; Sharkey et al. 2014) and impacting Black teens' long-term educational outcomes (Gershenson and Tekin 2015; Sharkey et al. 2012). Further, the impacts can spread at school to peers who live in different neighborhoods (Burdick-Will 2018). See also Ayers 2014; Caudillo and Torche 2014; Crowder and South 2003; Oosterhoff, Kaplow, and Layne 2018; Stewart, Stewart, and Simons 2007; Wodtke, Harding, and Elwert 2011.

14. Smith 2015; Umberson 2017; Umberson et al. 2017. Although adolescent friendship circles tend to be gendered, Black girls are often part of these extended social circles as well.

15. Currie 2020.

16. Omari would be fired from his job two weeks later for missing work for JahSun's memorial service.

17. Lubrano 2018.

18. At the time of this writing, public materials about the school have adjusted the college acceptance rate to 86 percent and the college enrollment and persistence rates to 76 percent.

19. The charter school movement is extremely polarizing—viewed by supporters

as a pathway to innovation and more specialized and equitable schooling and by critics as uneven, largely unsuccessful, and irreparably damaging to public schooling. See Berends 2015.

20. Golann 2015; Golann and Torres 2018; Whitman 2008.

21. Brown 2011; Howard 2014; Noguera 2009.

22. Whereas single-sex schooling for girls has long been an accepted intervention for improving girls' self-esteem and academic outcomes, changing gender-related education policies and increasing support for "school choice" have set the stage for the rapid spread of these "Black Male Academies." Research focusing on the effectiveness of single-sex schools for boys of color in improving student outcomes, however, has been mixed, if not disappointing. See Blume Oeur 2018; Fergus, Noguera, and Martin 2014; Lindsay 2018; Warren 2017; Williams 2016.

23. Urban Prep Academies 2012.

24. Blume Oeur 2018, 15.

25. Blume Oeur 2018, 6; see also Grundy 2022.

26. Blume Oeur 2018, 82.

27. Several of the nearby public schools were viewed by residents as unsafe (e.g., metal detectors lined their entrances and fights in the school building sometimes made local news), and they had increasingly struggled with enrollment.

28. Howard 2014, 14–15.

29. Philadelphia has the highest poverty rate (percentage of families living below the poverty line) among the twenty-five most populous cities in the United States (PEW 2018).

30. In *Scripting the Moves*, Golann (2021) writes about a "sense of urgency" present at no-excuses charter schools. The root of this feeling at Boys' Prep was similar — that students had a lot of catching up to do — but the effects were somewhat different. At Dream Academy, the no-excuses school documented by Golann, efforts to "eliminate inefficiencies and increase productivity" came at the expense of one-on-one time and relationship-building between students and teachers (104). At Boys' Prep, successful students often relied heavily on one-on-one attention from school staff, but this was a limited resource.

31. Other researchers have similarly found that schools focus on bodily comportment and dress as important components of social mobility training, particularly for students of color. See Blume Oeur 2018; Golann 2021; Harvey 2022; Morris 2005.

32. See the idea of "controlling images" from Collins 2000.

33. There is a rich empirical history within the subfield of the sociology of emotions that shows the way emotions are social and contextual experiences (see Hochschild 1979; 2002; Kang 2003; Wingfield 2012), as well as a small but growing focus among sociologists on grief (see Berns 2011; Fowlkes 1990; Goodrum 2008; Harris 2010; Jakoby 2012; Lofland 1985; Martin 2013; Walter 1999).

34. Hochschild 1979.
35. Disenfranchised grief, a concept developed by Kenneth Doka (1989), is the experience of suffering a loss but having "little or no opportunity to mourn publicly [because one does] not have a socially recognized right, role, or capacity to grieve" (3). Generally, the disenfranchisement of grief is exacerbated by social and structural inequalities, such that Black youth may experience not just public marginalization of their grief but also *punishment* for their grief displays, what thanatologist Tashel Bordere (2020) describes as "suffocated grief." See also Berns 2011; Granek and Peleg-Sagy 2017; Kersting et al. 2011; Klass 2013; Walter 2000.
36. Butler 2020.
37. "SAMHSA's Concept of Trauma and Guidance for a Trauma-Informed Approach" 2014, 7.
38. Alexander et al. 2004; Hirschberger 2018.
39. For example, Craig 2017; Dutil 2019; Dutro 2019; K. Gross 2020 (no relation); Rossen 2020; Wolfsdore, Wedlock, and Lo 2022; Zacarian, Alvarez-Ortiz, and Haynes 2017.
40. Cox 2023; Scheeringa 2021.
41. Fenwick 2022; K. Gross 2020.
42. Pandell 2022.
43. In 1996, Congress introduced the Dickey Amendment as part of the Omnibus Consolidated Appropriations Bill, which prohibited the use of federal funds to "advocate or promote gun control," effectively halting large-scale firearm-related research and severely limiting our understanding of gun violence. In 2018, Congress clarified that the amendment does not prohibit the study of the causes of gun violence and, in 2020, funding was finally allocated to the CDC and NIH for research on reducing gun-related deaths and injuries, marking the first such allocation in more than two decades.
44. Currie 2020.
45. Black children are often viewed as older than they are. For boys, this "adultification" can be confusing for identity development (Roy and Jones 2014; Stevenson 2004); have harmful consequences for their treatment within education, healthcare, and criminal-justice systems (Dancy 2014; Goff et al. 2014; Goyal et al. 2015); and contribute to a society in which Black boys are not seen as "worthy of protection" and Black *boyhood* itself becomes increasingly "unimaginable" (Dumas and Nelson 2016, 30).
46. I also must acknowledge that referring to the students as boys presumes a gender identity that cannot be fully known. Given that Boys' Prep is a school highly sought after by parents in the community and open only to male-identified students, and given that non-normative, more fluid gender performances in this

school and other contexts are often invisible, marginal, or policed in consequential ways, I simply cannot know how the term applies to all students and how each views his own gender identity at the time of the research or at any time before or after.

47. It is possible that the pseudonymized Instagram handles are being used by real people, but, if so, that is a coincidence and completely unrelated to this text.

Chapter Two

1. Bashir and JahSun have the same father but different mothers; however, Bashir always viewed JahSun as his brother and felt the "half" distinction did not reflect their actual bond. I therefore refer to them as brothers in the rest of the book.
2. Lauer 2021.
3. For more on the stigma that Black men and boys face around mental health support, see Cadaret and Speight 2018; Lindsey and Marcell 2012; Rosenblatt and Wallace 2005.
4. Majors and Billson 1992; Anderson 1999; Jackson 2018, 3. See also Hall and Pizarro 2010; hooks 2003; Stevenson 2003.
5. See Way 2013.
6. About the inequality of peer losses, see Smith 2015; Smith and Patton 2016; Umberson 2017; Umberson et al. 2017.
7. Collins 2004.

Chapter Three

1. It's not entirely clear why Mr. Hopkins did not consult the Philadelphia version of this handbook—though perhaps he did, and just did not remember in the blur of the crisis.
2. The US Office for Victims of Crime has created a model for these resources (Schonfeld and Newgass 2003). A related growing industry and set of resources focuses on school crisis management in the context of active shooter and mass shooting situations.
3. Fergus, Noguera, and Martin 2014, 24.
4. See Blume Oeur 2018.
5. Quotes from 2014 Fairbanks North Star Borough School District manual.
6. This text chat, renamed "JahWorld" by one of the boys, remained active throughout the school year whenever Ms. Bloom wanted to share information or offer support, or when the boys wished to include Ms. Bloom in their own peer communications.
7. Bereavement scholars find that there has been a recent emphasis on pursuing

"continuing bonds" with deceased loved ones rather than seeking closure (Klass and Steffen 2017; Mitchell et al. 2012; Neimeyer, Baldwin, and Gillies 2006; Walter et al. 2012). Physical memorials like locker decorations, t-shirts, car decals, or tattoos, as well as internet-based memorials, are some common approaches (Bordere 2009; Cann 2014; Jimerson 2014; Walter et al. 2012).

8.   Years later, Bashir recalled being deeply moved when he learned that his name was on the whiteboard during this meeting and that faculty had specifically discussed how they might support him.

Chapter Four

1.   For more on school reform and school closings in Philadelphia, see Cucchiara 2013; McWilliams 2019; Royal 2022.

2.   Boys' Prep averaged an attrition rate of 4 to 9 percent (or 18 to 41 students) each year. In 2017, the official reasons for students' withdrawal were: 52 percent left to attend "another local option," 28 percent moved "out of area," 16 percent were "undercredited," and 4 percent for disciplinary reasons. For a discussion of student attrition in charter schools, see Nichols-Barrer et al. 2016.

3.   This level of teacher turnover is not atypical in charter schools. See, for example, Guthery and Bailes 2022.

4.   Emotion management, as described in the sociological literature, is a response to situational *feeling rules*. It involves not just a deliberate modification of emotional displays to abide by those social rules, but inevitably a control of the emotions themselves. When practiced repeatedly, this can have long-term effects on a person's emotional life and identity—especially if there is an unequal power relationship between those prescribing the emotional displays and those fulfilling them (e.g., employer and employee or school institution and student). Over time, Hochschild (2002) argues, ongoing emotion work can result in a detachment from the self: "it affects the degree to which we listen to feeling and sometimes our very capacity to feel" (21). For research on Black men's emotion management practices, see Jackson 2018; Jackson and Wingfield 2013; White and Peretz 2010; Wilkins 2012; Wingfield 2007; 2012. For discussions of emotion management among Black students in school contexts, see Cox 2016; Dance 2002; Ferguson 2001; Gilmore 1985.

5.   As I discuss in chapter 5, several of the boys used marijuana as a coping mechanism to deal with their grief and other sources of distress. See Rich and Grey 2005.

6.   Suffocated grief is a concept developed by thanatologist Tashel Bordere (2020) to refer to expressions of grief that are punished in institutional contexts.

7.   Most teachers who fell into this category were white women, though given the

high percentage of white female teachers in the school, it is hard to qualify this as a pattern without further study.

8. Cann 2014, 2, 3.

9. Breen and O'Connor 2007; Doka 2017; Granek and Peleg-Sagy 2017; Walter 2000.

10. Bereavement leave is not mandated by any federal or state codes, and generally covers only up to three paid days for salaried workers and possibly no paid leave for hourly workers (Cann 2014). Some recent moves toward changing bereavement leave policies include Meta and several other major technology companies increasing the number of paid days off for bereavement leave (Brenoff 2017). About the "denial of death," see Aries 1981; Becker 1997.

Chapter Five

1. Berns 2011; Goodrum 2008; Harris 2010; Jakoby 2012; Klass 2013; Lofland 1985.

2. See Kübler-Ross 1969; Kübler-Ross and Kessler 2014. For an overview of dying and bereavement in contemporary Western culture, see Aries 1981; Cann 2014.

3. A diagnosis of Prolonged Grief Disorder, grief that inhibits a return to everyday activities more than one year after a loss, was added to the fifth edition of the *Diagnostic and Statistical Manual of Mental Disorders* (*DSM-5*) in 2022 amid great controversy (Barry 2022).

4. Bordere 2020.

5. Cacho 2007; Doka 1989; Fowlkes 1990; Martin 2013; Ralph 2015a; Walter 2000.

6. On the inequality of loss and grief, see Bindley et al. 2019; Kersting et al. 2011; Newson et al. 2011; Umberson et al. 2014. About differential access to supports, see Allen 2007; Martin 2005.

7. Cacho 2007; Lawson 2014; Martin 2010; Piazza-Bonin et al. 2015; Spungen 1997.

8. Martin 2013; see also Baker, Norris, and Cherneva 2021.

9. Rosenblatt and Wallace 2005.

10. Connell 2000; Creighton et al. 2013; Kenney 2003; Kimmel 2009; Newson et al. 2011; Stevenson 2003; Way 2013; Zinner 2000.

11. Doka and Martin 2010, 91.

12. Anderson 1999; Hall and Pizarro 2010; hooks 2003; Jackson 2018; Majors and Billson 1992; Stevenson 2003.

13. Doka 1989, 3; see also Bindley et al. 2019; Corr 1999.

14. Ralph 2015a, 33; Cacho 2007, 183; Leonard 2017. See also Bindley et al. 2019; Dutil 2019; Lawson 2014.

15. Bordere 2020.

16. Judith Butler (2004; 2020) describes grief in contexts of dehumanization as a "radical act." See Hochschild 2002 on emotion management.

17. Blume Oeur 2018, 185, 6; see also Brooms 2015; Fergus, Noguera, and Martin 2014.

18. For a brief history of the concept of "grit," see Ris 2015.

19. Interestingly, two years later, this teacher's perspective seemed to have shifted: at a memorial for another student killed in fall 2019, Mr. Leonard expressed frustration that just two days after his death, "Some teachers were already talking about the uniforms being messed up and cell phones out."

20. Pabon and Basile 2022.

21. Dancy 2014; Dumas and Nelson 2016.

22. My critique of a resilience framework is similar to the one made by Blume Oeur 2018 as well as larger critiques of the concept of grit by Goodman 2018 and Saltman 2014, among others.

23. Robson and Walter 2013.

24. I write in detail about this transition in our relationship in Gross 2022.

25. Many other students also found marijuana to be a useful coping practice, providing "quick" relief or helping them "calm" down when thinking about a loss. Marijuana use is common among American teenagers, and not unique to the population documented in this book. According to 2019 CDC data, 37 percent of US high school students reported having used marijuana, 22 percent within the past thirty days. For research on the way young men use drugs and/or alcohol to "mask, control, or justify" their emotions and expressions of grief, see Creighton et al. 2016, 236; Doka and Martin 2010; Rich and Grey 2005.

26. The deaths of peers can prompt fatalistic thinking and diminished expectations or aspirations for the future (Bluck et al. 2008; Ens and Bond 2007; Florian and Mikulincer 1997; Smith 2015). Studies estimate that between 6 percent and 15 percent of all youth anticipate their own early death at some point during adolescence (Borowsky, Ireland, and Resnick 2009; P. E. Jamieson and Romer 2008). These feelings are more common among Black male youth and those experiencing poverty (Swisher and Warner 2013; Warner and Swisher 2015). Anticipating one's own premature death, unsurprisingly, has negative implications for youths' criminal behaviors or school delinquency (Brezina, Tekin, and Topalli 2008; Caldwell, Wiebe, and Cleveland 2006), long-term health outcomes (Borowsky, Ireland, and Resnick 2009; Duke et al. 2011), and adult socioeconomic status (Nguyen et al. 2012). Further, youth can be impacted in these ways through their participation in peer groups with fatalistic attitudes (Haynie, Soller, and Williams 2014).

27. Although I frequently joined the students outside school for memorial events like vigils, balloon releases, and trips to the cemetery, this was the first (and only) time I was invited to join a more private gathering out of the building. I declined the boys' request that I purchase rolling papers for them and then,

later, that I smoke with them. While marijuana use among minors is illegal, personal possession and consumption of the drug was decriminalized in Philadelphia in 2014. I write more about some of the more complicated methodological choices in the Author's Note.

28. Walter (2000, 101) reminds us that this is nothing new: "In every society, the expression of grief is regulated by conventions and rituals which indicate how, and how much, mourners should speak about the dead and express their feelings." Just as in face-to-face interactions, online bereavement also has norms of expression and is susceptible to interpretations of a hierarchy of grief (DeGroot 2012; Robson and Walter 2013; Wagner 2018).

29. Cann 2014, 49 and 15.

30. Bordere 2009, 224; Cann 2014; Jimerson 2014; Johnson 2010, 368.

31. AP-NORC 2017.

32. There is a growing body of literature on digital or virtual grieving (see Cann 2014; Lingel 2013; Pearce 2017; Pennington 2013; Sofka, Cupit, and Gilbert 2012; Walter et al. 2012), particularly among urban Black youth who often have to navigate a complex online relationship between mourning and violent threats or escalations (see Gross 2023; Patton et al. 2018; 2017; Sandelson 2023; Stuart 2020a; 2020b).

33. Kaliq recalled that only two people regularly replied to his Instagram stories and checked in on him through the app: his grandmother and me, an adult researcher. Despite the limited interaction others had with his posts, Kaliq would sometimes call up a friend whose post suggested that he was really upset. I discuss one poignant example of this with Hazeem in Gross 2023.

34. I write in more detail about this finding in Gross 2023.

35. Dance 2002; Dumas 2014; Ferguson 2001; Lewis and Diamond 2015; Morris 2018; Rios 2011; Valenzuela 1999.

Chapter Six

1. Many scholars, journalists, novelists, and poets—far too many to list here—have written about the way death chases Black men and boys. Some of my favorites: Blow 2014; Coates 2009; Daniels 2021; Ellis 2011; Ward 2014.

2. Cookson and Persell 1987, 74.

3. Boys' Prep's emphasis on personal responsibility contrasts with, for example, the mission of another Black Male Academy that aims to "provide rigorous and culturally responsive curriculum and instruction to ensure that our Young Kings are prepared to successfully act as reflective agents of change to solve problems that impact their diaspora" (http://www.rbhsmonarchs.org/about-rbhs; accessed 2023). Despite their divergent orientations toward developing community-

engaged graduates, both schools experienced similar tensions between managing students' social-emotional needs related to their experiences with violence and prioritizing academic rigor and success (listen to the NPR podcast series for more: https://www.npr.org/series/557324733/a-year-at-ron-brown-high-school).

4. Like other Black Male Academies, and charter schools generally, the institution may gain recognition and esteem in contrast to local public schools, which are often viewed through a deficit lens. As Warren (2017) writes about Urban Prep, a BMA in Chicago, "while it is essential to counter anti-Blackness by actively and purposefully centering Blackness in the practices and organizational structure of a singular institution, it is equally necessary to attend to the ways a school's work/ ideologies improve or exacerbate the suffering of other Black people within and outside of the school building" (164).

5. In contrast are theories of highly *contextualized* education—such as community relevant, culturally relevant, or culturally sustaining pedagogy (see Duncan-Andrade 2022; Ladson-Billings 1995; Paris and Winn 2013)—or problem- or inquiry-based curricular models.

6. For example, the "code of the street" (Anderson 1999), "tough fronts" (Dance 2002), or the "cool pose" (Majors and Billson 1992).

7. Popular culture and pop psychology offer many examples of this approach: for example, "dress for the job you want" or the research that smiling can make one feel happier. In a more related context, Fader (2013) reports that young men in a juvenile detention center learned to "fake it to make it" to fulfill program requirements, but at the same time maintained their adherence to street codes in other ways (76). She argues that it would have been more beneficial to the young men to learn code switching.

8. Jeffrey Duncan-Andrade's (2022) metaphor of medicine offers one way to think about this. He writes: "practices that lead youth to know their histories, cultures, and traditions give them the gift of being in relationship with their own medicine. When these practices are extended to bring young people into relationship with others, it permits a mixing of medicines such that all of those involved have their respective medicines made even more powerful. Some of the things being taught in school are also forms of medicine in that they are cultural narratives and markers. But because so many children are asked to check their culture (their medicine) at the door, the opportunity to mix medicines in school is lost. What happens instead is that youth develop a relationship with school where the 'medicine' is shoved down their throats rather than shared with them and they are then told that it is good for their future. This approach does not make anybody feel well" (153–54).

9. Warren 2017. See also Grinage (2019) for a discussion of the effects of a "Euro-

centric curriculum" on the racial trauma and grief of Black students in a different kind of school context.

10. See Labaree 1997 for a clear summary of the competing goals of education. See Golann 2021 for one example of a school that promotes "worker-learners" who, as Ms. Abadi was arguing about Boys' Prep, are not being well prepared for intellectual or leadership roles.

11. More time outside, more interactions on the street, more free time for young people, and tempers exacerbated by heat are considered factors that contribute to a cyclical increase in homicides during spring and summer (Anderson 2001).

12. Though we might expect an "inoculation effect" from repeated exposure to trauma, researchers find that experiencing multiple traumatic events "can sensitize individuals, creating vulnerability to enhanced psychological and physiological distress following future adversity," and that even *indirect* exposure to collective traumatic events can be just as distressing to individuals (Andersen et al. 2013, 1, 2).

13. See Jones 2018 for a discussion of the way personal transformation is often a "group process" for young Black men.

14. Ralph (2014) describes something similar among those injured by gunfire as "renegade dreams."

15. This quote, with permission, comes from an interview conducted by Rodney's peers as part of a separate participatory project emerging from this research.

16. For discussions of the way opportunity gaps become achievement gaps, see Carter and Welner 2013; Ladson-Billings 2006.

17. In her book *Teaching on Days After*, Alyssa Dunn (2021) finds that in the immediate aftermath of major world and local events, school districts often advise that teachers stick to the curriculum; yet, students generally want to engage. Teaching for equity and justice, Dunn argues, demands that teachers respond to the moment.

18. Jackman (2002) alludes to the idea of social injuries in her discussion of the range of injurious outcomes of violence, including the physical, psychological, material, and social. She argues that "social injuries are the least likely to be acknowledged in discussions of violence" (395). A handful of other scholars have employed the term "social injury" to refer to related ideas of the effects of a harmful event on one's social standing or interpersonal relationships, or to mark injuries generally perceived to be private as collective (see Howe 1987; Osafo et al. 2011; Thornton 1989).

19. Harding 2010, 57. For a related body of literature on the way youths' aspirations are shaped by peers' experiences and group images, see Kao 2000; Oyserman, Bybee, and Terry 2006.

20. Hypervigilance is defined as "an intentional state of alertness and heightened awareness [in order] to anticipate and/or quickly react to danger" (Smith and Patton 2016, 219). Though practicing hypervigilance might offer some protection from the threat of violence, it is not without costs, including diverting energy and focus from other activities or distracting from efforts to draw motivation from loss.

21. On moral distress related to both teaching and nursing, where the concept was originally formulated, see Colnerud 2015; Hellawell 2015; Jameton 1984; Lützén et al. 2003; Severinsson 2003. Some recent attention has focused on the way both the COVID-19 pandemic and rising levels of gun violence strain teachers (see McMurdock 2023).

Chapter Seven

1. Sharkey 2022.
2. Cullen 2019, 9. Unless otherwise noted, my depiction of the aftermath of the Parkland shooting comes from Cullen's reporting.
3. All three ultimately survived the shooting, but one of the boys (the one Hazeem was closest to) was permanently paralyzed from the waist down.
4. See Beard et al. 2019 for a discussion of how mass shootings are defined.
5. Nass 2018.
6. Fueled by the work of the March for Our Lives youth activists, sixty pieces of gun-related legislation passed at the local level across the country in 2018 (Cullen 2019).
7. Based on my own calculations using data from Follman, Aronsen, and Pan 2023 and the Philadelphia Police Department. Note that this timeline does not even include a summer, when urban gun violence often peaks.
8. Butler 2009, 1; Leonard 2017. For instance, press reports on the murdered Boys' Prep students seemed to go to great lengths to describe them as having been "scholar athletes," "college-bound," or mention that they had "no prior contact with the police" or were "doing the right thing"—assurances that were never required for the victims, mainly white, of mass shootings.
9. Florida was one of only fourteen states to require both a civics course and an exam (Graham and Weingarten 2018; Shapiro and Brown 2018). However, Florida's approach to civic education shifted significantly under the leadership of Governor Ron DeSantis (see Najarro 2022).
10. Islam and Crego 2018.
11. Gurney 2018; Rosenblatt 2018.
12. Cullen 2019, 5. Teen activists from a more recent school shooting described their work as "fill[ing] that little hole that has been there" since the shooting (Mejia

2022). Of course, many Parkland survivors chose not to pursue activism (for example, Barbaro et al. 2019) or have since shared more complex reflections on that path and/or pulled back from their activist work (González 2023; Tarr 2021; 2022).

13. Yaja often includes me in his explanations of how he got through the period following JahSun's death. Having an extra adult hanging around the building who was interested in talking about grief, seemed to care, and had the time to listen made a difference during the tougher times.

14. Though numbness may be a protective response, it is also depoliticizing (Sandell and Bornäs 2017).

15. Some March for Our Lives leaders have since reflected on some blind spots in the early days of the movement and ways they could have been more inclusive of other forms of violence and of longtime activists of color working on these issues. See Blades 2018; A. Jamieson 2019; Tarr 2022.

16. I worked at North Lawndale College Prep, as I describe in the preface, long before Alex and D'Angelo were students, but I do vividly remember the founding years of the Peace Warriors and how exciting and promising it seemed even in its infancy. I share this as just one example of many successful youth anti-violence programs across the country.

17. Haga 2011; Irvine 2018.

18. Irvine 2018 and personal communication with Peace Warriors adult facilitators.

19. Hooker 2023, 11.

20. Cullen 2019; Posse Foundation 2018.

21. Ahmed 2021.

22. Butler 2020, 14; Hooker 2023.

23. Cheng 2001, 3; See also Crimp 1989; Ralph 2015a. Of course, grievances can also be dangerous, as when wielded by those with power to feign victimhood, which we see among white extremists, including some who become mass shooters (Hooker 2023).

24. Hooker 2023, 18, 19.

25. This has been true of many Black Lives Matter activists (see Hooker 2023). In the case of the Parkland students, some have reported, in retrospect, negative consequences of their involvement in the movement, and particularly of becoming celebrity activists: their stories of trauma being exploited as public commodities and their teenage years burdened with weighty responsibilities (González 2023; Tarr 2022; 2021). At the same time, for others, their abrupt foray into adolescent activism has launched promising careers in public service.

26. Baldwin 1963; Freire 2000; Love 2019; Seider and Graves 2020.

27. Duncan-Andrade 2022.

28. Seider and Graves (2020, 8) studied five urban charter schools, each with a dif-

ferent educational model but all with "youth civic development as a core part of their missions." They propose that the development of critical conscious-ness involves three components—social analysis, political agency, and social action—at least one of which they find centered at each school. The schools employed curricular models like a year-long first-year social engagement course, a sociology of change course, civics courses, African American history and lit-erature courses, culture circles and community meetings, exhibition nights for students to demonstrate their "habits of mind," community improvement proj-ects, explicit instruction in activism and participation in political demonstrations, formal invitations to suggest school policy changes, and senior projects and in-ternships.

29. Seider and Graves 2020, 3.
30. Freire 2000.
31. Duncan-Andrade 2009.
32. Ginwright 2016, 2 and 21.
33. Erikson 1994.
34. For further discussion of (school) uniforms and respectability politics in BMA contexts, see Clonan-Roy, Gross, and Jacobs 2021; Gross 2017; Oeur 2017. For more on student-teacher relationships, see Gross and Lo 2018.
35. Love 2019.
36. Golann 2015, 103.
37. Ben-Porath 2013.
38. I write more about this group, called Freedom to Speak, and its potential to make space for otherwise silenced emotional expression in Clonan-Roy, Gross, and Jacobs 2021.
39. Love 2019, 71.
40. Duncan-Andrade 2009, 182; Ginwright 2016; Goodman 2018.
41. hooks 1994, 207.
42. Ginwright 2007, 416.
43. Seider and Graves 2020, 3.
44. Duncan-Andrade 2009; Ginwright 2016.
45. For more on curricular models, see Dunn 2021; Seider and Graves 2020. On YPAR, see Bautista et al. 2013; Sandwick et al. 2018. On art, see Goodman 2018. On service learning, see Learn and Serve America 2020; NYLC 2020. On activ-ism, see Cohen 2012. On peer counseling and mediation, see Haga 2011; Reichert et al. 2012.
46. Harper, Terry, and Twiggs 2009.
47. See Duncan-Andrade 2022 for a discussion of wellness.
48. For scholarship on Black othermothers, see Collins 2000; Spruill et al. 2014; Stack and Burton 1993. The "othermothering" of gun violence victims' mothers

toward their child's friends has not, as far as I know, been discussed in prior research.

49. Carter (2019) refers to the way mothers of homicide victims continue to care for their children in death by marking their birthdays and death anniversaries as a kind of "*restorative* kinship, one that asserts the value of those who have been lost by restoring their position within the family and community, in this world and the next" (189). The boys in this study show the way friends and peers can play this role as well.

50. Some scholars have argued that in the Black community women often (have to) take on the role of "mourner in chief turned activist," which, while making their "grief legible to the broader public," also instrumentalizes it in ways that may not be personally beneficial (Hooker 2023, 187, 191). For more on Black mothers' responses to the deaths of their sons, see Carter 2019. For other powerful examples of intergenerational community activism for education justice, see Warren 2021.

51. In the cases of Tyhir, JahSun, and Bill, it was their mothers who were most visibly engaged in follow-ups with the school and their sons' peers. But this gendered imbalance may have had as much to do with societal stereotypes of less engaged Black fathers as with the men's actual level of involvement in the aftermath of their sons' murders. And, likewise, my focus on the mothers may be as much a reflection of my own biases and positional limits as anything else.

52. "School Counselors Matter" 2019; Whitaker et al. 2019.

53. The literature on trauma-informed education has grown too big to list here, but I'll offer a few examples: Craig 2017; Dutil 2019; Dutro 2019; K. Gross 2020; Rossen 2020; Wolfsdore, Wedlock, and Lo 2022; Zacarian, Alvarez-Ortiz, and Haynes 2017. The "Days After" curriculum also provides a useful approach to responding to traumatic events in the classroom (Dunn 2021). Schuurman and Mitchell's (2020) conceptualization of grief-informed practice includes, as a central tenet, the notion that "healthy adaptation to loss is fostered by personal empowerment and agency" (22).

54. Young people generally prefer to seek help from those with whom they already have established, trusted relationships (Harper, Terry, and Twiggs 2009; Lindsey and Marcell 2012).

55. As I see it, the most promising routes to reducing urban gun violence involve a combination of 1) focused violence prevention strategies that rely on local experts who understand the specificity of the community they are working within, put resources toward intervening on "hotspots" and "hot" people who are most likely to be involved in shootings, and prioritize supporting potential perpetrators toward pathways out of violence rather than into confinement (Abt 2019; Sharkey 2018); 2) both national and local poverty alleviation and racial equity-focused policies and programming (Doleac and Harvey 2022); and 3) more re-

strictive gun policies (Sharkey and Kang 2023). In relation to mass shootings, *The Violence Project* (Peterson and Densley 2021) offers a valuable starting point for prevention discussions.

Epilogue

1. Gramlich 2023.
2. Jay et al. 2023.
3. Vital City 2022.

Author's Note

1. The publication of Alice Goffman's now infamous *On the Run* (2014) offers a good example of the range of responses, debates, and critiques of scholarship on poverty and violence in Black communities—particularly when conducted by non-Black researchers. While enrolled at Ivy League universities, Goffman, a white woman from a privileged background, lived among and with her Black male participants in a low-income, racially segregated Philadelphia neighborhood while she studied their experiences contending with the criminal justice system. Some scholars and journalists critiqued her for sensationalizing the violence her participants engaged in and were surrounded by to pander to a middle-class audience, engaging in sloppy fact-checking or anonymizing practices, and confessing in the methodological appendix to what some viewed as a federal crime (see Lewis-Kraus 2016 for a good overview of the saga). Several powerful critiques from scholars of color like Robin Autry (2020), Laurence Ralph (2015b), Victor Rios (2015), and Christina Sharpe (2014) pointed to Goffman's work as an example of larger reifications of white supremacy embedded in urban ethnography.

    In addition to these important discussions of researcher racial positionality, the book's publication also prompted—or, perhaps, reignited—a debate about long-held social scientific conventions of anonymity as well as ethnographic "evidence." In recent years, the call has been mounting for figurative "ethnographic trials" that would require ethnographers to offer more proof of their claims. At the forefront of these calls for reform is legal scholar Steven Lubet (2017), who argues in his book *Interrogating Ethnography* that qualitative methodology would benefit from approaches more aligned with "fact-based" disciplines such as journalism and law, including dropping the use of pseudonyms as the default. See Jerolmack and Murphy (2019) and Reich (2015) for arguments in favor of rethinking ethnographic conventions of anonymity and Pugh and Mosseri (2020) and Reyes (2018) for convincing rebukes of this "credibility crisis" in ethnography as well as proposals for how to best protect research participants from harm.

2. Some of the most powerful of these conversations have to do with whether re-search centers damage and deficit rather than young people's desires or strengths (Howard 2013; Tuck 2009) and whether ethnographic writing relies on a "jungle book trope" that sensationalizes violence and dehumanizes research participants (Betts 2014; Paris and Winn 2013; Rios 2011). White researchers—and perhaps all researchers to some degree—are prone to under-theorizing racism as an ex-planation for observations in the field (Bonilla-Silva and Baiocchi 2008; War-ren 2000) due to the colorblindness we have been socialized into (Bonilla-Silva 2013; Frankenberg 1993). There is also a long and somewhat troubled history of white ethnographers studying the "everydayness of low income African Amer-ican people," and then sharing this "new knowledge" (and perhaps receiving praise for it) with a "distant audience" (Young 2008, 197, 196).

3. For example, Bourgois 2003; Desmond 2017; Duneier 2000; Edin and Nelson 2013; Goffman 2014; Harding 2010; Liebow 1967; Venkatesh 2008.

4. Despite this personal identification with teachers, I was often aware of feeling more on the "side" of the students (Becker 1967).

5. Bourgois 2003, 204–5.

6. Certainly, my identity as a relatively young woman played a role in my research relationships with teenage male participants who were heterosexual. Particu-larly in a school with no girls their own age, I may have seemed just old enough to be a mysterious older (but not *old*) woman who was also not their teacher. When students occasionally made comments about my appearance, I would shut down their advances as gently and playfully as possible. I did not want to mislead any student into thinking he had a chance for a different kind of relationship, but I also did not want to make him feel embarrassed in ways that might hinder a continued research relationship. Generally, rather than address the underlying question of whether I could be romantically interested, I diverted the conversa-tion to something self-deprecating about my age—how I was *so* old and lame. When I discovered that I was, in fact, the same age as one student's mother, I realized I could drop that detail humorously in opportune moments. (Both Pascoe [2011] and Fader [2013], in their ethnographic research with young men and teenage boys, describe a similar approach to rejecting sexual advances while maintaining strong research relationships.)

7. Mandell 1988; Pascoe 2011.

8. Lareau 2021, 50.

9. Hammersley and Atkinson 2007, 74.

10. Carter 2008; Mac an Ghaill 1994; Pascoe 2011; Tyson 2003.

11. Member checks are also sometimes referred to as "respondent validation" (Ravitch and Carl 2016).

12. For each participating student, there was an assent form (for minors) and a pa-

rental consent form, both of which allowed them to agree to a range of research activities, including observations, in-person and text-based interviews, social media observations, and the retrieval of school records. I also had a passive consent process for schoolwide observations: the principal sent a letter home to all families explaining my role and offering the opportunity to opt out. In total, four families returned the opt-out form.

13. My approach to interviews was guided by Josselson 2013; Lamont and Swidler 2014; Rubin 1992; Schensul and LeCompte 2013; Vaughan 1990; Weiss 1995. I also conducted follow-up interviews with several participants drawing on techniques from Hammersley and Atkinson 2007; Harding 2010; Young 2004.

14. Though I use the term "sampling bias" and considered issues of variation and representativeness in my sample, I certainly do not claim anything close to objectivity in this research. Further, as many ethnographers and qualitative researchers—and, increasingly, critical quantitative scholars—would say, objectivity is not the goal. Rather, I aim to present the complex and nuanced experiences of my participants and the larger patterns they point to, while also, as much as I can, accounting for the subjectivity of my perspective. There is a thoughtful discussion of bias, objectivity, and complexity in ethnographic research in the methodological appendix of *Human Targets* (Rios 2017).

15. I write more about the complex evolution of my research relationship with Yaja in Gross 2022.

16. Over time, I did become the de facto adult supervisor for a student-led club, Freedom to Speak, since their official advisor was often tied up in meetings. I would unlock the classroom door for them and spend the lunch period observing and participating in their conversations. This group also became a key space both for recruiting interview participants and for talking through my emerging research discoveries and questions. I write more about this group in Clonan-Roy, Gross, and Jacobs 2021.

17. My colleagues and I describe the concept of care-based research more fully in our book *Care-Based Methodologies* (Vasudevan et al. 2022).

18. Jackson 2010.

19. Laura 2013, 291.

20. Jackson 2013; Reich 2015.

21. I applied for and was issued a Certificate of Confidentiality by the NIH, which provides some protection to researchers who collect sensitive data from forced disclosure about participants in a legal proceeding. Thankfully, I never had to invoke it.

22. Though more traditional advice might be to *not* intervene in participants' lives as a researcher, several ethnographers have written about the near-impossibility,

even when desired, of actually impacting participants' trajectories in any meaningful way through interventions made during research. For instance, in their
study of college students, Armstrong and Hamilton (2013, 276) describe being
"struck by how much intervention it takes to redirect someone's fate . . . We generally could not override the powerful influences of funds, family, peer culture,
and the organizational structure of the university."

23. I was moved by a comment from Isabel Wilkerson at a public lecture in 2021.
In response to a question about how she cares for herself while researching unimaginable racial traumas, she calmly responded, according to my not-verbatim
notes, *If the people who suffered endured what they did, surely I can endure researching,*
analyzing, writing, talking about it, and we can all honor them by witnessing and listening.
I wholeheartedly agree. At the same time, I also advise researchers embarking on
emotionally taxing projects to consider how they will build self-care and support
into their long-term research plans. For me, useful practices have included ther-
apy, collegial research/writing communities, finding joy and pleasure in activities
outside my research/work, and holding myself accountable to promises I made
to my participants to make the work as meaningful and impactful as possible.

24. Other scholars have written about the role of personal grief in fieldwork (see
Behar 1996; Gillespie and Lopez 2019; Mitchell-Eaton 2019) and the political
power of grief in research contexts (see Butler 2004; Persson 2023).

25. Just as I was finalizing this manuscript, Herc made an eerie discovery that
I learned about through his Instagram post: Bill is in the background of a photograph I took, more than a year before his death, of a cafeteria Uno game between
Herc, Kaliq, Latrell, and Jonquett. His face is caught in an almost ghostly blur as
he walks past the table.

26. Sweeting and Gilhooly 1990.

27. Sharkey 2018.

28. Pew 2018.

29. Schott Foundation 2015.

30. Elijah Anderson (1999), W. E. B. Du Bois (1967), Kathryn Edin and Maria
Kefalas (2011), Jamie Fader (2013), Alice Goffman (2014), Marcus Anthony
Hunter (2013), and Nikki Jones (2009), among others.

31. I do not believe a revisit to this school would provide any more value than an
exploration of related research questions in a *similar* school, such as those written about by scholars like Blume Oeur 2018; Fergus, Noguera, and Martin 2014;
Nagarajan 2018; Nelson 2016; or Warren 2017. My perspective here emerged,
in part, from my reading of another piece of ethnographic work conducted at
the school I have called Boys' Prep about ten years before mine. While I learned
a great deal from this author's investigation and findings, it became clear that

schools—as mini cultural contexts—evolve so much within even a few years as staff change, policies evolve, and student demographics shift that a revisit would be unlikely to provide the opportunity to reconfirm or replicate earlier findings.

32. Pugh and Mosseri 2020, 18.

33. Reyes 2018, 207.

34. Ubiñas 2017. For example, Bashir, Irell, Khalil, Rajae, Rodney, Sean, and Sybrii come from this list.

35. Weiss 1995.

36. In a small community like Boys' Prep, it is likely that despite these efforts, some characters will still be internally recognizable.

37. Once I made the decision to use JahSun's, Tyhir's, and Bill's real names, their mothers and I decided that it would feel strange and disorienting not to also use their names. Additionally, Maxayn, Tanisha, and Williesha's names are easily found online in connection with their sons' deaths, so disguising them felt unnecessary to them. Bashir, however, is a pseudonym, since he was a living minor at the time of the research. Since we never know the potential long-term impacts of a work, there did not seem to be a need to expose his real identity.

38. On a practical level, it also became clear that to fully disguise the identities of these murder victims—about whom dozens of newspaper articles have been written—would require a host of alterations to the facts of their lives and deaths (e.g., dates, locations, event details), all of which might threaten the integrity of my analysis.

39. For other deceased boys represented in this text, I use pseudonyms because I was not able to discuss the decision with their families. I chose to keep Jonquett's name as a pseudonym since his appearances in this book are all from his life.

40. Jason De León (2015) made a similar decision to include the faces of the dead in photographs in his anthropological text about suffering and death at the US border. He writes that it was important to his participants that he convey "the realness" of their stories (19).

References

Abt, Thomas. 2019. *Bleeding Out: The Devastating Consequences of Urban Violence—and a Bold New Plan for Peace in the Streets.* New York: Basic Books.

Ahmed, Sara. 2021. *Complaint!* Durham, NC: Duke University Press.

Alexander, Jeffrey C., Ron Eyerman, Bernard Giesen, Neil J. Smelser, and Piotr Sztompka. 2004. *Cultural Trauma and Collective Identity.* Berkeley: University of California Press.

Allen, Chris. 2007. "The Poverty of Death: Social Class, Urban Deprivation, and the Criminological Consequences of Sequestration of Death." *Mortality* 12 (1): 79–93. https://doi.org/10.1080/13576270601088392.

Andersen, Judith Pizarro, Roxane Cohen Silver, Brandon Stewart, Billie Koperwas, and Clemens Kirschbaum. 2013. "Psychological and Physiological Responses Following Repeated Peer Death." *PLOS ONE* 8 (9): e75881. https://doi.org/10.1371/journal.pone.0075881.

Anderson, Craig A. 2001. "Heat and Violence." *Current Directions in Psychological Science* 10 (1): 33–38. https://doi.org/10.1111/1467-8721.00109.

Anderson, Elijah. 1999. *Code of the Street: Decency, Violence, and the Moral Life of the Inner City.* New York: W. W. Norton & Company.

Ansell, David A. 2017. *The Death Gap: How Inequality Kills.* Chicago: University of Chicago Press.

AP-NORC. 2017. "Instagram and Snapchat Are the Most Popular Social Networks for Teens; Black Teens Are Most Active on Social Media, Messaging Apps." University of Chicago: The Associated Press-NORC Center for Public Affairs Research.

Aries, Philippe. 1981. *The Hour of Our Death: The Classic History of Western Attitudes Toward Death over the Last One Thousand Years.* Translated by Helen Weaver. New York: Vintage Books.

Armstrong, Elizabeth A., and Laura T. Hamilton. 2013. *Paying for the Party: How College Maintains Inequality*. Cambridge, MA: Harvard University Press.

Autry, Robin. 2020. "Urban Ethnographers Do Harm in Speaking for Black Communities | Aeon Essays." *Aeon*, November 26. https://aeon.co/essays/urban-ethnographers-do-harm-in-speaking-for-black-communities.

Ayers, Rick. 2014. *An Empty Seat in Class: Teaching and Learning After the Death of a Student*. New York: Teachers College Press.

Baker, David, Dana Norris, and Veroniki Cherneva. 2021. "Disenfranchised Grief and Families' Experiences of Death After Police Contact in the United States." *OMEGA—Journal of Death and Dying* 83 (2): 239–56. https://doi.org/10.1177/00 30222819846420.

Baldwin, James. 1963. "A Talk to Teachers." *The Saturday Review*, December 21. https://www.zinnedproject.org/materials/baldwin-talk-to-teachers/.

Balk, David E., Donna Zaengle, and Charles A. Corr. 2011. "Strengthening Grief Support for Adolescents Coping with a Peer's Death." *School Psychology International* 32 (2): 144–62. https://doi.org/10.1177/0143034311400826.

Barbaro, Michael, Clare Toeniskoetter, Alexandra Leigh Young, and Lisa Tobin, dirs. 2019. "The Parkland Students, One Year Later." *The Daily* (podcast). *New York Times*. https://www.nytimes.com/2019/02/14/podcasts/the-daily/parkland-stoneman-douglas-school-shooting.html.

Barry, Ellen. 2022. "How Long Should It Take to Grieve? Psychiatry Has Come Up with an Answer." *New York Times*, March 18, sec. Health. https://www.nytimes.com/2022/03/18/health/prolonged-grief-disorder.html.

Bautista, Mark A., Melanie Bertrand, Ernest Morrell, D. Scorza, and Corey Matthews. 2013. "Participatory Action Research and City Youth: Methodological Insights from the Council of Youth Research." *Teachers College Record* 115 (10): 1–23.

Beard, Jessica H., Shelby Resnick, Zoe Maher, Mark J. Seamon, Christopher N. Morrison, Carrie A. Sims, Randi N. Smith, Lars O. Sjoholm, and Amy J. Goldberg. 2019. "Clustered Arrivals of Firearm-Injured Patients in an Urban Trauma System: A Silent Epidemic." *Journal of American College of Surgeons* 229 (3): 236–43.

Becker, Ernest. 1997. *The Denial of Death*. New York: Free Press.

Becker, Howard S. 1967. "Whose Side Are We On?" *Social Problems* 14 (3): 239–47.

Beckett, Lois, and Abené Clayton. 2022. "'An Unspoken Epidemic': Homicide Rate Increase for Black Women Rivals That of Black Men." *The Guardian*, June 25. https://www.theguardian.com/world/2022/jun/25/homicide-violence-against-black-women-us.

Beeghley, Leonard. 2003. *Homicide: A Sociological Explanation*. Lanham, MD: Rowman & Littlefield.

Behar, Ruth. 1996. *The Vulnerable Observer: Anthropology That Breaks Your Heart*. Boston: Beacon Press.

Bell, Carl C., and Esther J. Jenkins. 1993. "Community Violence and Children on Chicago's Southside." *Psychiatry* 56 (1): 46–54.

Ben-Porath, Sigal. 2013. "Deferring Virtue: The New Management of Students and the Civic Role of Schools." *Theory and Research in Education* 11 (2): 111–28. https://doi.org/10.1177/1477878513485172.

Berends, Mark. 2015. "Sociology and School Choice: What We Know After Two Decades of Charter Schools." *Annual Review of Sociology* 41 (1): 159–80. https://doi.org/10.1146/annurev-soc-073014-112340.

Berns, Nancy. 2011. *Closure: The Rush to End Grief and What It Costs Us*. Philadelphia: Temple University Press.

Betts, Dwayne. 2014. "Alice Goffman's *On the Run*: She Is Wrong about Black Urban Life." Slate. July 10. https://slate.com/news-and-politics/2014/07/alice-goffmans-on-the-run-she-is-wrong-about-black-urban-life.html.

Bindley, Kristin, Joanne Lewis, Joanne Travaglia, and Michelle DiGiacomo. 2019. "Disadvantaged and Disenfranchised in Bereavement: A Scoping Review of Social and Structural Inequity Following Expected Death." *Social Science & Medicine* 242 (December): 112599. https://doi.org/10.1016/j.socscimed.2019.112599.

Blades, Lincoln Anthony. 2018. "Black Teens Have Been Fighting for Gun Reform for Years." *Teen Vogue*, February 23. https://www.teenvogue.com/story/black-teens-have-been-fighting-for-gun-reform-for-years.

Blow, Charles M. 2014. *Fire Shut Up in My Bones*. Boston: Houghton Mifflin Harcourt.

Bluck, Susan, Judith Dirk, Michael M. MacKay, and Ashley Hux. 2008. "Life Experience with Death: Relation of Death Attitudes and to the Use of Death-Related Memories." *Death Studies* 32: 524–49.

Blume Oeur, Freeden. 2018. *Black Boys Apart: Racial Uplift and Respectability in All-Male Public Schools*. Minneapolis: University of Minnesota Press.

Bonilla-Silva, Eduardo. 2013. *Racism without Racists: Color-Blind Racism and the Persistence of Racial Inequality in America*. 4th ed. Lanham, MD: Rowman & Littlefield.

Bonilla-Silva, Eduardo, and Gianpaolo Baiocchi. 2008. "Anything but Racism: How Sociologists Limit the Significance of Racism." In *White Logic, White Methods: Racism and Methodology*, by Tukufu Zuberi and Eduardo Bonilla-Silva, 137–51. Lanham, MD: Rowman & Littlefield.

Bordere, Tashel C. 2009. "'To Look at Death Another Way': Black Teenage Males' Perspectives on Second-Lines and Regular Funerals in New Orleans." *OMEGA—Journal of Death and Dying* 58 (3): 213–32. https://doi.org/10.2190/OM.58.3.d.

———. 2020. "Suffocated Grief, Resilience and Survival among African American Families." In *Exploring Grief: Towards a Sociology of Sorrow*, ed. Michael Hviid Jacobsen and Anders Petersen, 188–204. New York: Routledge.

Borowsky, Iris W., Marjorie Ireland, and Michael D. Resnick. 2009. "Health Status and Behavioral Outcomes for Youth Who Anticipate a High Likelihood of Early Death." *Pediatrics* 124 (1): e81–88.

Bourgois, Philippe. 2003. *In Search of Respect: Selling Crack in El Barrio.* 2nd ed. Cambridge: Cambridge University Press.

Breen, L. J., and M. O'Connor. 2007. "The Fundamental Paradox in the Grief Literature: A Critical Reflection." *OMEGA—Journal of Death and Dying* 55 (3): 199–218. https://doi.org/10.2190/OM.55.3.c.

Brenoff, Ann. 2017. "Bereavement Leave Shouldn't Be A Luxury." *Huffington Post*, November 15. https://www.huffpost.com/entry/bereavement-leave_n _59e8dc5ae4b06b440e447db6?guccounter=1.

Brezina, Timothy, Erdal Tekin, and Volkan Topalli. 2008. "Might Not Be a Tomorrow: A Multi-Methods Approach to Anticipated Early Death and Youth Crime." IZA Discussion Papers No. 3831. Germany: Institute for the Study of Labor (IZA). http://hdl.handle.net/10419/35370.

Brooms, Derrick R. 2015. "'We Didn't Let the Neighborhood Win': Black Male Students' Experiences in Negotiating and Navigating an Urban Neighborhood." *Journal of Negro Education* 84 (3): 14.

Brown, Anthony L. 2011. "'Same Old Stories': The Black Male in Social Science and Educational Literature, 1930s to the Present." *Teachers College Record* 113 (9): 2047–79.

Burdick-Will, Julia. 2018. "Neighborhood Violence, Peer Effects, and Academic Achievement in Chicago." *Sociology of Education* 91 (3): 205–23. https://doi.org /10.1177/0038040718779063.

Butler, Judith. 2004. *Precarious Life: The Powers of Mourning and Violence.* London: Verso.

———. 2009. *Frames of War: When Is Life Grievable?* London: Verso.

———. 2020. "Between Grief and Grievance, A New Sense of Justice." In *Grief and Grievance: Art and Mourning in America,* ed. Okwui Enwezor, Naomi Beckwith, and Massimiliano Gioni, 11–15. New York: Phaidon Press.

Cacho, Lisa Marie. 2007. "'You Just Don't Know How Much He Meant': Deviancy, Death, and Devaluation." *Latino Studies* 5 (2): 182–208. https://doi.org/10.1057 /palgrave.lst.8600246.

Cadaret, Michael C., and Suzette L. Speight. 2018. "An Exploratory Study of Attitudes Toward Psychological Help Seeking Among African American Men." *Journal of Black Psychology* 44 (4): 347–70. https://doi.org/10.1177/009 5798418774655.

Caldwell, Roslyn M., Richard P. Wiebe, and H. Harrington Cleveland. 2006. "The Influence of Future Certainty and Contextual Factors on Delinquent Behavior and School Adjustment Among African American Adolescents." *Journal of Youth and Adolescence* 35 (4): 587–98.

Cann, Candi K. 2014. *Virtual Afterlives: Grieving the Dead in the Twenty-First Century*. Lexington: University Press of Kentucky.

Carter, Dorinda. 2008. "Achievement as Resistance: The Development of a Critical Race Achievement Ideology among Black Achievers." *Harvard Educational Review* 78 (3): 466–97.

Carter, Prudence L., and Kevin G. Welner, eds. 2013. *Closing the Opportunity Gap: What America Must Do to Give Every Child an Even Chance*. Oxford: Oxford University Press.

Carter, Rebecca Louise. 2019. *Prayers for the People: Homicide and Humanity in the Crescent City*. Chicago: University of Chicago Press.

Caudillo, Mónica L., and Florencia Torche. 2014. "Exposure to Local Homicides and Early Educational Achievement in Mexico." *Sociology of Education* 87 (2): 89–105. https://doi.org/10.1177/0038040714523795.

Cheng, Anne Anlin. 2001. *The Melancholy of Race: Psychoanalysis, Assimilation, and Hidden Grief*. New York: Oxford University Press.

Clonan-Roy, Katherine, Nora Gross, and Charlotte Jacobs. 2021. "Safe Rebellious Places: The Value of Informal Spaces in Schools to Counter the Emotional Silencing of Youth of Color." *International Journal of Qualitative Studies in Education* 34 (4): 330–52.

Coates, Ta-Nehisi. 2009. *The Beautiful Struggle: A Memoir*. Reprint ed. New York: Spiegel & Grau.

Cohen, Cathy J. 2012. *Democracy Remixed: Black Youth and the Future of American Politics*. New York: Oxford University Press.

Collins, Patricia Hill. 2000. *Black Feminist Thought: Knowledge, Consciousness, and the Politics of Empowerment*. New York: Routledge.

Collins, Randall. 2004. *Interaction Ritual Chains*. Princeton, NJ: Princeton University Press.

Colnerud, Gunnel. 2015. "Moral Stress in Teaching Practice." *Teachers and Teaching* 21 (3): 346–60. https://doi.org/10.1080/13540602.2014.953820.

Connell, Raewyn. 2000. *The Men and the Boys*. Berkeley: University of California Press.

Cookson, Peter W. Jr., and Caroline Hodges Persell. 1987. *Preparing for Power: America's Elite Boarding Schools*. New York: Basic Books.

Corr, C. A. 1999. "Enhancing the Concept of Disenfranchised Grief." *OMEGA— Journal of Death and Dying* 38 (1): 1–20. https://doi.org/10.2190/LD26-42A6 -1EAV-3MDN.

Cox, Amanda Barrett. 2016. "Correcting Behaviors and Policing Emotions: How Behavioral Infractions Become Feeling-Rule Violations: Correcting Behaviors and Policing Emotions." *Symbolic Interaction* 39 (3): 484–503. https://doi.org/10 .1002/symb.239.

Cox, Ana Marie. 2023. "We Are Not Just Polarized. We Are Traumatized." *The*

New Republic, September 14. https://newrepublic.com/article/175311/america
-polarized-traumatized-trump-violence.

Cox, John Woodrow. 2021. *Children Under Fire: An American Crisis*. New York: Ecco.

Craig, Susan E. 2017. *Trauma-Sensitive Schools for the Adolescent Years: Promoting Resiliency and Healing, Grades 6–12*. New York: Teachers College Press.

Creighton, Genevieve, John L. Oliffe, Shauna Butterwick, and Elizabeth Saewyc. 2013. "After the Death of a Friend: Young Men's Grief and Masculine Identities." *Social Science & Medicine* 84 (May): 35–43. https://doi.org/10.1016/j.socscimed.2013.02.022.

Creighton, Genevieve, John Oliffe, Jennifer Matthews, and Elizabeth Saewyc. 2016. "'Dulling the Edges': Young Men's Use of Alcohol to Deal with Grief Following the Death of a Male Friend." *Health Education & Behavior* 43 (1): 54–60. https://doi.org/10.1177/1090198115596164.

Crimp, Douglas. 1989. "Mourning and Militancy." *October* 51: 3–18. https://doi.org/10.2307/778889.

Crowder, Kyle, and Scott J. South. 2003. "Neighborhood Distress and School Dropout: The Variable Significance of Community Context." *Social Science Research* 32 (4): 659–98. https://doi.org/10.1016/S0049-089X(03)00035-8.

Cucchiara, Maia Bloomfield. 2013. *Marketing Schools, Marketing Cities: Who Wins and Who Loses When Schools Become Urban Amenities*. Chicago: University of Chicago Press.

Cullen, Dave. 2019. *Parkland: Birth of a Movement*. New York: Harper.

Currie, Elliott. 2020. *A Peculiar Indifference: The Neglected Toll of Violence on Black America*. New York: Metropolitan Books.

Dance, L. Janelle. 2002. *Tough Fronts: The Impact of Street Culture on Schooling*. New York: Routledge.

Dancy, T. Elon III. 2014. "The Adultification of Black Boys: What Educational Settings Can Learn from Trayvon Martin." In *Trayvon Martin, Race, and American Justice: Writing Wrong*, ed. Kenneth J. Fasching-Varner, Rema E. Reynolds, Katrice Albert, and Lori Latrice Martin, 49–55. Rotterdam, The Netherlands: Sense Publishers. http://dx.doi.org/10.1007/978-94-6209-842-8.

Daniels, Joél Leon. 2021. "As a Black Man in America, I Feel Death Looming Every Day." *New York Times*, December 5, sec. Opinion. https://www.nytimes.com/2021/12/05/opinion/culture/virgil-abloh-black-mortality.html.

DeGroot, Jocelyn M. 2012. "Maintaining Relational Continuity with the Deceased on Facebook." *OMEGA—Journal of Death and Dying* 65 (3): 195–212. https://doi.org/10.2190/OM.65.3.c.

De León, Jason. 2015. *The Land of Open Graves: Living and Dying on the Migrant Trail*. With photographs by Michael Wells. Oakland: University of California Press.

Desmond, Matthew. 2017. *Evicted: Poverty and Profit in the American City.* New York: Broadway Books.

Doka, Kenneth J. 1989. *Disenfranchised Grief: Recognizing Hidden Sorrow.* Lexington, MA: Lexington Books.

———. 2017. "Complicated Grief Is Complicated." *Psychology Today,* January 3. https://www.psychologytoday.com/blog/good-mourning/201701 /complicated-grief-is-complicated.

Doka, Kenneth J., and Terry L. Martin. 2010. *Grieving Beyond Gender: Understanding the Ways Men and Women Mourn.* Rev. ed. New York: Routledge.

Doleac, Jennifer, and Anna Harvey. 2022. "Stemming Violence by Investing in Civic Goods." *Vital City,* March 2. https://www.vitalcitynyc.org/articles/stemming -violence-investing-in-civic-goods.

Du Bois, W. E. B. 1967. *The Philadelphia Negro: A Social Study.* New York: Schocken Books.

Duke, Naomi N., Iris W. Borowsky, Sandra L. Pettingell, Carol L. Skay, and Barbara J. McMorris. 2011. "Adolescent Early Death Perception: Links to Behavioral and Life Outcomes in Young Adulthood." *Journal of Pediatric Health Care* 25 (4): 224–34. https://doi.org/10.1016/j.pedhc.2010.03.004.

Dumas, Michael J. 2014. "'Losing an Arm': Schooling as a Site of Black Suffering." *Race Ethnicity and Education* 17 (1): 1–29. https://doi.org/10.1080/13613324 .2013.850412.

Dumas, Michael J., and Joseph Derrick Nelson. 2016. "(Re) Imagining Black Boyhood: Toward a Critical Framework for Educational Research." *Harvard Educational Review* 86 (1): 27–47.

Duncan-Andrade, Jeffrey M. R. 2009. "Note to Educators: Hope Required When Growing Roses in Concrete." *Harvard Educational Review* 79 (2): 181–94. https:// doi.org/10.17763/haer.79.2.nu3436017730384w.

———. 2022. *Equality or Equity: Toward a Model of Community-Responsive Education.* Cambridge, MA: Harvard Education Press.

Duneier, Mitchell. 2000. *Sidewalk.* New York: Farrar, Straus & Giroux.

Dunn, Alyssa Hadley. 2021. *Teaching on Days After: Educating for Equity in the Wake of Injustice.* New York: Teachers College Press.

Dutil, Stacey. 2019. "Adolescent Traumatic and Disenfranchised Grief: Adapting an Evidence-Based Intervention for Black and Latinx Youths in Schools." *Children & Schools* 41 (3): 179–87. https://doi.org/10.1093/cs/cdz009.

Dutro, Elizabeth. 2019. *The Vulnerable Heart of Literacy: Centering Trauma as Powerful Pedagogy.* New York: Teachers College Press.

Edin, Kathryn, and Maria J. Kefalas. 2011. *Promises I Can Keep: Why Poor Women Put Motherhood Before Marriage.* Berkeley: University of California Press.

Edin, Kathryn, and Timothy J. Nelson. 2013. *Doing the Best I Can: Fatherhood in the Inner City*. Berkeley: University of California Press.

Ellis, Aimé J. 2011. *If We Must Die: From Bigger Thomas to Biggie Smalls*. Detroit: Wayne State University Press.

Ens, Carla, and John B. Bond. 2007. "Death Anxiety in Adolescents: The Contributions of Bereavement and Religiosity." OMEGA—*Journal of Death and Dying* 55 (3): 169–84.

Erikson, Erik H. 1994. *Identity and the Life Cycle*. Rev. ed. New York: W. W. Norton & Company.

Everytown for Gun Safety. 2021. "Gun Violence and COVID-19 in 2020: A Year of Colliding Crises." https://everytownresearch.org/report/gun-violence-and-covid-19-in-2020-a-year-of-colliding-crises/.

Ewing, Eve L. 2018. *Ghosts in the Schoolyard: Racism and School Closings on Chicago's South Side*. Chicago: University of Chicago Press.

Fader, Jamie J. 2013. *Falling Back: Incarceration and Transitions to Adulthood among Urban Youth*. New Brunswick, NJ: Rutgers University Press.

Fenwick, Julie. 2022. "The Rise of 'TraumaTok': When Does Sharing Trauma Online Become Unhealthy?" VICE, May 19. https://www.vice.com/en/article/k7wm9w/the-rise-of-traumatok-when-does-sharing-trauma-online-become-unhealthy.

Fergus, Edward, Pedro A. Noguera, and Margary Martin. 2014. *Schooling for Resilience: Improving the Life Trajectory of Black and Latino Boys*. Cambridge, MA: Harvard Education Press.

Ferguson, Ann Arnett. 2001. *Bad Boys: Public Schools in the Making of Black Masculinity*. Ann Arbor: University of Michigan Press.

Florian, Victor, and Mario Mikulincer. 1997. "Fear of Personal Death in Adulthood: The Impact of Early and Recent Losses." *Death Studies* 21: 1–24.

Follman, Mark, Gavin Aronsen, and Deanna Pan. 2023. "US Mass Shootings, 1982–2023: Data from Mother Jones' Investigation." *Mother Jones* (blog), August 27. https://www.motherjones.com/politics/2012/12/mass-shootings-mother-jones-full-data/.

Fowlkes, Martha R. 1990. "The Social Regulation of Grief." *Sociological Forum* 5 (4): 635–52.

Frankenberg, Ruth. 1993. *White Women, Race Matters: The Social Construction of Whiteness*. Minneapolis: University of Minnesota Press.

Freire, Paulo. 2000. *Pedagogy of the Oppressed*. 30th anniversary ed. New York: Continuum.

Gershenson, Seth, and Erdal Tekin. 2015. "The Effect of Community Traumatic Events on Student Achievement: Evidence from the Beltway Sniper Attacks." National Bureau of Economic Research. http://www.nber.org/papers/w21055.

Gillespie, Kathryn, and Patricia J. Lopez, eds. 2019. *Vulnerable Witness: The Politics of Grief in the Field.* Oakland: University of California Press.

Gilmore, Perry. 1985. "'Gimme Room': School Resistance, Attitude, and Access to Literacy." *Journal of Education* 167 (1): 111–28.

Ginwright, Shawn. 2007. "Black Youth Activism and the Role of Critical Social Capital in Black Community Organizations." *American Behavioral Scientist* 51 (3): 403–18. https://doi.org/10.1177/0002764207306068.

———. 2016. *Hope and Healing in Urban Education: How Urban Activists and Teachers Are Reclaiming Matters of the Heart.* New York: Routledge.

Glass, Ira, dir. 2013. "Harper High School, Part One." Podcast. *This American Life.* Chicago: WBEZ. https://www.thisamericanlife.org/radio-archives/episode/487/harper-high-school-part-one.

Goff, Phillip Atiba, Matthew Christian Jackson, Brooke Allison Lewis Di Leone, Carmen Marie Culotta, and Natalie Ann DiTomasso. 2014. "The Essence of Innocence: Consequences of Dehumanizing Black Children." *Journal of Personality and Social Psychology* 106 (4): 526–45.

Goffman, Alice. 2014. *On the Run: Fugitive Life in an American City.* Chicago: University of Chicago Press.

Golann, Joanne W. 2015. "The Paradox of Success at a No-Excuses School." *Sociology of Education* 88 (2): 103–19. https://doi.org/10.1177/0038040714567866.

———. 2021. *Scripting the Moves: Culture and Control in a "No-Excuses" Charter School.* Princeton, NJ: Princeton University Press.

Golann, Joanne W., and A. Chris Torres. 2018. "Do No-Excuses Disciplinary Practices Promote Success?" *Journal of Urban Affairs*, February, 1–17. https://doi.org/10.1080/07352166.2018.1427506.

Goldstick, Jason E., Rebecca M. Cunningham, and Patrick M. Carter. 2022. "Current Causes of Death in Children and Adolescents in the United States." *New England Journal of Medicine* 386 (20): 1955–56. https://doi.org/10.1056/NEJMc2201761.

González, X. 2023. "The Education of X González." *The Cut*, January 3. https://www.thecut.com/article/x-gonzalez-parkland-shooting-activist-essay.html.

Goodman, Steven. 2018. *It's Not About Grit: Trauma, Inequity, and the Power of Transformative Teaching.* New York: Teachers College Press.

Goodrum, Sarah. 2008. "When the Management of Grief Becomes Everyday Life: The Aftermath of Murder." *Symbolic Interaction* 31 (4): 422–42. https://doi.org/10.1525/si.2008.31.4.422.

Goyal, Monika K., Nathan Kuppermann, Sean D. Cleary, Stephen J. Teach, and James M. Chamberlain. 2015. "Racial Disparities in Pain Management of Children with Appendicitis in Emergency Departments." *JAMA Pediatrics* 169 (11): 996–1002.

Graham, Bob, and Randi Weingarten. 2018. "The Power of Active Citizenship:

A Renewed Focus on Teaching Civics Education." *American Educator: A Journal of Educational Equity, Research, and Ideas* 42 (2): 4–7.

Gramlich, John. 2023. "What the Data Says about Gun Deaths in the U.S." *Pew Research Center* (blog), April 26. https://www.pewresearch.org/short-reads/2023/04/26/what-the-data-says-about-gun-deaths-in-the-u-s/.

Granek, Leeat, and Tal Peleg-Sagy. 2017. "The Use of Pathological Grief Outcomes in Bereavement Studies on African Americans." *Transcultural Psychiatry* 54 (3): 384–99. https://doi.org/10.1177/1363461517708121.

Grinage, Justin. 2019. "Endless Mourning: Racial Melancholia, Black Grief, and the Transformative Possibilities for Racial Justice in Education." *Harvard Educational Review* 89 (2): 227–50. https://doi.org/10.17763/1943-5045-89.2.227.

Gross, Karen. 2020. *Trauma Doesn't Stop at the School Door: Strategies and Solutions for Educators, PreK–College.* New York: Teachers College Press.

Gross, Nora. 2017. "#IfTheyGunnedMeDown: The Double Consciousness of Black Youth in Response to Oppressive Media." *Souls* 19 (4): 416–37. https://doi.org/10.1080/10999949.2018.1441587.

———. 2022. "A 'Friend' or an 'Experiment'? The Paradox of Ethnographic Relationships with Youth." In *Care-Based Methodologies: Reimagining Qualitative Research with Youth in US Schools*, ed. Veena Vasudevan, Nora Gross, Pavithra Nagarajan, and Katherine Clonan-Roy, 133–46. London: Bloomsbury Academic.

———. 2023. "#LongLiveDaGuys: Online Grief, Solidarity, and Emotional Freedom for Black Teenage Boys after the Gun Deaths of Friends." *Journal of Contemporary Ethnography* 52 (2): 261–89. https://doi.org/10.1177/08912416221105869.

Gross, Nora, and Cassandra Lo. 2018. "Relational Teaching and Learning after Loss: Evidence from Black Adolescent Male Students and Their Teachers." *School Psychology Quarterly* 33 (3): 381–89. https://doi.org/10.1037/spq0000285.

Grundy, Saida. 2022. *Respectable: Politics and Paradox in Making the Morehouse Man.* Oakland: University of California Press.

Gurney, Kyra. 2018. "Last Fall, They Debated Gun Control in Class. Now, They Debate Lawmakers on TV." *Miami Herald*, February 23. https://www.miamiherald.com/news/local/education/article201678544.html.

Guthery, Sarah, and Lauren P. Bailes. 2022. "Patterns of Teacher Attrition by Preparation Pathway and Initial School Type." *Educational Policy* 36 (2): 223–46. https://doi.org/10.1177/0895904819874754.

Haga, Kazu. 2011. "Chicago's Peace Warriors." *Rethinking Schools* 26 (2). https://www.rethinkingschools.org/articles/chicagos-peace-warriors.

Hall, Ronald E., and Jesenia M. Pizarro. 2010. "Cool Pose: Black Male Homicide and the Social Implications of Manhood." *Journal of Social Service Research* 37 (1): 86–98. https://doi.org/10.1080/01488376.2011.524530.

Hammersley, Martyn, and Paul Atkinson. 2007. *Ethnography: Principles in Practice*. 3rd ed. London: Routledge.

Harding, David J. 2009. "Collateral Consequences of Violence in Disadvantaged Neighborhoods." *Social Forces* 88 (2): 757–84.

———. 2010. *Living the Drama: Community, Conflict, and Culture among Inner-City Boys*. Chicago: University of Chicago Press.

Harper, Frederick D., Linda M. Terry, and Rashida Twiggs. 2009. "Counseling Strategies with Black Boys and Black Men: Implications for Policy." *Journal of Negro Education* 78 (3): 216–32.

Harris, Darcy. 2010. "Oppression of the Bereaved: A Critical Analysis of Grief in Western Society." *OMEGA—Journal of Death and Dying* 60 (3): 241–53. https://doi.org/10.2190/OM.60.3.c.

Hartman, Saidiya. 2008. *Lose Your Mother: A Journey Along the Atlantic Slave Route*. New York: Farrar, Straus & Giroux.

Harvey, Peter Francis. 2022. "'Make Sure You Look Someone in the Eye': Socialization and Classed Comportment in Two Elementary Schools." *American Journal of Sociology* 127 (5): 1417–59. https://doi.org/10.1086/719406.

Haynie, Dana L., Brian Soller, and Kristi Williams. 2014. "Anticipating Early Fatality: Friends', Schoolmates' and Individual Perceptions of Fatality on Adolescent Risk Behaviors." *Journal of Youth and Adolescence* 43 (2): 175–92.

Hellawell, Beate. 2015. "Ethical Accountability and Routine Moral Stress in Special Educational Needs Professionals." *Management in Education* 29 (3): 119–24. https://doi.org/10.1177/0892020615584106.

Hemenway, David, and Eliot Nelson. 2020. "The Scope of the Problem: Gun Violence in the USA." *Current Trauma Reports* 6 (1): 29–35. https://doi.org/10.1007/s40719-020-00182-x.

Hirschberger, Gilad. 2018. "Collective Trauma and the Social Construction of Meaning." *Frontiers in Psychology* 9: 1–14.

Hochschild, Arlie Russell. 1979. "Emotion Work, Feeling Rules, and Social Structure." *American Journal of Sociology* 85 (3): 551–75.

———. 2002. *The Managed Heart: Commercialization of Human Feeling*. 2nd ed. Berkeley: University of California Press.

Holloway, Karla F. C. 2003. *Passed On: African American Mourning Stories: A Memorial*. Durham, NC: Duke University Press.

Hooker, Juliet. 2023. *Black Grief/White Grievance: The Politics of Loss*. Princeton, NJ: Princeton University Press.

hooks, bell. 1994. *Teaching to Transgress: Education as the Practice of Freedom*. New York: Routledge.

———. 2003. *We Real Cool: Black Men and Masculinity*. New York: Routledge.

Howard, Tyrone C. 2013. "How Does It Feel to Be a Problem? Black Male Students,

Schools, and Learning in Enhancing the Knowledge Base to Disrupt Deficit Frameworks." *Review of Research in Education* 37: 54–86.

———. 2014. *Black Male(d): Peril and Promise in the Education of African American Males.* New York: Teachers College Press.

Howe, Adrian. 1987. "Social Injury Revisited: Towards a Feminist Theory of Social Justice." *International Journal of the Sociology of Law* 15 (4): 423–38.

Hunter, Marcus Anthony. 2013. *Black Citymakers: How The Philadelphia Negro Changed Urban America.* Oxford: Oxford University Press.

Irvine, Martha. 2018. "Peace Warriors—Gen Z's ode to SNCC." *Chicago Sun Times,* May 16. https://chicago.suntimes.com/2018/5/16/18348340/peace-warriors -gen-z-s-ode-to-sncc.

Islam, Frank, and Ed Crego. 2018. "Why Are Parkland Students So Articulate? Because They Were Taught Civics in Middle School." *Washington Monthly*, March 5. https://washingtonmonthly.com/2018/03/05/the-civic-education-program -that-trained-the-parkland-student-activists/.

Jackman, Mary R. 2002. "Violence in Social Life." *Annual Review of Sociology* 28 (1): 387–415. https://doi.org/10.1146/annurev.soc.28.110601.140936.

Jackson, Brandon A. 2018. "Beyond the Cool Pose: Black Men and Emotion Management Strategies." *Sociology Compass* 12 (4): e12569. https://doi.org/10.1111 /soc4.12569.

Jackson, Brandon A., and Adia Harvey Wingfield. 2013. "Getting Angry to Get Ahead: Black College Men, Emotional Performance, and Encouraging Respectable Masculinity: Getting Angry to Get Ahead." *Symbolic Interaction* 36 (3): 275–92. https://doi.org/10.1002/symb.63.

Jackson, John L. Jr. 2010. "On Ethnographic Sincerity." *Current Anthropology* 51 (S2): S279–87. https://doi.org/10.1086/653129.

———. 2013. *Thin Description: Ethnography and the African Hebrew Israelites of Jerusalem.* Cambridge, MA: Harvard University Press.

Jacoby, Sara F., John A. Rich, Jessica L. Webster, and Therese S. Richmond. 2018. "'Sharing Things with People That I Don't Even Know': Help-Seeking for Psychological Symptoms in Injured Black Men in Philadelphia." *Ethnicity & Health* (April): 1–19. https://doi.org/10.1080/13557858.2018.1455811.

Jakoby, Nina R. 2012. "Grief as a Social Emotion: Theoretical Perspectives." *Death Studies* 36 (8): 679–711. https://doi.org/10.1080/07481187.2011.584013.

Jameton, Andrew. 1984. *Nursing Practice: The Ethical Issues.* Englewood Cliffs, NJ: Prentice-Hall.

Jamieson, Amber. 2019. "March for Our Lives Knows They Got One Big Thing Wrong. As They Head into 2020, They're Fixing It." *BuzzFeed News*, August 6, sec. USNews. https://www.buzzfeednews.com/article/amberjamieson/march -for-our-lives-parkland-mfol-diversity-gun-violence.

Jamieson, Patrick E., and Dan Romer. 2008. "Unrealistic Fatalism in U.S. Youth Ages 14 to 22: Prevalence and Characteristics." *Journal of Adolescent Health* 42 (2): 154–60. https://doi.org/10.1016/j.jadohealth.2007.07.010.

Jay, Jonathan, Rachel Martin, Manish Patel, Kristal Xie, Faizah Shareef, and Jessica T. Simes. 2023. "Analyzing Child Firearm Assault Injuries by Race and Ethnicity During the COVID-19 Pandemic in 4 Major US Cities." *JAMA Network Open* 6 (3): e233125. https://doi.org/10.1001/jamanetworkopen.2023.3125.

Jerolmack, Colin, and Alexandra K. Murphy. 2019. "The Ethical Dilemmas and Social Scientific Trade-Offs of Masking in Ethnography." *Sociological Methods & Research* 48 (4): 801–27. https://doi.org/10.1177/0049124117701483.

Jimerson, Lanette. 2014. "The Literacy of Loss: Youth Creation of RIP T-Shirts." In *An Empty Seat in Class: Teaching and Learning After the Death of a Student*, by Rick Ayers, 23–25. New York: Teachers College Press.

Johnson, Celeste M. 2010. "When African American Teen Girls' Friends Are Murdered: A Qualitative Study of Bereavement, Coping, and Psychosocial Consequences." *Families in Society: The Journal of Contemporary Social Services* 91 (4): 364–70.

Jones, Nikki. 2009. *Between Good and Ghetto: African American Girls and Inner-City Violence*. New Brunswick, NJ: Rutgers University Press.

———. 2018. *The Chosen Ones: Black Men and the Politics of Redemption*. Oakland: University of California Press.

Josselson, Ruthellen. 2013. *Interviewing for Qualitative Inquiry: A Relational Approach*. New York: Guilford Press.

Kang, Miliann. 2003. "The Managed Hand: The Commercialization of Bodies and Emotions in Korean Immigrant–Owned Nail Salons." *Gender & Society* 17 (6): 820–39. https://doi.org/10.1177/0891243203257632.

Kao, Grace. 2000. "Group Images and Possible Selves among Adolescents: Linking Stereotypes to Expectations by Race and Ethnicity." *Sociological Forum* 15: 407–30. http://link.springer.com/article/10.1023/A:1007572209544.

Kenney, J. Scott. 2003. "Gender Roles and Grief Cycles: Observations on Models of Grief and Coping in Homicide Cases." *International Review of Victimology* 10 (1): 19–47.

Kersting, Anette, Elmar Brähler, Heide Glaesmer, and Birgit Wagner. 2011. "Prevalence of Complicated Grief in a Representative Population-Based Sample." *Journal of Affective Disorders* 131 (1–3): 339–43. https://doi.org/10.1016/j.jad.2010.11.032.

Kimmel, Michael. 2009. *Guyland: The Perilous World Where Boys Become Men*. Reprint ed. New York: Harper Perennial.

Klass, Dennis. 2013. "Sorrow and Solace: Neglected Areas in Bereavement Research." *Death Studies* 37 (7): 597–616.

Klass, Dennis, and Edith Maria Steffen, eds. 2017. *Continuing Bonds in Bereavement.* New York: Routledge.

Knopov, Anita, Michael Siegel, and Molly Pahn. 2017. "Gun Violence in the US Kills More Black People and Urban Dwellers." *The Conversation*, November 8. http://theconversation.com/gun-violence-in-the-us-kills-more-black-people-and-urban-dwellers-86825.

Kotlowitz, Alex. 2020. *An American Summer: Love and Death in Chicago.* New York: Anchor.

Krivo, Lauren J., María B. Vélez, Christopher J. Lyons, Jason B. Phillips, and Elizabeth Sabbath. 2018. "Race, Crime, and the Changing Fortunes of Urban Neighborhoods, 1999–2013." *Du Bois Review: Social Science Research on Race* 15 (1): 47–68. https://doi.org/10.1017/S1742058X18000103.

Kübler-Ross, Elisabeth. 1969. *On Death and Dying: What the Dying Have to Teach Doctors, Nurses, Clergy and Their Own Families.* New York: Scribner.

Kübler-Ross, Elisabeth, and David Kessler. 2014. *On Grief and Grieving: Finding the Meaning of Grief Through the Five Stages of Loss.* New York: Simon and Schuster.

Kubrin, Charis E. 2005. "'I See Death around the Corner': Nihilism in Rap Music." *Sociological Perspectives* 48 (4): 433–59.

Labaree, David F. 1997. "Public Goods, Private Goods: The American Struggle over Educational Goals." *American Educational Research Journal* 34 (1): 39–81.

Ladson-Billings, Gloria. 1995. "Toward a Theory of Culturally Relevant Pedagogy." *American Educational Research Journal* 32 (3): 465–91. https://doi.org/10.2307/1163320.

———. 2006. "From the Achievement Gap to the Education Debt: Understanding Achievement in U.S. Schools." *Educational Researcher* 35 (7): 3–12. https://doi.org/10.3102/0013189X035007003.

Lamont, Michèle, and Ann Swidler. 2014. "Methodological Pluralism and the Possibilities and Limits of Interviewing." *Qualitative Sociology* 37 (2): 153–71.

Lareau, Annette. 2021. *Listening to People: A Practical Guide to Interviewing, Participant Observation, Data Analysis, and Writing It All Up.* Chicago: University of Chicago Press.

Lauer, Claudia. 2021. "Grief Counselors in Short Supply with Gun Violence Rising." *AP NEWS*, July 12, sec. COVID-19. https://apnews.com/article/health-government-and-politics-shootings-violence-coronavirus-pandemic-bab192f9358aecd055c39971a60ab72c.

Laura, Crystal T. 2013. "Intimate Inquiry: Love as 'Data' in Qualitative Research." *Cultural Studies ↔ Critical Methodologies* 13 (4): 289–92.

Lawson, Erica. 2014. "Disenfranchised Grief and Social Inequality: Bereaved African Canadians and Oppositional Narratives about the Violent Deaths of Friends

and Family Members." *Ethnic and Racial Studies* 37 (11): 2092–109. https://doi
.org/10.1080/01419870.2013.800569.

Learn and Serve America. 2020. "National Service-Learning Clearinghouse."
https://community-wealth.org/content/national-service-learning-clearing
house.

Lee, Jooyoung. 2012. "Wounded: Life after the Shooting." *The ANNALS of the American Academy of Political and Social Science* 642 (1): 244–57. https://doi.org/10.1177
/0002716212438208.

Leonard, David J. 2017. "Illegible Black Death, Legible White Pain: Denied Media,
Mourning, and Mobilization in an Era of 'Post-Racial' Gun Violence—David J.
Leonard, 2017." *Cultural Studies ↔ Critical Methodologies* 17 (2): 101–9.

Lewis, Amanda E., and John B. Diamond. 2015. *Despite the Best Intentions: How Racial
Inequality Thrives in Good Schools*. New York: Oxford University Press.

Lewis-Kraus, Gideon. 2016. "The Trials of Alice Goffman." *New York Times*, January
12, sec. Magazine. https://www.nytimes.com/2016/01/17/magazine/the-trials
-of-alice-goffman.html.

Liebow, Elliott. 1967. *Tally's Corner: A Study of Negro Streetcorner Men*. Lanham, MD:
Rowman & Littlefield.

Lindsay, Keisha. 2018. *In a Classroom of Their Own: The Intersection of Race and Feminist
Politics in All-Male Black Schools*. Urbana: University of Illinois Press.

Lindsey, Michael A., and Arik V. Marcell. 2012. "'We're Going Through a Lot of
Struggles That People Don't Even Know About': The Need to Understand
African American Males' Help-Seeking for Mental Health on Multiple Levels."
American Journal of Men's Health 6 (5): 354–64. https://doi.org/10.1177/15579883
12441520.

Lingel, Jessa. 2013. "The Digital Remains: Social Media and Practices of Online
Grief." *The Information Society* 29 (3): 190–95. https://doi.org/10.1080/019722
43.2013.777311.

Lofland, Lyn H. 1985. "The Social Shaping of Emotion: The Case of Grief." *Symbolic
Interaction* 8 (2): 171–90.

Lohmon, Jonathan. 2006. "A Memorial Wall in Philadelphia." In *Spontaneous Shrines
and the Public Memorialization of Death*, ed. Jack Santino, 177–214. New York: Pal-
grave Macmillan.

Love, Bettina. 2019. *We Want to Do More Than Survive: Abolitionist Teaching and the
Pursuit of Educational Freedom*. Boston: Beacon Press.

Lubet, Steven. 2017. *Interrogating Ethnography: Why Evidence Matters*. Oxford: Oxford
University Press.

Lubrano, Alfred. 2018. "New Census Figures on Philly Neighborhoods Show
Inequality, High Numbers of Whites Living in Poverty." *WHYY-PBS*, De-

cember 6. https://whyy.org/articles/new-census-figures-on-philly
-neighborhoods-show-inequality-high-numbers-of-whites-living-in-poverty/.

Lützén, Kim, Agneta Cronqvist, Annabella Magnusson, and Lars Andersson. 2003.
"Moral Stress: Synthesis of a Concept." *Nursing Ethics* 10 (3): 312–22. https://doi
.org/10.1191/0969733003ne6080a.

Mac an Ghaill, Mairtin. 1994. *Making of Men: Masculinities, Sexualities and Schooling.*
Buckingham: Open University Press.

Majors, Richard, and Janet Mancini Billson. 1992. *Cool Pose: The Dilemmas of Black
Manhood in America.* New York: Touchstone.

Mandell, Nancy. 1988. "The Least-Adult Role in Studying Children." *Journal of Contemporary Ethnography* 16 (4): 433–67.

Martin, Daniel D. 2005. "Acute Loss and the Social Construction of Blame." *Illness,
Crisis, & Loss* 13 (2): 149–67.

———. 2010. "Identity Management of the Dead: Contests in the Construction of
Murdered Children." *Symbolic Interaction* 33 (1): 18–40.

———. 2013. *The Politics of Sorrow: Families, Victims, and the Micro-Organization of
Youth Homicide.* Burlington, VT: Routledge.

McMurdock, Marianna. 2023. "What One NYC Educator's Grief Reveals About
Teachers' Mental Health Struggles." February 4. https://www.the74million
.org/article/what-one-educators-grief-reveals-about-the-mental-health
-challenges-facing-teachers-now/.

McWilliams, Julia A. 2019. *Compete or Close: Traditional Neighborhood Schools Under
Pressure.* Cambridge, MA: Harvard Education Press.

Mejia, Mercedes, dir. 2022. "Oxford, One Year Later: The Student Activists." *Michigan Radio.* NPR. https://www.michiganradio.org/show/stateside/2022-11-28
/oxford-aubrey-greenfield-zoe-touray.

Mitchell, Lisa M., Peter H. Stephenson, Susan Cadell, and Mary Ellen Macdonald.
2012. "Death and Grief On-Line: Virtual Memorialization and Changing Concepts of Childhood Death and Parental Bereavement on the Internet." *Health
Sociology Review* 21 (4): 413–31.

Mitchell-Eaton, Emily. 2019. "Grief as Method: Topographies of Grief, Care, and
Fieldwork from Northwest Arkansas to New York and the Marshall Islands."
Gender, Place & Culture 26 (March): 1–21. https://doi.org/10.1080/0966369X
.2018.1553865.

Morris, Edward W. 2005. "'Tuck in That Shirt!' Race, Class, Gender, and Discipline
in an Urban School." *Sociological Perspectives* 48 (1): 25–48. https://doi.org/10
.1525/sop.2005.48.1.25.

Morris, Monique. 2018. *Pushout: The Criminalization of Black Girls in Schools.* New York:
The New Press.

Nagarajan, Pavithra. 2018. "Chutes, Not Ladders: The Control and Confinement of Boys of Color through School Discipline." *Boyhood Studies* 11 (2): 114–30.

Najarro, Ileana. 2022. "Revamped Florida Civics Education Aims for 'Patriotism.' Will It Catch on Elsewhere?" *Education Week*, July 12, sec. Social Studies. https://www.edweek.org/teaching-learning/revamped-florida-civics-education-aims-for-patriotism-will-it-catch-on-elsewhere/2022/07.

Nass, Daniel. 2018. "Parkland Generated Dramatically More News Coverage Than Most Mass Shootings." *The Trace*, May 17, sec. Data. https://www.thetrace.org/2018/05/parkland-media-coverage-analysis-mass-shooting/.

Neimeyer, Robert A., Scott A. Baldwin, and James Gillies. 2006. "Continuing Bonds and Reconstructing Meaning: Mitigating Complications in Bereavement." *Death Studies* 30 (8): 715–38. https://doi.org/10.1080/07481180600848322.

Nelson, Joseph D. 2016. "Relational Teaching with Black Boys: Strategies for Learning at a Single-Sex Middle School for Boys of Color." *Teachers College Record* 118 (6): 130.

Newson, Rachel S., Paul A. Boelen, Karin Hek, Albert Hofman, and Henning Tiemeier. 2011. "The Prevalence and Characteristics of Complicated Grief in Older Adults." *Journal of Affective Disorders* 132 (1–2): 231–38.

Nguyen, Quynh C., Jon M. Hussey, Carolyn T. Halpern, Andres Villaveces, Stephen W. Marshall, Arjumand Siddiqi, and Charles Poole. 2012. "Adolescent Expectations of Early Death Predict Young Adult Socioeconomic Status." *Social Science & Medicine* 74 (9): 1452–60.

Nichols-Barrer, Ira, Philip Gleason, Brian Gill, and Christina Clark Tuttle. 2016. "Student Selection, Attrition, and Replacement in KIPP Middle Schools." *Educational Evaluation and Policy Analysis* 38 (1): 5–20. https://doi.org/10.3102/0162373714564215.

Noguera, Pedro A. 2009. *The Trouble With Black Boys . . . And Other Reflections on Race, Equity, and the Future of Public Education*. San Francisco: Jossey-Bass.

NYLC. 2020. "National Youth Leadership Council." https://www.nylc.org/.

Oeur, Freeden. 2017. "The Respectable Brotherhood: Young Black Men in an All-Boys Charter High School." *Sociological Perspectives* 60 (6): 1063–81.

Oosterhoff, Benjamin, Julie B. Kaplow, and Christopher M. Layne. 2018. "Links between Bereavement Due to Sudden Death and Academic Functioning: Results from a Nationally Representative Sample of Adolescents." *School Psychology Quarterly* 33 (3): 372–80. https://doi.org/10.1037/spq0000254.

Osafo, Joseph, Heidi Hjelmeland, Charity Sylvia Akotia, and Birthe Loa Knizek. 2011. "Social Injury: An Interpretative Phenomenological Analysis of the Attitudes towards Suicide of Lay Persons in Ghana." *International Journal of Qualitative Studies on Health and Well-Being* 6: 1–10. https://doi.org/10.3402/qhw.v6i4.8708.

Oyserman, Daphna, Deborah Bybee, and Kathy Terry. 2006. "Possible Selves and Academic Outcomes: How and When Possible Selves Impel Action." *Journal of Personality and Social Psychology* 91 (1): 188–204. https://doi.org/10.1037/0022 -3514.91.1.188.

Pabon, Amber Jean-Marie, and Vincent Basile. 2022. "It Don't Affect Them Like It Affects Us: Disenfranchised Grief of Black Boys in the Wake of Peer Homicide." *The Urban Review* 54 (1): 67–82. https://doi.org/10.1007/s11256-021-00605-2.

Pandell, Lexi. 2022. "How Trauma Became the Word of the Decade." *Vox*, January 17. https://www.vox.com/the-highlight/22876522/trauma-covid-word -origin-mental-health.

Paris, Django, and Maisha T. Winn, eds. 2013. *Humanizing Research: Decolonizing Qualitative Inquiry With Youth and Communities.* Thousand Oaks, CA: SAGE Publications.

Pascoe, C. J. 2011. *Dude, You're a Fag: Masculinity and Sexuality in High School.* 2nd ed. Berkeley: University of California Press.

Patton, Desmond U., Jamie MacBeth, Sarita Schoenebeck, Katherine Shear, and Kathleen McKeown. 2018. "Accommodating Grief on Twitter: An Analysis of Expressions of Grief Among Gang Involved Youth on Twitter Using Qualitative Analysis and Natural Language Processing." *Biomedical Informatics Insights* 10 (January): 1–9. https://doi.org/10.1177/1178222618763155.

Patton, Desmond U., Ninive Sanchez, Dale Fitch, Jamie Macbeth, and Patrick Leonard. 2017. "I Know God's Got a Day 4 Me: Violence, Trauma, and Coping Among Gang-Involved Twitter Users." *Social Science Computer Review* 35 (2): 226–43. https://doi.org/10.1177/0894439315613319.

Pearce, Jessica S. 2017. "Lafayette Strong: A Content Analysis of Grief and Support Online Following a Theater Shooting." *Illness, Crisis & Loss* (November): 105413731774223. https://doi.org/10.1177/1054137317742234.

Peña, Mauricio. 2022. "A Chicago School Confronts a Wave of Grief after Losing 2 Students to Gun Violence." *Chalkbeat Chicago*, September 7. https://chicago .chalkbeat.org/2022/9/7/23339990/simeon-career-academy-chicago-public -schools-shootings-gun-violence-trauma-help.

Pennington, Natalie. 2013. "You Don't De-Friend the Dead: An Analysis of Grief Communication by College Students Through Facebook Profiles." *Death Studies* 37 (7): 617–35. https://doi.org/10.1080/07481187.2012.673536.

Persson, Asha. 2023. "Heart Cracked Open: From Personal Loss to Radical Mourning." *Mortality* 28 (1): 189–203. https://doi.org/10.1080/13576275.2021 .1918075.

Peterson, Jillian, and James Densley. 2021. *The Violence Project: How to Stop a Mass Shooting Epidemic.* New York: Harry N. Abrams.

Pew. 2018. "Philadelphia 2018: The State of the City." Pew Charitable Trusts, April. https://pew.org/2q4Uf8c.

Philadelphia Department of Public Health and Mayor's Office of Public Engagement. 2019. "Brotherly Love: Health of Black Men and Boys in Philadelphia." City of Philadelphia. https://www.phila.gov/media/20190314105459/Brotherly-Love_Health-Of-Black-Men-And-Boys_3_19.pdf.

Piazza-Bonin, Elizabeth, Robert A. Neimeyer, Laurie A. Burke, Meghan E. McDevitt-Murphy, and Amanda Young. 2015. "Disenfranchised Grief Following African American Homicide Loss: An Inductive Case Study." *OMEGA—Journal of Death and Dying* 70 (4): 404–27.

The Posse Foundation. 2018. "Scholar Speaks at D.C. March, Joins Parkland Calls for Peace." *The Posse Foundation* (blog), Spring. https://www.possefoundation.org/news-and-events/scholar-speaks-at-d-c-march-joins-parkland-calls-for-peace.

Pugh, Allison J., and Sarah Mosseri. 2020. "Trust-Building versus 'Just Trust Me': Reliability and Resonance in Ethnography." Unpublished manuscript.

Rajan, Sonali, Charles C. Branas, Dawn Myers, and Nina Agrawal. 2019. "Youth Exposure to Violence Involving a Gun: Evidence for Adverse Childhood Experience Classification." *Journal of Behavioral Medicine* 42 (4): 646–57. https://doi.org/10.1007/s10865-019-00053-0.

Ralph, Laurence. 2014. *Renegade Dreams: Living through Injury in Gangland Chicago.* Chicago: University of Chicago Press.

———. 2015a. "Becoming Aggrieved: An Alternative Framework of Care in Black Chicago." *RSF: The Russell Sage Foundation Journal of the Social Sciences* 1 (2): 31–41.

———. 2015b. "The Limitations of a 'Dirty' World." *Du Bois Review: Social Science Research on Race* 12 (02): 441–51. https://doi.org/10.1017/S1742058X1500 020X.

Rankine, Claudia. 2015. "The Condition of Black Life Is One of Mourning." *New York Times Magazine*, June 22, sec. Magazine. https://www.nytimes.com/2015/06/22/magazine/the-condition-of-black-life-is-one-of-mourning.html.

Ravitch, Sharon M., and Nicole C. Mittenfelner Carl. 2016. *Qualitative Research: Bridging the Conceptual, Theoretical, and Methodological.* Los Angeles: SAGE Publications.

Reich, Jennifer A. 2015. "Old Methods and New Technologies: Social Media and Shifts in Power in Qualitative Research." *Ethnography* 16 (4): 394–415. https://doi.org/10.1177/1466138114552949.

Reichert, Michael, Joseph Nelson, Janet Heed, Roland Yang, and Wyatt Benson. 2012. "'A Place to Be Myself': The Critical Role of Schools in Boys' Emotional Development." *Thymos Journal of Boyhood Studies* 6 (1): 55–75.

Reyes, Victoria. 2018. "Three Models of Transparency in Ethnographic Research:

Naming Places, Naming People, and Sharing Data." *Ethnography* 19 (2): 204–26. https://doi.org/10.1177/1466138117733754.

Rich, John A. 2011. *Wrong Place, Wrong Time: Trauma and Violence in the Lives of Young Black Men*. Baltimore: Johns Hopkins University Press.

Rich, John A., and Courtney M. Grey. 2005. "Pathways to Recurrent Trauma Among Young Black Men: Traumatic Stress, Substance Use, and the 'Code of the Street.'" *American Journal of Public Health* 95 (5): 816–24. https://doi.org/10.2105/AJPH.2004.044560.

Richardson, Joseph B., Christopher St. Vil, Tanya Sharpe, Michael Wagner, and Carnell Cooper. 2016. "Risk Factors for Recurrent Violent Injury among Black Men." *Journal of Surgical Research* 204 (1): 261–66. https://doi.org/10.1016/j.jss.2016.04.027.

Rios, Victor M. 2011. *Punished: Policing the Lives of Black and Latino Boys*. New York: New York University Press.

———. 2015. "Decolonizing the White Space in Urban Ethnography: Decolonizing the White Space in Urban Ethnography." *City & Community* 14 (3): 258–61. https://doi.org/10.1111/cico.12122.

———. 2017. *Human Targets: Schools, Police, and the Criminalization of Latino Youth*. Chicago: University of Chicago Press.

Ris, Ethan W. 2015. "Grit: A Short History of a Useful Concept." *Journal of Educational Controversy* 10 (1): 1–18.

Robson, P., and T. Walter. 2013. "Hierarchies of Loss: A Critique of Disenfranchised Grief." *OMEGA—Journal of Death and Dying* 66 (2): 97–119. https://doi.org/10.2190/OM.66.2.a.

Rojas, Rick. 2021. "One High School, Five Students Fatally Shot." *New York Times*, April 23, sec. U.S. https://www.nytimes.com/2021/04/23/us/knoxville-anthony-thompson.html.

Rosenblatt, Kalhan. 2018. "He Taught Parkland Students about the NRA. Then the Shots Rang Out." *NBC News*, March 13, sec. U.S. News. https://www.nbcnews.com/news/us-news/he-taught-parkland-students-about-nra-then-gunshots-rang-out-n856266.

Rosenblatt, Paul C., and Beverly R. Wallace. 2005. *African American Grief*. New York: Routledge.

Rossen, Eric, ed. 2020. *Supporting and Educating Traumatized Students: A Guide for School-Based Professionals*. New York: Oxford University Press.

Roy, Kevin, and Nikki Jones. 2014. "Theorizing Alternative Pathways Through Adulthood: Unequal Social Arrangements in the Lives of Young Disadvantaged Men: Theorizing Alternative Pathways Through Adulthood." *New Directions for Child and Adolescent Development* 2014 (143): 1–9. https://doi.org/10.1002/cad.20051.

Royal, Camika. 2022. *Not Paved for Us: Black Educators and Public School Reform in Phila-delphia.* Cambridge, MA: Harvard Education Press.

Rubin, Lillian. 1992. *Worlds of Pain.* 2nd ed. New York: Basic Books.

Saltman, Kenneth J. 2014. "Neoliberalism and Corporate School Reform: 'Failure' and 'Creative Destruction.'" *Review of Education, Pedagogy, and Cultural Studies* 36 (4): 249–59. https://doi.org/10.1080/10714413.2014.938564.

"SAMHSA's Concept of Trauma and Guidance for a Trauma-Informed Approach." 2014. SAMHSA's Trauma and Justice Strategic Initiative. https://s3.amazonaws .com/static.nicic.gov/Library/028436.pdf.

Sandell, Kerstin, and Hanna Bornäs. 2017. "Functioning Numbness Instead of Feel-ings as a Direction: Young Adults' Experiences of Antidepressant Use." *Sociology* 51 (3): 543–58. https://doi.org/10.1177/0038038515591947.

Sandelson, Jasmin. 2023. *My Girls: The Power of Friendship in a Poor Neighborhood.* Oak-land: University of California Press.

Sandwick, Talia, Michelle Fine, Andrew Cory Greene, Brett G. Stoudt, María Elena Torre, and Leigh Patel. 2018. "Promise and Provocation: Humble Reflections on Critical Participatory Action Research for Social Policy." *Urban Education* 53 (4): 473–502. https://doi.org/10.1177/0042085918763513.

Scheeringa, Michael. 2021. *The Trouble with Trauma.* Las Vegas: Central Recovery Press.

Schensul, Jean J., and Margaret D. LeCompte. 2013. *Essential Ethnographic Methods: A Mixed Methods Approach.* 2nd ed. Lanham, MD: AltaMira Press.

Schonfeld, David J., and Scott Newgass. 2003. "School Crisis Response Initiative." Office for Victims of Crime Bulletin. Office of Justice Programs, U.S. Depart-ment of Justice. https://doi.org/10.1037/e532222006-001.

"School Counselors Matter." 2019. The Education Trust. https://www.school counselor.org/getmedia/b079d17d-6265-4166-a120-3b1f56077649/School -Counselors-Matter.pdf.

Schott Foundation. 2015. "Black Lives Matter: The Schott 50 State Report on Public Education and Black Males." Schott Foundation for Public Education.

Schuurman, Donna L, and Monique B. Mitchell. 2020. "Becoming Grief-Informed: A Call to Action." Dougy Center: The National Grief Center for Children & Families.

Seider, Scott, and Daren Graves. 2020. *Schooling for Critical Consciousness: Engaging Black and Latinx Youth in Analyzing, Navigating, and Challenging Racial Injustice.* Cam-bridge, MA: Harvard Education Press.

Severinsson, Elisabeth. 2003. "Moral Stress and Burnout: Qualitative Content Analysis." *Nursing & Health Sciences* 5 (1): 59–66. https://doi.org/10.1046/j.1442 -2018.2003.00135.x.

Shapiro, Sarah, and Catherine Brown. 2018. "A Look at Civics Education in the

United States." *American Educator: A Journal of Educational Equity, Research, and Ideas* 42 (2): 10–13.

Sharkey, Patrick. 2010. "The Acute Effect of Local Homicides on Children's Cognitive Performance." *Proceedings of the National Academy of Sciences* 107 (26): 11733–38. https://doi.org/10.1073/pnas.1000690107.

———. 2018. *Uneasy Peace: The Great Crime Decline, the Renewal of City Life, and the Next War on Violence.* New York: W. W. Norton.

———. 2022. "How Long Are Americans Sad and Angry about Mass Shootings? Four Days." *Washington Post*, May 26. https://www.washingtonpost.com /outlook/2022/05/26/uvalde-school-shooting-emotions-guns/.

Sharkey, Patrick, and Megan Kang. 2023. "The Era of Progress on Gun Mortality: State Gun Regulations and Gun Deaths from 1991 to 2016." *Epidemiology* 34 (6): 786. https://doi.org/10.1097/EDE.0000000000001662.

Sharkey, Patrick, and Alisabeth Marsteller. 2022. "Violence and Urban Inequality." *Vital City*, March 2. https://www.vitalcitynyc.org/articles/violence-and-urban -inequality.

Sharkey, Patrick, Amy Ellen Schwartz, Ingrid Gould Ellen, and Johanna Lacoe. 2014. "High Stakes in the Classroom, High Stakes on the Street: The Effects of Community Violence on Student's Standardized Test Performance." *Sociological Science* 1: 199–220. https://doi.org/10.15195/v1.a14.

Sharkey, Patrick, Nicole Tirado-Strayer, Andrew V. Papachristos, and C. Cybele Raver. 2012. "The Effect of Local Violence on Children's Attention and Impulse Control." *American Journal of Public Health* 102 (12): 2287–93. https://doi.org/10 .2105/AJPH.2012.300789.

Sharpe, Christina. 2014. "Black Life, Annotated." *The New Inquiry* (blog), August 8. https://thenewinquiry.com/black-life-annotated/.

———. 2016. *In the Wake: On Blackness and Being.* Durham, NC: Duke University Press.

Sklar, Fred, and Shirley F. Hartley. 1990. "Close Friends as Survivors: Bereavement Patterns in a 'Hidden' Population." *OMEGA—Journal of Death and Dying* 21 (2): 103–12. https://doi.org/10.2190/3Y94-G16J-D8MY-5P9M.

Smith, Jocelyn R. 2015. "Unequal Burdens of Loss: Examining the Frequency and Timing of Homicide Deaths Experienced by Young Black Men across the Life Course." *American Journal of Public Health* 105 (S3): S483–90.

Smith, Jocelyn R., and Desmond U. Patton. 2016. "Posttraumatic Stress Symptoms in Context: Examining Trauma Responses to Violent Exposures and Homicide Death among Black Males in Urban Neighborhoods." *American Journal of Orthopsychiatry* 86 (2): 212–23. https://doi.org/10.1037/ort0000101.

Sofka, Carla J., Illene Noppe Cupit, and Kathleen R. Gilbert, eds. 2012. *Dying, Death, and Grief in an Online Universe: For Counselors and Educators.* New York: Springer.

Spruill, Ida J., Bernice L. Coleman, Yolanda M. Powell-Young, Tiffany H. Williams, and Gayenell Magwood. 2014. "Non-Biological (Fictive Kin and Othermothers): Embracing the Need for a Culturally Appropriate Pedigree Nomenclature in African-American Families." *Journal of the National Black Nurses Association* 25 (2): 23–30.

Spungen, Deborah. 1997. *Homicide: The Hidden Victims: A Resource for Professionals.* Thousand Oaks, CA: SAGE Publications.

Stack, Carol B., and Linda M. Burton. 1993. "Kinscripts." *Journal of Contemporary Family Studies* 24 (2): 157–70.

Stevenson, Howard C. 2003. *Playing with Anger: Teaching Coping Skills to African American Boys Through Athletics and Culture.* Westport, CT: Praeger.

———. 2004. "Boys in Men's Clothing: Racial Socialization and Neighborhood Safety as Buffers to Hypervulnerability in African American Males." In *Adolescent Boys: Exploring Diverse Cultures of Boyhood,* by Niobe Way and Judy Y. Chu, 59–77. New York: New York University Press.

Stewart, Endya B., Eric A. Stewart, and Ronald L. Simons. 2007. "The Effect of Neighborhood Context on the College Aspirations of African American Adolescents." *American Educational Research Journal* 44 (4): 896–919.

Stuart, Forrest. 2020a. *Ballad of the Bullet: Gangs, Drill Music, and the Power of Online Infamy.* Princeton, NJ: Princeton University Press.

———. 2020b. "Code of the Tweet: Urban Gang Violence in the Social Media Age." *Social Problems* 67: 191–207. https://doi.org/10.1093/socpro/spz010.

Sweeting, Helen N., and Mary L. M. Gilhooly. 1990. "Anticipatory Grief: A Review." *Social Science & Medicine* 30 (10): 1073–80. https://doi.org/10.1016/0277-9536 (90)90293-2.

Swisher, Raymond R., and Tara D. Warner. 2013. "If They Grow Up: Exploring the Neighborhood Context of Adolescent and Young Adult Survival Expectations." *Journal of Research on Adolescence* 23 (4): 678–94.

Szymkowiak, Dorota, and Giridhar Mallya. 2015. "Vital Statistics Report: Philadelphia 2012." City of Philadelphia, Department of Public Health.

Tarr, Delaney. 2021. "The Life Cycle Of A Youth Activist." *The Pavlovic Today,* July 20. http://thepavlovictoday.com/the-life-cycle-of-a-youth-activist/.

———. 2022. "Youth Gun Violence Activists Can't Be Asked to Save the World." *Teen Vogue,* December 7. https://www.teenvogue.com/story/delaney-tarr -youth-gun-violence-activists-december-2022-special-issue.

Thornton, Margaret. 1989. "Pornography as Social Injury Sex, Violence and Censorship." *Current Issues in Criminal Justice* 1 (1): 140–48.

Tuck, Eve. 2009. "Suspending Damage: A Letter to Communities." *Harvard Educational Review* 79 (3): 409–28.

Tyson, Karolyn. 2003. "Notes from the Back of the Room: Problems and Paradoxes in the Schooling of Young Black Students." *Sociology of Education* 76 (4): 326. https://doi.org/10.2307/1519869.

Ubiñas, Helen. 2017. "Look at the Faces of Our Dead." *Philadelphia Inquirer*, November 22. https://www.inquirer.com/columnists/inq/look-faces-our-dead-children-helen-ubias-20171122.html.

Umberson, Debra. 2017. "Black Deaths Matter: Race, Relationship Loss, and Effects on Survivors." *Journal of Health and Social Behavior* 58 (4): 405–20.

Umberson, Debra, Julie Skalamera Olson, Robert Crosnoe, Hui Liu, Tetyana Pudrovska, and Rachel Donnelly. 2017. "Death of Family Members as an Overlooked Source of Racial Disadvantage in the United States." *Proceedings of the National Academy of Sciences* 114 (5): 915–20. https://doi.org/10.1073/pnas.1605599114.

Umberson, Debra, Kristi Williams, Patricia A. Thomas, Hui Liu, and Mieke Beth Thomeer. 2014. "Race, Gender, and Chains of Disadvantage Childhood Adversity, Social Relationships, and Health." *Journal of Health and Social Behavior* 55 (1): 20–38.

Urban Prep Academies. 2012. "About Urban Prep." http://www.urbanprep.org/about.

Valenzuela, Angela. 1999. *Subtractive Schooling: U.S.-Mexican Youth and the Politics of Caring*. Albany: State University of New York Press.

Vasudevan, Veena, Nora Gross, Pavithra Nagarajan, and Katherine Clonan-Roy, eds. 2022. *Care-Based Methodologies: Reimagining Qualitative Research with Youth in US Schools*. London: Bloomsbury Academic.

Vaughan, Diane. 1990. *Uncoupling: Turning Points in Intimate Relationships*. New York: Vintage.

Venkatesh, Sudhir. 2008. *Gang Leader for a Day: A Rogue Sociologist Takes to the Streets*. Reprint ed. New York: Penguin Books.

Vital City. 2022. "Gun Violence in New York City: The Data." *Vital City*. https://www.vitalcitynyc.org/vital_signs/gun-violence-in-new-york-city-the-data.

Wagner, Anna J. M. 2018. "Do Not Click 'Like' When Somebody Has Died: The Role of Norms for Mourning Practices in Social Media." *Social Media + Society* 4 (1): 1–11. https://doi.org/10.1177/2056305117744392.

Walter, Tony. 1999. *On Bereavement: The Culture of Grief*. Buckingham, UK: Open University Press.

———. 2000. "Grief Narratives: The Role of Medicine in the Policing of Grief." *Anthropology & Medicine* 7 (1): 97–114. https://doi.org/10.1080/136484700109377.

Walter, Tony, Rachid Hourizi, Wendy Moncur, and Stacey Pitsillides. 2012. "Does the Internet Change How We Die and Mourn? Overview and Analysis." *OMEGA—Journal of Death and Dying* 64 (4): 275–302.

Ward, Jesmyn. 2014. *Men We Reaped: A Memoir*. Reprint ed. London: Bloomsbury USA.

Warner, Tara D., and Raymond R. Swisher. 2015. "Adolescent Survival Expectations
Variations by Race, Ethnicity, and Nativity." *Journal of Health and Social Behavior*
56 (4): 478–94.

Warren, Chezare A. 2017. *Urban Preparation: Young Black Men Moving from Chicago's
South Side to Success in Higher Education*. Cambridge, MA: Harvard Education
Press.

Warren, Jonathan W. 2000. "Masters in the Field: White Talk, White Privilege,
White Biases." In *Racing Research, Researching Race: Methodological Dilemmas in Crit-
ical Race Studies*, ed. France Winddance Twine and Jonathan W. Warren, 135–64.
New York: New York University Press.

Warren, Mark R. 2021. *Willful Defiance: The Movement to Dismantle the School-to-Prison
Pipeline*. New York: Oxford University Press.

Way, Niobe. 2013. *Deep Secrets: Boys' Friendships and the Crisis of Connection*. Cambridge, MA: Harvard University Press.

Weiss, Robert S. 1995. *Learning From Strangers: The Art and Method of Qualitative Interview Studies*. New York: Free Press.

Whitaker, Amir, Sylvia Torres-Guillen, Michelle Morton, Harold Jordan, Stefanie
Coyle, Angela Mann, and Wei-Ling Sun. 2019. "Cops and No Counselors."
American Civil Liberties Union. https://www.aclu.org/issues/juvenile-justice
/school-prison-pipeline/cops-and-no-counselors.

White, Aaronette M., and Tal Peretz. 2010. "Emotions and Redefining Black Masculinity: Movement Narratives of Two Profeminist Organizers." *Men and Masculinities* 12 (4): 403–24. https://doi.org/10.1177/1097184X08326007.

Whitman, David. 2008. *Sweating the Small Stuff: Inner-City Schools and the New Pater-
nalism*. Washington, DC: Thomas B. Fordham Institute.

Wilkins, Amy. 2012. "'Not Out to Start a Revolution': Race, Gender, and Emotional
Restraint among Black University Men." *Journal of Contemporary Ethnography* 41
(1): 34–65.

Williams, Juliet A. 2016. *The Separation Solution? Single-Sex Education and the New Politics of Gender Equality*. Oakland: University of California Press.

Wingfield, Adia Harvey. 2007. "The Modern Mammy and the Angry Black Man:
African American Professionals' Experiences with Gendered Racism in the
Workplace." *Race, Gender & Class* 14 (1/2): 196–212.

———. 2012. *No More Invisible Man: Race and Gender in Men's Work*. Philadelphia:
Temple University Press.

Wintemute, Garen J. 2015. "The Epidemiology of Firearm Violence in the Twenty-
First Century United States." *Annual Review of Public Health* 36 (1): 5–19.

Wodtke, G. T., D. J. Harding, and F. Elwert. 2011. "Neighborhood Effects in Temporal Perspective: The Impact of Long-Term Exposure to Concentrated Disadvantage on High School Graduation." *American Sociological Review* 76 (5): 713–36. https://doi.org/10.1177/0003122411420816.

Wolfers, Justin, David Leonhardt, and Kevin Quealy. 2015. "1.5 Million Missing Black Men." *New York Times,* April 20. https://www.nytimes.com/interactive /2015/04/20/upshot/missing-black-men.html.

Wolfsdore, Adam, Kristen Park Wedlock, and Cassandra Lo. 2022. *Navigating Trauma in the English Classroom.* Champaign, IL: National Council of Teachers of English.

Woodbine, Onaje X. O. 2016. *Black Gods of the Asphalt: Religion, Hip-Hop, and Street Basketball.* New York: Columbia University Press.

Wright, Anna W., Makeda Austin, Carolyn Booth, and Wendy Kliewer. 2016. "Exposure to Community Violence and Physical Health Outcomes in Youth: A Systematic Review." *Journal of Pediatric Psychology* (October): jsw088. https:// doi.org/10.1093/jpepsy/jsw088.

Young, Alford A. Jr. 2004. *The Minds of Marginalized Black Men: Making Sense of Mobility, Opportunity, and Future Life Chances.* Princeton, NJ: Princeton University Press.

———. 2008. "White Ethnographers on the Experiences of African American Men: Then and Now." In *White Logic, White Methods: Racism and Methodology,* by Tukufu Zuberi and Eduardo Bonilla-Silva, 179–200. Lanham, MD: Rowman & Littlefield.

Zacarian, Debbie, Lourdes Alvarez-Ortiz, and Judie Haynes. 2017. *Teaching to Strengths: Supporting Students Living with Trauma, Violence, and Chronic Stress.* Alexandria, VA: ASCD.

Zinner, Ellen S. 2000. "Being a Man about It: The Marginalization of Men in Grief." *Illness, Crisis & Loss* 8 (2): 181–88. https://doi.org/10.1177/10541373000080 0206.

Index

Page numbers in italics refer to figures and tables.